TRUTH IN A TIME OF DISINFORMATION

TRUTH IN A TIME OF DISINFORMATION

Psychoanalytic Insights

Edited by
Jean Arundale

KARNAC
firing the mind

First published in 2027 by
Karnac Books Limited
62 Bucknell Road
Bicester
Oxfordshire OX26 2DS

British Library Cataloguing in Publication Data

A C.I.P. for this book is available from the British Library

ISBN: 978-1-80013-471-3 (paperback)
ISBN: 978-1-80013-473-7 (e-book)
ISBN: 978-1-80013-472-0 (PDF)

Typeset by vPrompt eServices Pvt Ltd, India

www.firingthemind.com

MIX
Paper | Supporting responsible forestry
FSC® C011748

Karnac Books is committed to a sustainable future for our business, our readers, and our planet. This book is made from Forest Stewardship Council® certified paper.

To my children, Lindsey and Scott, our love sustains me.

To my esteemed colleagues in psychoanalysis,
whose work continues to inspire.

To everyone who seeks Goodness, Truth, and Beauty.

Contents

Acknowledgements

I give warm thanks to the authors who have contributed chapters to this book. I'm hugely grateful for their interest and enthusiasm for the topic and it has been a delight working together on the book.

Much gratitude is due to the publisher, Kate Pearce at Karnac Books, who enabled the production with brio, along with Izzy Da Silva's nimble assistance, always willing to answer queries.

I owe special thanks to Riccardo Steiner for his interest and helpful suggestions, and to John Morton for his thoughtful comments.

To Heidi Gaffney, my assistant and alter ego, who has been an indispensable part of the infrastructure of this book, I give warm thanks. I could not have managed without her patience, reliability, techno-knowledge, humour, and good sense.

I am immensely grateful to friends and family for their kind support and interest.

I am very grateful that Ron Britton, shortly before he died in August 2025, so kindly agreed to contribute a chapter to this book.

I owe thanks to the publisher, Taylor & Francis, who have given permission to reprint the following material:

Thomas Ogden (2016). Language and truth in psychoanalysis. *Psychoanalytic Quarterly*, *85*: 411–426.

Ronald Britton (1998). *Belief and Imagination: Explorations in Psychoanalysis* (Chapter 1). London: Routledge.

Mark Solms (2003). Do unconscious phantasies really exist? In: R. Steiner (Ed.), *Unconscious Phantasy* (Chapter 3). London: Karnac.

David Bell (2009). Is truth an illusion? Psychoanalysis and post-modernism. *British Journal of Psychotherapy, 90*(2): 331–345.

Hanna Segal (1989). Psychoanalysis and freedom of thought. In: J. Sandler (Ed.), *Dimensions of Psychoanalysis* (Chapter 4). London: Karnac.

John Steiner (2016). Illusion, disillusion, and irony in psychoanalysis. *Psychoanalytic Quarterly, 85*: 427–447.

Thank you to the *Journal of the American Psychoanalytic Association* for giving permission to reprint:

Giuseppe Civitarese (2023). On Bion's concept of truth in an extra-moral sense. *American Journal of Psychoanalysis, 83*: 495–519.

Finally, thank you to The Marsh Agency Ltd, on behalf of the Estate of W. R. Bion, for giving permission to reprint the Grid.

About the editor and contributors

Jorge L. Ahumada is a distinguished fellow of the British Psychoanalytical Society since 1999, and a training and supervising analyst at the Argentinian Psychoanalytic Association. He received the Mary Sigourney Award in New York in 1996, and the Konex Prize in Buenos Aires in 2006. He was the main speaker at the celebration of Freud's 150th birthday at Frankfurt University in 2006, and speaker of the "Meet the Analyst" conference at the International Psychoanalytical Association Prague Congress in 2013. His papers on the method and the epistemology of psychoanalysis, on the changes in the psychopathologies, and on autism have been published in nine languages. His books published in English are *The Logics of the Mind. A Clinical View* (Karnac, 2001), *Insight: Essays on Psychoanalytic Knowing* (Routledge, 2011), and, with Luisa C. Busch de Ahumada, *Contacting the Autistic Child: Five Successful Early Psychoanalytic Interventions* (Routledge, 2017).

Jean Arundale, PhD, is a training and supervising analyst for the British Psychoanalytic Association. In the BPA, she recently served as president, was chair of the Scientific Committee for six years, and worked on many other committees since the BPA was founded in 2010. Primarily in private practice in North West London, Jean was a consultant psychotherapist working part-time in the National Health Service for more than forty years, supervising groups of psychotherapy trainees at Guy's Hospital, London. She has taught widely and presented papers at UCL, EPF, and IPA conferences, and published papers and books on psychoanalysis, the most recent being *The Omnipotent State of Mind*, published by Routledge in 2022. Jean is presently serving on the *International Journal of Psychoanalysis*' editorial board.

Elias Mallet da Rocha Barros is a supervising and training analyst at the Brazilian Association of Psychoanalysis of São Paulo; a distinguished fellow of the British Psychoanalytical Society and Institute; a past editor for Latin America of the *International Journal of Psychoanalysis*; and co-chair for Latin America of the *IPA Encyclopaedic Dictionary of Psychoanalysis*. Elias received the Sigourney Award in 1999. He is also a member of the editorial boards of several journals.

David Bell is a past president of the British Psychoanalytical Society. He is well known for his writing and his lectures on the work of Freud, Klein, and Bion. Throughout his career he has been deeply involved in interdisciplinary studies—psychoanalysis and literature, philosophy, and sociopolitical theory. He retired in 2021 after twenty-five years as a consultant at the Tavistock and Portman NHS Foundation Trust, where he led a specialist service (the Fitzjohn's Unit) for complex cases. His 2018 report on the Tavistock Gender Development Service for children and adolescents (GIDS) was part of the chain of events leading to the Cass Review and subsequently the closure of the service. He is a leading psychiatric expert in immigration/asylum/human rights. His most recent paper "Some psychoanalytic reflections on the events in Gaza" was published in *Psychoanalytic Psychotherapy*. His books include *Reason and Passion, Psychoanalysis and Culture: A Kleinian Perspective*, and *On the Border: Psychotic Processes in Individuals, Couples and Groups*.

Christopher Bollas is a member of the British Psychoanalytical Society. A former director of education of the Austen Riggs Center, Stockbridge, MA, former professor of English literature at the University of Massachusetts, and former professor of psychoanalysis at the University of Rome (1978–1998), Bollas is in private practice. Much of his work is by "tele-analysis" or zoom workshops.

Ronald Britton (1933–2025) was a distinguished fellow and former president of the British Psychoanalytical Society, and widely recognised as one of the most original and influential psychoanalytic thinkers of his generation. A leading figure in post-Kleinian theory, he was known for his illuminating explorations of belief, imagination, and the struggle between internal and external reality. Formerly a consultant psychiatrist at the Tavistock Clinic in London, Britton was the author of several seminal works, including *Belief and Imagination* (1998), *Sex, Death, and the Superego* (2003), and *Between Mind and Brain* (2015), which remain touchstones in contemporary psychoanalytic thought.

Giuseppe Civitarese is a psychiatrist and training and supervising analyst of the Italian Psychoanalytic Society (SPI), and a member of the American Psychoanalytic Association (APsA). He works in private practice, in Pavia, Italy. In 2022, he received the Sigourney Award. Among his books are: *The Intimate Room: Theory and Technique of the Analytic Field*; *The Violence of Emotions: Bion and Post-Bionian Psychoanalysis*; *The Necessary Dream: New Theories and Techniques of Interpretation*; *Losing Your Head: Abjection, Aesthetic Conflict and Psychoanalytic Critics*; *The Analytic Field and Its Transformations* (with A. Ferro*); Truth and the Unconscious*; *An Apocryphal Dictionary of Psychoanalysis*; *Sublime Subjects: Aesthetic Experience and Intersubjectivity in Psychoanalysis*; *Vitality and Play in Psychoanalysis* (with A. Ferro); *Psychoanalytic Field Theory: Limits of Interpretation*; *The Psychoanalytic Approach*; *The Bion Tradition: Lines of Development—Evolution of Theory and Practice over the Decades*; and *Advances in Psychoanalytic Field Theory. The Hour of Birth: Psychoanalysis of the Sublime and Contemporary Art* is in press.

Sara Collins is a fellow of the British Psychoanalytic Association and its past director of training. She is a supervising and training psychoanalyst at the BPA, BPF, and University of Exeter. Sara has contributed book chapters and published articles in the *International Journal of Psychoanalysis* and the *Psychoanalytic Quarterly*. She has taught widely and presented papers at international conferences. She has written on wide psychoanalytic subjects including "authenticity in psychoanalysis and literature", "memory and historical truth", "psychic time and enactment", "psychoanalytic clinical writing", and "psychoanalytic training". Sara lives and works in private practice in London. Previously she worked in the National Health Service in North London including at the Tavistock and Portman Clinic. She is currently the book review editor of the *International Journal of Psychoanalysis* as well as its board member.

Gregorio Kohon is a distinguished fellow and training analyst of the British Psychoanalytical Society. Originally from Argentina, he moved to England in 1970, where he worked with R. D. Laing in the anti-psychiatry movement and trained as an analyst. For eight years he lived in Australia, where he co-founded (together with Valli Shaio Kohon) The Brisbane Centre for Psychoanalytic Studies. He was a visiting professor at the San Francisco Centre for Psychoanalysis, and a visiting professorial fellow at Birkbeck, University in London. His books include *No Lost Certainties to be Recovered*; *Reflections on the Aesthetic Experience—Psychoanalysis and the Uncanny*; and *Considering the Nature of Psychoanalysis.* He co-edited: *The British School of Psychoanalysis—The Independent Tradition*; *The Dead Mother*; *Love and Its Vicissitudes* (with André Green); *The Greening of Psychoanalysis*; and *British Psychoanalysis—New Perspectives in the Independent Tradition.* His work has been translated into seven languages. His has written a novel, *Red Parrot, Wooden Leg*, and books of poetry, *Odetta in Babylon*, *The Canada Express*, and others.

Alessandra Lemma is a fellow of the British Psychoanalytical Society and a chartered clinical and counselling psychologist, a visiting professor in the Psychoanalysis Unit, University College London, a consultant, Anna Freud Centre, and visiting professor, Centro Winnicott, Rome. For sixteen years she worked at the Tavistock Clinic where she was, at different stages, head of psychology and professor of psychological therapies in conjunction with Essex University. She was a recipient of the 2022 Sigourney Award in recognition of her theoretical and clinical contributions to understanding body modification practices, the impacts of technology on psychic functioning and transgender identities, as well as for her efforts in developing and disseminating worldwide a brief psychoanalytic intervention for mood disorders. She is the former general editor of the New Library of Psychoanalysis book series and former chair of the *International Journal of Psychoanalysis*' management board. She has published extensively on psychoanalysis, trauma, the body, transgender identities, and ethics.

David Howell Morgan worked as a consultant psychotherapist in the NHS for more than twenty-five years, mainly at the Tavistock and Portman Clinic. He is now in full-time private practice in North London. He is a training analyst and supervisor for most trainings and a fellow of the British Psychoanalytical Society. He is chair of the Political Minds Seminars at the Institute of Psychoanalysis, the Poetic Mind at the British Psychoanalytic Association, and has presented a podcast called Frontier Psychoanalyst on Resonance Radio. He has written and edited three books: *Violence Perversion and Delinquency* (with Stan Ruszczynski), *The Unconscious in Social and Political Life*, and *A Deeper Cut: Further Reflections on Social and Political Life*. He also works as a consultant to several sociopolitical organisations and to whistleblowers.

Thomas H. Ogden is a graduate of the Yale School of Medicine and served as an associate psychiatrist at the Tavistock Clinic, London. He is currently a supervising and personal analyst at the Psychoanalytic Institute of Northern California. He has published thirteen books on psychoanalytic theory and practice, including *What Alive Means*; *Coming to Life in the Consulting Room*; *Reclaiming Unlived Life*; and *Creative Readings: Essays on Seminal Analytic Works*. In addition, he has published three novels: *The Parts Left Out*; *The Hands of Gravity and Chance*; and *This Will Do* ...; and a collection of short stories, *Aunt Birdie and Other Stories*. His work has been published in more than twenty-five languages. Dr Ogden teaches, practises, and supervises psychoanalysis in San Francisco, where he also teaches creative writing.

Eran J. Rolnik is a training and supervising analyst with the Israel Psychoanalytic Society and the Frankfurt Psychoanalytic Institute. He teaches at the Max Eitingon Institute for Psychoanalysis, the

Tel-Aviv University Medical School, the Frankfurt Psychoanalytic Institute, and, since 2024, the Sigmund Freud Institute in Frankfurt. Rolnik has published more than seventy journal papers and authored, edited, or translated more than twenty books. His book *Freud in Zion* is widely regarded as a landmark in psychoanalytic historiography, widely translated. In 2019 he published a collection of Freud's letters, a non-fiction bestseller in Israel for nearly a year. His latest book, *Psychoanalytic Objects Near and Far: Talking Cure* (Routledge, 2025), grew out of lectures delivered to clinicians during the Covid-19 lockdown. Rolnik lectures and teaches, while maintaining private practices in Tel-Aviv and Frankfurt. A regular contributor to the Haaretz opinion section, he has been a leading voice in Israel's mental health community's protests against the judicial overhaul.

Hanna Segal (1918–2011) was a Polish British psychoanalyst and one of the most influential figures in post-war psychoanalysis. A leading member of the British Psychoanalytical Society, she was a close collaborator of Melanie Klein and became one of the foremost exponents of Kleinian theory. Segal's work focused on the nature of symbol formation, phantasy, and artistic creativity, as well as the role of truth and freedom of thought in psychoanalytic practice. She extended Klein's ideas into the study of psychosis and creativity and wrote seminal texts including *Introduction to the Work of Melanie Klein* (1964) and *Dream, Phantasy and Art* (1991). Beyond the clinic, she also applied psychoanalytic thought to politics, war, and the dangers of nuclear conflict, becoming an influential public intellectual. Segal's clear teaching style and clinical insight made her a central figure in transmitting Kleinian thought to later generations.

Mark Solms is a member of the British Psychoanalytical Society and the American and South African Psychoanalytic Associations. He is director of neuropsychology at the Neuroscience Institute of the University of Cape Town. He is an honorary fellow of the American College of Psychiatrists. He has received numerous honours and awards, including the Sigourney Prize. He has published 350 scientific papers, and eight books, the latest being *The Only Cure* (Weidenfeld & Nicolson, 2026). He is the authorised editor and translator of the

Revised Standard Edition of the Complete Psychological Works of Sigmund Freud (24 volumes) and the forthcoming *Complete Neuroscientific Works of Sigmund Freud* (4 volumes).

John Steiner is a training analyst of the British Psychoanalytical Society, who was formerly a psychiatrist at the Maudsley Hospital and a psychotherapist at the Tavistock Clinic. He has now retired from clinical practice but continues to supervise and write. He is the author of *Psychic Retreats* (1993), *Seeing and Being Seen* (2011), and *Illusion, Disillusion and Irony in Psychoanalysis* (2020). He has also edited and written introductions to: *The Oedipus Complex Today* (1989), *Psychoanalysis, Literature and War*, by Hanna Segal (1997), *Rosenfeld in Retrospect* (2008), and *Melanie Klein's 1936 Lectures on Technique* (2017). He is currently working on a collection of papers on mourning.

Introduction

Jean Arundale

"Beauty is truth, truth beauty." Keats' enigmatic line from "Ode on a Grecian urn" opens up a vista, alluding to truth not as a bare proposition or fact but as something radiant and alive. When it joins with other patterns of understanding, it reveals an elegance, a coherence that feels unmistakably beautiful. It is an attempt to gather fragments of human experience, uniting with the whole. At its height, truth rises towards the sublime; when lies creep in the result is ugliness.

Seeking truth is intrinsic to humans as they work to find their place in the world. Cicero (44 BC) wrote that "Nature has planted in our minds an insatiable longing to see the truth." From the ancient Platonic ideals of Goodness, Truth, and Beauty, to the Enlightenment's devotion to reason, truth has been the foundation of trust, knowledge, and civilisation. It enables societies to make informed choices, build relationships, and stay connected to what is real. Without truth, the human mind and human culture descend into delusion and chaos.

This book has its origins in a profound concern about the state of truth in today's world, a situation in which lies and misinformation have become a dangerous virus, masquerading as ordinary life, that is invading global cultural foundations. Misinformation is spreading into the public discourse, many false narratives and downright lies being perpetrated, invading institutions that were established under the rule of law; the corrupting attacks on truth are having serious consequences for the pillars of our society and to the zeitgeist. The phrase "post-truth era" has become a cliché, yet it describes a grave condition. Lies repeated by politicians and amplified by media are mistaken for veracity. Trust in institutions erodes; facts compete with conspiracy; cynicism becomes the first reflex in public discourse. As Hannah Arendt warned, "The ideal subject of totalitarian rule is not the convinced Nazi or the dedicated Communist, but people for whom the distinction between fact and fiction, true and false, no longer exists" (Arendt, 1951, p. 474).

This movement is driven by narcissism, power, and greed. The narcissist, intoxicated by omnipotence, refutes reality itself, turning what *is* into what he wishes it to be. This tyranny of the mind, when enacted on a collective scale, becomes disastrous. The most powerful nations now shrug at evidence and dismiss reason, as if facts themselves are lost.

The measure of truth in these narcissistic times has morphed into feeling states. If what is right or true depends only on what people *feel*, we have moved beyond the boundaries of civilisation. The collective search for truth gives way to narcissistic self-creations: "my truth", "my story", "my reality". This cultural shift, from shared reality to subjective authenticity, has fractured public life into tribes and echo chambers.

Philosophers such as Jean-François Lyotard (1984) saw this coming. He wrote that modern societies have lost faith in "grand narratives", the overarching stories that once unified knowledge and meaning. Truth, he argued, had become local and plural, shaped by language games and internal rules rather than universal principles. Today, social media is the theatre of this fragmentation, a hall of mirrors where every reflection claims authority.

Nietzsche (1906) had already warned that all "facts" are really interpretations; whichever interpretation prevails at a given time is a function of power, not truth. In our era, that prophecy has come to pass. Truth has been subordinated to demagoguery.

Truth has become subjective: Fukuyama (2018) pointed out that those who urge "Be who you are", from Nietzsche to Ayn Rand and others, inadvertently were central to the cultural disintegration leading to the radical individualism that flourished over the nineteenth and twentieth centuries, laying the foundation for today's identity politics. This primacy of identity has meant that to question another's "truth" is now seen as a transgression, a moral assault on their being. Societies retreat into tribes, unwilling to hear one another, regressing into a shouting match between competing realities. Democracy, which depends upon compromise and persuasion, struggles to survive in such a climate. The consequences are visible: tribalism, inequality widening into anger, public institutions losing legitimacy, and leaders who thrive not on solutions but on division. Austerity, greed, and the worship of wealth have replaced civic responsibility. Many ask: where are the bold ideas? Where are the leaders willing to hold the centre? Who is able to stand up and articulate the truth without fear?

When we lose touch with reality, we lose our orientation in the world. This distortion of truth begins early: the first lie a child tells his parent marks the dawning sense that his mind is private, boundaried, distinct. Lies, paradoxically, are part of the development of subjectivity. Yet the mind's capacity to create illusion can also destroy its grasp on the real.

Another force now destabilising our sense of reality is the rapid advance of AI and its ability to fabricate convincing images and texts that circulate widely. Combined with the flood of lies and misinformation on social media, it creates a world in which trust grows increasingly tenuous.

Psychoanalysis has long studied the defences against the truth: denial, projection, splitting, wishful thinking, turning a blind eye, and the repetition compulsion that binds a person to their suffering. Only when inner truth becomes conscious can it be thought about, acted upon, and allow change.

Winnicott's (1971) distinction between the true and false self recognised the importance of authenticity, being true to oneself. To find oneself, one must clear away the inner debris, trauma, narcissism, ego rigidity, conflicts, that distort the personality. But psychoanalysis, too, has been infected by the cultural fragmentation. Schools of thought, too, have formed silos, subscribing to their own language and models, rejecting others. How can we afford to ignore the range of insights from the different traditions that can helpfully inform us? The analytic community mirrors the political world: tribal, defensive, reluctant to engage with difference. Was Freud himself partly responsible for this inward turn that mistakenly prioritises emotion and feeling? His revolutionary discovery of psychic reality shifted the cultural focus from external truth to inner consciousness. That insight liberated the modern self, yet it may have inadvertently laid the groundwork for our current predicament, where subjective feeling is treated as ultimate authority.

There are many possible ways to interrogate psychoanalysis and culture for their truth value. The chapters in this book will explore psychic truth, the unconscious, phantasies, dreams, our theoretical framework, truth in the consulting room, reality, and more, all in the search for truthful representations, methods, and models.

A very brief history of our concepts of truth

Before focusing on psychoanalytic questions, a very brief history of the quest for truth will remind us of what we have gained and what now may be imperilled in the evolution of civilisation. Truth has a long and complex history across philosophy, religion, science, politics, art, and language.

Turning to the philosophers, a nineteenth-century German legend said, "Philosophy bakes no bread." Hegel (1821) famously replied, "True, philosophy does not bake bread, yet it provides something higher—it nourishes the spirit." From antiquity onwards, thinkers have negotiated this tension between the practical and the ideal. Socrates sought truth through dialectical enquiry in conversation with people in Athens, foreshadowing the psychoanalytic method. For Plato, truth existed in eternal and immutable ideas; to find the truth, one must emerge from the cave, the walls of which display a false world of appearance, and step into the light of perfect forms, where truth resides. Aristotle went on to offer the first formal definition of truth: the correspondence theory—truth corresponds to reality, external correlations.

Losing a grip on sense data as reality, in medieval thought, religious belief prevailed; Christian, Islamic, and Jewish philosophers blended philosophy with theology in which truth was often identified with the will of God. The early modern period, by contrast, divided along the lines of rationalism and empiricism. Descartes' *cogito* epitomised the former, grounding truth in the thinking subject, while Locke and Hume championed observation, measurement, data collection, and experience as the foundations of knowledge. Kant subsequently proposed that truth emerges from the interplay between mind and world: we cannot know things-in-themselves but only appearances structured by our inbuilt categories of perception and cognition. Hegel reimagined truth as a dynamic historical process, the progressing of the human spirit through the joining of opposites, whereas Marx quite differently jumped to materialism as the ultimate truth, the dynamics of production and social conflict, warning against the ills of capitalism with its excess profit.

In the nineteenth and twentieth centuries, philosophers proposed several competing theories to define truth. The traditional correspondence theory held that truth reflects reality, while the coherence theory claimed that truth is found in the consistency within systems of belief. Pragmatic theory, championed by thinkers like James and Dewey, saw truth as what proves useful or effective in practice. In contrast, deflationary or minimalist theories argued that to call a statement true is merely to affirm it, not to add anything beyond the statement itself. Challenging them all, Nietzsche rejected the notion of objective truth altogether, viewing it as a human construct shaped by language, perspective, and power.

In the contemporary landscape, analytic philosophy has pursued truth through the logical analysis of concepts, seeking clarity and logical precision, while Continental thinkers such as Foucault and Derrida recapitulated Nietzsche, questioning the very objectivity of truth, highlighting how power and language shape what we accept as true. Science and artificial intelligence have shifted attention towards models, prediction, and utility, eschewing metaphysical questions altogether. Common sense realism also put in its bid for the truth.

Meanwhile, postmodernism describes our present predicament, the loss of ideas of universal or objective truths, seeing only the operations of power in determining what counts as real, and the importance of the cultural concerns of the individual.

Thus, in this rapid trip through its history, truth has evolved from a metaphysical ideal (Plato), to a logical concept (Aristotle), to a theological principle, medieval thinkers, to the great Germans' systems (Kant and Hegel), to a practical or linguistic construct (modern and postmodern thinkers). Its definition varies across cultures and disciplines, but truth remains a central concern in our quest to understand reality.

Our cultural heritage

From the birth of ideas and throughout the history of philosophy we have built and developed our minds and humanity: to mention a few, detecting reality from appearance, the need for external correlates, inherent internal perceptual structures, logic, ethics, the influence of dynamic social realities, class struggle, practicality, common sense, the postmodern dilemma, all these are embedded in our contemporary thinking.

Kant (1784) observed that all truth is representation; there cannot be a final word. In the history of thought, we can see that in all the sciences, in philosophy, in the arts, truth is not only represented by empirical facts but by metaphor, analogy, simile, and parable. As we strive towards better representations, each era of philosophical investigation, with its methods and models, has contributed to the cultural richness of human thought that are relevant today. In this age of misinformation, we need not lose, indeed we are inextricably entwined with, the insights and methods from the rich sources of knowledge from our cultural past. Ultimately, the climate of lies and narcissistic fantasies cannot wipe out these truths.

Can we afford to be tribal, living in silos or halls of mirrors, engaging only with the echo of our own beliefs and shutting out the new ideas discovered by our neighbours? Can interest groups or nations afford to exist when treating one another as hostile, disagreeable adversaries? There is a price.

Psychoanalysis also faces these risks: loyalties to particular ideologies or leaders can limit our openness to learning from the wider field.

Psychoanalysis joins with philosophy to supply tools to help us to analyse and understand what's happening in the world. They help us to question our assumptions, recognise the limits of our knowledge, and explore how meaning is created between people.

The chapters in this book offer different perspectives, yet they also demonstrate the value of thinking together. This holds true, whether in clinical work, scientific inquiry, or cultural debate; creative dialogue is the way to understanding and growth.

Psychoanalytic truth

Although Freud did not develop the idea, he wrote of an epistemophilic instinct, an innate drive to know, originating in the sexual curiosity of infancy and childhood, later gradually expanding into scientific and intellectual inquiry. What begins as a derivative of sexuality and scopophilia becomes redirected towards mastery, comprehension, and the pursuit of knowledge (Freud, 1909b, p. 245; 1916–17, pp. 327–328).

Melanie Klein's (1928) adaptation of this was to connect it to the child's curiosity about the inside of the mother's body and having to contend with the attendant aggression and guilt. Wilfred Bion (1965) transformed the concept into K, the desire for knowledge, one of his three drivers of the psyche, along with love and hate. Bion held that the human need for truth is as crucial as the need for the nourishment of food. Building on Klein's thoughts about curiosity and object relations, for Bion, pivotally, the epistemophilic instinct is foundational to the development of thinking: thinking about experience.

Despite his descriptions of instincts (*trebes*), recently retranslated as drives, Freud was a rationalist, writing and testing his theories against rational argument; however, it is also true that Freud was a positivist, arising as he did from a cultural period in Vienna that was infused with logical positivism.

Positivism is a philosophical viewpoint that asserts that genuine knowledge is exclusively derived from empirical observation of clinical phenomena and scientific evidence. Logical positivism holds that meaningful statements must be empirically verifiable by logical necessity, rejecting metaphysical claims as without meaning. Freud was clear that true propositions arise from the clinical situation, from the patient, not imposed by the analyst's theoretical presumptions, lopping off bits of the patient that do not fit the paradigm, a Procrustean Bed. Although he claimed to be an empiricist, his early written case histories often did not show clinical evidence for the theories that he was developing. In the theoretical edifice he was building, it was left to his followers to require clinical evidence to more rigorously substantiate the truth: that is, what is actually going on with the patient as it emerges from the unconscious in the analytic dialogue.

Psychoanalysis has been the target of volumes of criticism from its detractors in attempts to demonstrate that it is neither a natural nor an empirical science, as it has obstacles that militate against scientific principles: namely the principle of predictability, unable, as it is, to make formulations that cannot be refuted or replicated (Fonagy, 2003). Due to the concept of overdetermination, which Freud used frequently, particularly in *The Interpretation of Dreams* (1900a)—the idea that any given statement, symptom, dream, or action can have multiple underlying threads of meaning—there is ambiguity. That is to say, a single expression can be the result of several unconscious motives, defences, desires, or conflicts converging together, including lies. So how can psychoanalysts do their work of making the unconscious conscious, interpreting unconscious phantasy, without falling short of scientific acceptability?

The rationalist within Freud—and in my view as well—would argue that rational necessity underpins the formulations and interpretations of unconscious content. Within the analytic session, the analyst's accumulated knowledge of the patient, combined with an intense yet freely floating attention to the utterances and behaviours emerging in the here and now of the consulting room, converge to form a field of meaning. This agglomeration of information, with high probability, points towards an unconscious significance that serves as the missing link—the bridge that connects and renders coherent the patient's dilemma, position, or character. Logic dictates that this particular unconscious phantasy or meaning, and no other, is the one indicated at that moment.

Psychoanalysts accept this interpretive anomaly as the generative source of working hypotheses, which can, of course, be refuted by the patient or accepted as clarifying insights that advance the analytic process. Intuition plays a powerful role in this interpretive act, yet it is continually tested against reason and logical consistency. Equally crucial is pattern recognition, one of the most essential capacities an analyst must cultivate, through which the analyst detects recurring motifs or unconscious configurations that organise the patient's psychic life.

In this way, new ideas can emerge directly from the clinical encounter. In the attempt to understand and to break new ground, hypotheses are formed in response to the unfolding material. Joseph Sandler proposed that truth and new ideas originate within the unconscious, and that the analyst's task is to listen for their emergence. As Sandler (1983, p. 38) suggested, "research should be directed towards making explicit the implicit concepts of practising psychoanalysts. This process may contribute to the development of new ideas and refinements in psychoanalytic theory." He further insisted that "the investigation of the implicit, private theories of clinical psychoanalysis opens a major new door in psychoanalytic research. Exploring these private formulations can lead to innovation and the generation of novel conceptual insights" (Sandler, 1983, p. 39).

From this perspective, we arrive at the crucial conclusion that the single case study is scientifically respectable, verified by eminent researchers such as Skinner (1938), Luria (1968), Allport (1942), and Kazdin (2011), bringing together behavioural and psychoanalytic methodology. The single case study is intrinsic to psychoanalytic tradition, training, theory, and practice, as the bearer of psychoanalytic truth. This view aligns with the broader coherence of psychoanalytic thought in which the detailed case study serves not just as an illustration but as the living ground from which psychoanalytic knowledge grows.

Psychoanalytic truth: The arguments

Apropos of the single case study, Thomas Ogden in Chapter 1 explores the way language shapes and reveals emotional, experiential truth, not only through verbal discourse but also through the breaks, silences, and disjunctions, moments when communication falters or shifts unexpectedly. He identifies three distinct forms of analytic dialogue: direct discourse, tangential discourse, and discourse of non sequiturs, different ways of co-creating experiential truth. Through detailed clinical examples, Ogden shows how language communicates and is the lived emotional process through which truth emerges. He concludes that the analyst and patient "dream" truth into being together through their evolving ways of speaking and listening, turning the analytic encounter into a space where previously unbearable or "unlived" experiences can finally be felt and articulated.

In his theory of truth, Ronald Britton in Chapter 2 proposes we all have shared assumptions, which he describes as *natural belief*, an ordinary, taken-for-granted belief system formed in childhood, that underlies and shapes how individuals perceive reality; for instance, belief in the existence of the external world, of other minds, or a stable self. As the mind grows, these beliefs, along with a multitude of new phantasies, notions, ideas, thoughts arising from experience, imbued with emotion, form what is called the internal world or psychic reality. Britton conveys his essential work on the Oedipus complex and the development of the "third position", a mental space from which one can observe and reflect upon experience. When beliefs are taken as facts, the analytic session offers a place where they can be scrutinised and tested for their truth value, revising them when necessary. When beliefs fail the reality test, they must be mourned and relinquished. Importantly, Britton posits a knowledge-drive alongside the drives of love and aggression, a dynamic psychic function that shapes psychic reality.

In Chapter 3, Mark Solms addresses the fundamental question of whether unconscious phantasies genuinely "exist". Solms maintains that unconscious phantasies are basic mental structures that underpin all thought and emotion, the instinctual drives, and object relations. Whether in symbolic form, non-verbal, or as visual images, all unable to be measured, Solms argues they are no less real, saying that the criterion for existence should be causal efficacy, their ability to shape experience and behaviour. Unconscious phantasies function as dynamic, organising models of internal life, valuable for their explanatory and therapeutic power rather than for their metaphysical status. These hidden unconscious phantasies, if connection can be made, circumvent the ego and its defences, the internal enemies of truth such as projective identification, transference, denial, wishful thinking, turning a blind eye, clinging to hope over evidence. Founded in clinical observation, in the immediacy of the moment, they are real because they matter.

Jorge L. Ahumada's article, Chapter 4, discusses how the concept of truth has evolved from ancient science and philosophy to modern psychoanalysis. From thinkers such as Pythagoras, Aristotle, and Descartes to modern scientists like Einstein and Poincaré, the concept of truth has moved from absolute universals to recognising the role of intuition, unconscious thought, and fallibility. Ahumada argues that gaining self-awareness goes against our natural tendencies and involves a painful but necessary shift from seeking pleasure to facing reality.

Through observational vignettes of infant behaviour, he shows how the earliest experience gives shape to the infant's life. Ahumada indicates the importance of working through deep, often preverbal emotional realities, requiring us to rethink what we mean by knowing, understanding, and healing in the human mind.

In Chapter 5, David Bell explores the philosophical and psychoanalytic implications of postmodern relativism and the fate of truth in its remit. Bell argues that while postmodernism's critique of authority and absolute truth has merit, its denial of objective truth undermines the foundations of psychoanalysis, which depends on a distinction between reality and illusion. He situates psychoanalysis firmly within the modernist tradition, emphasising its commitment to uncovering deeper realities beneath appearances and its belief that knowledge, though limited, can liberate. Through clinical examples, Bell illustrates how denying objective truth leads to psychological fragmentation and solipsism, and how its prioritising of subjectivity can mask a form of narcissism. In contrast, psychoanalysis acknowledges the painful but necessary struggle towards greater objectivity and self-knowledge. Ultimately, Bell contends that truth—imperfect and provisional though it may be—is indispensable to both psychoanalytic theory and human understanding.

In the context of increasing demands for empirical evidence-based scientific validation within mental health disciplines, Gregorio Kohon in Chapter 6 critically examines the relationship between psychoanalysis and the concept of research. The qualities inherent in psychoanalysis such as indeterminacy, undecidability, overdetermination, and hypercomplexity, Kohon asserts, mean that psychoanalysis, operating as it does within a realm of uncertainty that resists fixed truths or universal conclusions, cannot be an exact science, featuring outcome studies or standardised measurements. He compares psychoanalytic interpretation to a musical performance: improvisational, intuitive, and deeply subjective. But there is no fixed score, and the analyst's role involves creativity, emotional resonance, and responsiveness to each patient's uniqueness. He concludes that psychoanalysis can be studied by examining detailed single cases, with its theory and body of knowledge, as its guide, preserving the distinctive epistemological character of psychoanalysis.

Responding to Kohon's reflections on the uneasy relationship between psychoanalysis and research, Alessandra Lemma in Chapter 7 agrees with Kohon in ascertaining that reliable, reparable truths cannot be supplied by psychoanalysis. She agrees with Kohon's critique of the dominance of scientific paradigms, particularly the privileging of randomised controlled trials (RCTs) as the "gold standard", which is not in a position to grasp the complexity and singularity central to psychoanalytic work. Drawing on her own experience in the NHS during the rise of evidence-based therapy initiatives like Improving Access to Psychological Therapies (IAPT), Lemma highlights how research can become an idealised tool that simplifies mental health care for political or economic reasons, ignoring the messy reality of psychic suffering. While she agrees with Kohon's caution against "scientism", nevertheless she believes research remains essential in order to advance psychoanalytic knowledge and accountability. Lemma stresses that single case studies, though valuable for capturing individuality, must be written with methodological rigour to avoid bias, and she points to the possibility of combining psychoanalytic and empirical perspectives in a "space of conjunction", a potential for interdisciplinary dialogue that can enrich both, thus securing the place of psychoanalysis in the wider mental health landscape.

The whole truth and nothing but the truth?

As an advocate of the whole truth, in this encompassing and beautifully written paper, Hanna Segal in Chapter 8 presents a vision of the analytic process that has the ring of truth, that captures the fabric of work in the consulting room. She speaks cogently in favour of Freud's great project of abandoning dogma in the medical world and establishing truth. There is a struggle in every analysis to find what is true about the patient; there are resistances, as the patient fights against the knowledge of unpalatable truths about themselves, such as shame, guilt, hate, greed, selfishness, unwarranted aggression. Finding out what is real although undesirable is an important part of growing up, also in analysis. Often there are cherished beliefs that have been lifelong comforts but at the same time have inhibited growth and development. These must be mourned and relinquished. Omnipotence and delusions must be overcome by reality testing. When there are internal attacks against knowledge and truth, particularly in angry and aggressive patients, these must be acknowledged and understood. As unwanted parts of the self are revealed, the patient is in a position to choose to face the truth and the possibility of modification. In accepting difficult aspects of one's personality, the reward is greater mental freedom, the capacity to move about in an expanded mind.

In Chapter 9, John Steiner explores the parallels between psychoanalysis and classical drama, using Ibsen's *The Wild Duck* and Sophocles' *Oedipus the King* in order to exemplify how denial, illusion, and avoidance can maintain a false but comforting status quo until the truth emerges and comfort collapses. To find the truth, he argues that both analysts and audiences need to navigate a dual role: emotionally engaged participants and detached observers. The ironic stance, Steiner suggests, allows acknowledgement of both the need for illusions and the harshness, sometimes unbearable, of truth. Through these plays, Steiner illustrates how the determined pursuit of truth, without empathy or timing, can lead to tragedy. While truth is essential in psychoanalysis, it must be tempered with kindness, empathy, and self-reflection. Irony allows for this balance, helping analysts avoid the rigidity, allowing a compassionate balance between confronting reality and sensitivity to the patient's capacity to bear it.

In Chapter 10, Elias da Rocha Barros explores in a vivid and stirring paper the impact of trauma on the individual's psychic life and how this can be ameliorated. Whether the trauma is physical or emotional, it profoundly affects, damages, and partly destroys the mind; it affects the capacity to symbolise and integrate experiences, creating a "hole of vulnerability". It metastasises, it operates like a psychic sepsis, diminishing the will to live, with a sense of home and belonging lost. When trauma remains unrepresented there will be repetitive suffering. Trauma can only be metabolised when given meaning and place, time, and a narrative frame. The author makes an important shift in focus, away from the original traumatic event, to memories, dreams, linked events, re-significations, and related emotional experiences. Da Rocha Barros presents two fascinating case studies that show the work on metabolisation; truth is not presented to the patient by the analyst but is co-constructed in a shared emotional experience.

Sara Collins in Chapter 11 argues that Freud's later work marks a shift from viewing analytic reconstruction as the recovery of an objectively knowable past to understanding it as a matter of psychological probability. Freud's early archaeological metaphor suggested that analysts could piece together fragments of memory like pottery shards to reveal a true childhood history, but he gradually recognised that memory is unreliable and that objective proof is mostly unattainable. Collins points out that Freud's reflections in *Moses and Monotheism* (1939a) demonstrate this transition, relying not on factual certainty but on "psychological probabilities". She proposes that contemporary psychoanalysis should move away from the pursuit of historical truth and instead embrace authenticity, an account of the past that is emotionally credible and emerges within the analytic relationship. In this view, change occurs not through uncovering factual events but through the co-creation of meanings that feel real, coherent, and transformative for the patient. Two case studies are presented.

The particularity of truth

Guiseppe Civitarese in Chapter 12 examines Bion's unconventional concept of truth in an extra-moral, emotional, and intersubjective sense. Civitarese explains that for Bion, truth is not a factual proposition but a form of emotional nourishment essential for psychic growth. Lies, correspondingly, are not always moral failures but defensive operations that block contact with emotional reality. Bion's ideas such as *truth as food for the mind, thoughts without a thinker*, and the centrality of "O", ultimate being, challenge positivist views of the mind. Clinically, Bion shifts the focus from detecting factual truth to the development of the capacity to think. Post-Bionian analytic field theory radicalises this further, bringing in the "we" of a shared emotional field, instead of individual statements by analyst and patient. Civitarese shows that Bion offers a profoundly non-moralistic, intersubjective, and dynamic vision of truth that reshapes psychoanalytic theory and technique.

In his Chapter 13, Eran Rolnik writes movingly about the experience of practising psychoanalysis in the midst of political upheaval and threats towards freedom of thought, arguing that analytic practice cannot be insulated from political reality. Rolnik traces a historical lineage from Freud's advice to Ferenczi to contemporary debates about neutrality, showing how psychoanalysts have long grappled with authoritarian pressures and the temptation to withdraw from politics. Drawing on both theory and personal testimony from Israel amid democratic backsliding, Rolnik demonstrates how threats to democracy undermine not only public institutions but also the analytic setting, constraining free association, truth-seeking, and psychic integrity. He proposes that psychoanalysis and democracy are parallel projects of *parrhesia*, fearless truth-telling, that mutually reinforce one another, and that analysts must acknowledge the political conditions that shape mental life and their own capacity to think and work freely.

David Howell Morgan in Chapter 14 explores the profound relationship between poetry and psychoanalysis, arguing that both disciplines serve as gateways to unconscious truth. Drawing on Freud, Bion, Winnicott, and a range of poets like Heaney, Lorca, and Hughes, Howell Morgan contends that poetry has often anticipated psychoanalytic insight, accessing the unconscious through metaphor, symbol, and tone in ways that psychoanalysis later attempts to name and structure. A capacity for engaging with the complex and a deep respect for metaphor as the voice of the unconscious are at its heart. The access to unconscious truths through metaphor, ambiguity, and form rather than direct explanation is illustrated in clinical vignettes in which patients speak in metaphor, revealing the analyst's task as one of listening, holding, and waiting rather than explaining. Symbolic imagination is vital to both poetry and analysis; both require patience, openness to uncertainty, and a reverence for what remains unsaid.

In the context around untruth in the child sexual abuse scandal, Christopher Bollas in Chapter 15 begins by reflecting on the rise of questionable abuse allegations in the 1970s and 80s, when inexperienced therapists and social pressure led to a wave of false memories and exaggerated claims of childhood abuse. Drawing on Freud's theory of deferred trauma, when genuine traumatic shock is experienced belatedly after cognition matures, the author emphasises that trauma often manifests later in life, triggered by seemingly unrelated events, and can be difficult to differentiate from individuals who genuinely struggle with true traumatic memories. "False memories" can become self-reinforcing narratives, a form of self-traumatisation, where the individual perpetuates their suffering through identification with victimhood. This process of identification with the life of another is illustrated through a case study, illustrating what Bollas names as *appropriative identification*, as an extreme form of *pathological envy*: individuals unconsciously "steal" others' identities, qualities, and social worlds, amounting to psychological identity theft. This process can be convincing on the surface but is, at its core, a *deluded invasion*, a destructive fusion, taking over the other's individuality, and demands careful clinical handling.

In Chapter 16, Jean Arundale writes of the link between truth and freedom: the desire for personal and social freedom is universal and ageless. However, at the present time, these social freedoms are threatened and require protection in the face of political movements towards autocracy. Personal, internal freedom is equally threatened by living within false narratives and inauthenticity. This chapter explores the vital importance of facing truth in both the public discourse and the internal world. Defensive refusal to recognise psychic truth can limit or enslave the individual. Insights into personal truth, achieved through the psychoanalytic method, it is argued, facilitate emotional and intellectual freedom and development. Citing the theories of Bion, Freud, Segal, Civitarese, and Klein, Arundale contends that psychoanalysis also proposes to free the mind from undue psychic suffering, promoting thinking, authenticity and self-determination, the freedom to speak out, and for the patient to be unafraid of things as they are. Arundale provides material from two analytic patients whose encounters with unconscious truth were liberating.

End note to the Introduction

Seeking truth is not only a fascinating pursuit in itself but also a vital instinct for the survival of democracy and civilisation, enabling discovery and progress. Orwell's *1984* warned of a world where the very concept of objective truth could be erased under authoritarian rule—are we moving towards such a reality? How can we preserve a mindset grounded in truth that has external correlates and evidence-based foundations? We need people who can fearlessly stand up and articulate the truth.

Truth possesses a beauty of its own, its elegance reflects authenticity and integrity, with the power to transform both inner and collective realities. Debate and argument are indispensable means of finding truth when differences arise among people or schools of thought. Psychoanalysis, in particular, offers a unique model for thinking and working together. Truth arises in any field when serious discussion takes place to find it.

This question of which psychoanalytic theories best represent truth of the mind was at the heart of the book *The Freud–Klein Controversies 1941–45* by Pearl King and Riccardo Steiner (1991). The Controversial Discussions were a prolonged series of meetings of the British Psychoanalytical Society between 1942 and 1944, when the Viennese school led by Anna Freud and the followers of Melanie Klein debated fundamental theoretical divisions. Such conflicts are inevitable where differing models coexist, yet they also mark the vitality of a living science.

The Discussions ended on a note of tolerance while still maintaining a need to debate differences, alongside an agreement to share equally in the tasks of training and governing the society. Riccardo Steiner (2025) reminds us of the concluding words of Klein:

> As long as this Society has any claim to be called a scientific society there must be disagreement ... though it need not be embittered by personal animosity. A scientific society is a group of people who are seeking to discover new truths, not a group who are resting content at any stage in the search for knowledge ... (King & Steiner, 1991, p. 204)

Further to this, Marjorie Brierley, who played a mediating role in the debate, wrote in 1942:

> Scientific truth can never be absolute because hypotheses are formulated in the light of contemporary knowledge. In consequence, as knowledge grows, older hypotheses become inadequate and have to be revised, expanded, or reformulated to contain new facts ... a continuous process of adaptation of theory to continually expanding facts. (Brierley, 1942, quoted by Steiner, 2025, p. 669)

This book presents efforts to reveal truth, not final and immutable but as hypotheses, formulations, and insights that are the best attainable at the time, open to debate, to be tested, developed, disagreed with, or refuted.

After the wildest beauty in the world,
For by my glee might many men have laughed,
And of my weeping something had been left,
Which must die now. I mean the truth untold …

Wilfred Owen, "Strange meeting" (1919)

References

Allport, G. (1942). *The Use of Personal Documents in Psychological Science*. New York: Social Science Research Council.

Arendt, H. (1951). *The Origins of Totalitarianism*. New York: Harcourt, Brace.

Bion, W. R. (1965). *Transformations: Change from Learning to Growth*. London: Heinemann.

Brierley, M. (1942). Internal objects and theory. *International Journal of Psychoanalysis*, *23*: 107–112.

Cicero, M. T. (44 BC). *On Duties (De Officiis)*. W. Miller (Trans.). Loeb Classical Library. Cambridge, MA: Harvard University Press, 1913. Book I, §4.

Fonagy, P. (2003). Psychoanalysis today. *World Psychiatry*, *2*(2): 73–80.

Freud, S. (1900a). *The Interpretation of Dreams*. *S. E.*, *4–5*. London: Hogarth.

Freud, S. (1909b). Analysis of a phobia in a five-year-old boy. *S. E.*, *10*: 3–149. London: Hogarth.

Freud, S. (1916–17). *Introductory Lectures on Psycho-Analysis*. *S. E.*, 15–16. London: Hogarth.

Freud, S. (1939a). *Moses and Monotheism*. *S. E.*, *23*. London: Hogarth.

Fukuyama, F. (2018). *Identity: The Demand for Dignity and the Politics of Resentment*. New York: Farrar, Straus and Giroux.

Hegel, G. W. F. (1821). *Elements of the Philosophy of Right*. H. B. Nisbet (Trans.), A. W. Wood (Ed.). Cambridge: Cambridge University Press, 1991.

Kant, I. (1784). An answer to the question: What is enlightenment? In: M. J. Gregor (Ed. & Trans.), *Practical Philosophy*. Cambridge: Cambridge University Press, 1996.

Kazdin, A. (2011). *Single-Case Research Designs: Methods for Clinical and Applied Settings* (2nd edn). New York: Oxford University Press.

Keats, J. (1819). Ode on a Grecian urn. In: *Complete Poems.* J. Stillinger (Ed.). Cambridge, MA: Harvard University Press, 1982.
King, P., & Steiner, J. (Eds.) (1991). *The Freud–Klein Controversies, 1941–45.* London: Routledge.
Klein, M. (1928). Early stages of the Oedipus complex. *International Journal of Psycho-Analysis, 9*: 167–180.
Luria, A. (1968). *The Mind of a Mnemonist: A Little Book About a Vast Memory.* Trans. L. Solotaroff (Trans.). New York: Basic Books.
Lyotard, J.-F. (1984). *The Postmodern Condition: A Report on Knowledge.* G. Bennington & B. Massumi (Trans.). Minneapolis, MN: University of Minnesota Press.
Nietzsche, F. (1906). *The Will to Power.* W. Kaufmann & R. J. Hollingdale (Trans.), W. Kaufmann (Ed.). New York: Vintage, 2968.
Orwell, G. (1949). *Nineteen Eighty-Four.* London: Secker & Warburg.
Owen, W. (1919). Strange meeting. In: J. Stallworthy (Ed.), *Poems of Wilfred Owen.* London: Chatto & Windus, 1985.
Sandler, J. (1983). Reflections on some relations between psychoanalytic concepts and psychoanalytic practice. *International Journal of Psychoanalysis, 64*(1): 35–45.
Skinner, B. F. (1938). *The Behavior of Organisms: An Experimental Analysis.* New York: Appleton-Century.
Steiner, R. (2025). Some notes on Marjorie Brierley and the part she played during the Freud–Klein Controversies. *Bulletin of the British Psychoanalytical Society, 61*(1): 40–55.
Winnicott, D. W. (1971). *Playing and Reality.* London: Tavistock.

Part I

Psychoanalytic truth: The arguments

CHAPTER 1

On language and truth in psychoanalysis*

Thomas H. Ogden

Psychoanalysis as a therapeutic process centres much of its energy on helping the patient experience, and give voice to, a truth that has been disturbing him for much of his life, a truth that he has been unable to think or feel because it has been too much to bear. Language plays a pivotal role in bringing to life the emotional truth of previously unbearable experience in the analytic session.

The patient and analyst develop ways of talking to one another and use those ways of talking to get at the truth as it is lived in the session. I discuss three ways that my patients and I have talked to one another, which I call direct discourse, tangential discourse, and discourse in non sequiturs.

The language that patient and analyst use in talking with one another is an inherent part of the experience of the truth, and the truth of the experience, of any session. To put it in slightly different words, the ways in which patients and analysts talk to one another, including all that is

* This chapter was originally published as Ogden, T. H. (2016). On language and truth in psychoanalysis. *The Psychoanalytic Quarterly*, 85(2): 411–426. https://doi.org/10.1002/psaq.12079, copyright © *The Psychoanalytic Quarterly*, 2016, reprinted by permission of Informa UK Limited, trading Taylor & Francis Group, https://www.tandfonline.com on behalf of *The Psychoanalytic Quarterly*.

not said but expressed in tone of voice or in what is left to the imagination, are an integral part of what is happening in the session.

I take as a starting point for this discussion the idea that human beings are fundamentally truth-seeking animals, though we are afraid of the truth in almost, but not quite, equal measure. I will be discussing particular forms of discourse that enable the patient to experience with the analyst the truth that the patient has previously been unable to think or feel, much less put into words, on his own. Often the truth of the session involves events that the patient has not yet been able to experience (Winnicott, 1974) and consequently remain "unlived" (Ogden, 2014) aspects of the patient's life.

There are innumerable forms of discourse (a term I use interchangeably with dialogue and conversation). I will be addressing only the three I mentioned: direct discourse, tangential discourse, and discourse in the form of non sequiturs. (I have invented the names for these types of discourse as a form of shorthand with which to discuss the similarities and differences among these ways of conversing.) All three of these forms derive their shape from the very structure of language, a structure that inherently involves an active interplay of manifest and implicit meaning.

In the analytic setting, the experience of the truth is shaped, coloured, textured, structured, and so on, by language. Patient and analyst develop forms of discourse that not only serve as the medium in which the truth is conveyed; the discourse itself is a critical part of the truth of what is occurring at any given moment of a session. Each form of discourse is expressive of a truth that bears its mark. In the present paper, I am not simply illustrating three different forms of analytic discourse; I am hoping to convey a sense of the ways in which three of my patients and I developed different ways of talking with one another that were unique to the work I did with each of them, and allowed us to bring to life the truth of what was occurring between us.

While each of the three forms of discourse that I will discuss serves to express the truth in its own distinctive way, all three, to my mind, hold in common the following quality: the medium for the communication of the truth is not to be found primarily in the declaratives, in the story being told, but in the parts left out, in the breaks in the discourse. What I have in mind when I refer to the breaks in the discourse are the places where there is disjunction—sometimes a lack of correspondence between the words and their usual meanings, at other times a seemingly incomprehensible gap between what one person says and how the other responds, and at still other times a divide between the feeling or idea that is expected and the one that is actually stated or implied.

When these and other sorts of disjunctions occur in the discourse between patient and analyst, an emotional climate is generated in which both participants experience some degree of feeling lost, confused, perplexed, at sea, and almost always mystified. Mystified because patient and analyst, at points of break in expected coherence of dialogue, not only feel shaken; they also experience a feeling of marvel in the face of the unknown, in the face of unanticipated possibilities. The analytic pair can no longer rely on what they thought they knew, for what they have known no longer feels sufficient to meaningfully contain the elements of experience now in play. They must either attempt to deaden, obscure, and ignore what is occurring in the break, or attempt to make themselves open and vulnerable to something of the reality, the truth, of what is happening.

The truth sensed in the breaks is merely suggested, as if perceived through a mist in which discernible shapes are vague, but doubtlessly real, doubtlessly true. The imperfectly perceived truth leaves the individual feeling a combination of amazement and fear. The truth of the individual's experience that is nascent in the moment cannot be passively "taken in" in a moment of epiphany; unconscious psychological work must be done. What is true to that moment must be created psychically—"dreamt up"—as patient and analyst together engage in the conscious and unconscious experience of being changed by the truth of the moment, a truth that is always on the move, accruing verbally symbolic meanings as it goes.

The analytic setting—with its unstructured mode of conversation; the maximisation of the role of language and sound by means of the patient's use of the couch; the effort to release analyst and patient from the hegemony of secondary process thinking, and, in so doing, allowing waking dreaming (reverie) to become a form of intrasubjective and intersubjective communication—all of this together is designed to help the analytic pair enter into a state of mind in which an experience of the truth, and the truth of the experience, may unfold, both in the form of what is said and what is left out.

Before proceeding to a detailed discussion of different forms of discourse, I would like to offer three clarifications. First, when I speak of patient and analyst "dreaming" together, I am referring to their unconsciously thinking and feeling, individually and collectively, the truth of an experience that was, for the patient, previously unthinkable. To my mind, this overlap of the dreaming of patient and analyst lies at the heart of the analytic experience (see Ogden, 1997, 2004, 2007, for discussions and illustrations of patient and analyst "dreaming up" the truth of an experience together).

Second, the unconscious, in the way I understand the term, is an aspect of mind capable of realistically perceiving internal and external reality and encompassing the two in the process of generating a form of psychic reality that I think of as the psychic truth of one's experience.

Third, it is essential not to overvalue the names I have given to the three forms of discourse that I will discuss. I am not wedded to the terminology, nor do I see clear dividing lines that indicate precisely when a segment of dialogue ceases to be direct discourse and becomes tangential discourse, and when tangential discourse begins to be discourse of non sequiturs.

Direct discourse

The manifest level of a conversation consisting of a series of direct responses appears to limit itself strictly to questions and statements pertaining to the subject at hand. I think of this exchange as direct discourse because of its form—a series of declarative sentences and questions with little in the way of metaphor, visual imagery, irony, wit, syntactical variety, and so on. And yet direct discourse may succeed in conveying a truth that can only be created in this form of exchange.

I will now turn to an analytic experience in which direct discourse played a prominent role in creating an experience of the truth, which evolved in the course of the analysis.

In the early stages of analytic work, Ms V described the neglect and verbal abuse that she had received at the hands of her mother, and the isolation she experienced in response to the absence of her father, who was home only briefly between lecture tours. Once she had given me all the "history" that she could "recall", she felt at a loss regarding "what more to say". She then adopted a pattern of describing in detail the events that had occurred in the interval between her sessions.

After more than a year of this five-sessions-per-week analysis, I was reminded, as Ms V was talking, of a comment made by a beloved, deceased mentor of mine who had said that when this sort of description of daily life went on too long, he felt tempted to say, "And how much salt, Mrs Jones, did you say you put on your green beans?" I was struck for the first time, as the remark came to me during this session with Ms V, that it was addressed to "Mrs Jones", an imaginary patient—it was a joke, after all—but the fact that it was not addressed to a real patient caught my attention.

The deprecating nature of my mentor's comment also struck me in a way that was different from the ways it had before, in that it resonated with my already growing feeling that Ms V's listing of her activities was meant to provoke anger in me. It seemed to me that the patient was unable to experience feelings of her own and was trying to evoke them in me in her stead—most prominently, feelings of anger and despair. The importance of my recalling my mentor's comment at that particular juncture, in conjunction with intense feelings of missing him, led me to bring into focus for myself how lonely I felt while sitting with Ms V.

As these thoughts and feelings came to me during the course of the second year of analysis, I found myself talking to Ms V in a way that was unusual for me. I repeatedly asked her to tell me what she was feeling during one of the seemingly endless series of events she was describing—for example, by enquiring, "How did you feel when J [a man she had been dating for six months] was yelling at you?"

The patient would give me one-word replies to my questions, such as "angry", "scared", "disappointed", and "horrified". I said to Ms V in exasperation at one point, "You're naming a feeling, and then saying nothing further about it, feels as if you're trying to provoke anger in me, which would result in my feeling something that would substitute for your having a feeling of your own."

Ms V said, without pause, "That's right. I do that a lot." This response seemed to me at the time to be a continuation of the patient's provocations. I recognised that, in my persistent questioning of Ms V, I was trying to get blood from a stone, just as she had attempted in vain to extract love from her mother and father. Even though my comment was in some ways accurate, it failed to capture the truth of the moment because it was spoken in a way that was belittling of the patient.

One day during this period of analysis, in response to the patient telling me she felt "sad" when a friend said she was unable to attend an event with her, I asked, "Did you really feel sad?"

Ms V was silent for some time, which was unusual for her. She then said, "When you ask me how I'm feeling, I say what I think a person should feel, or what I think you think I should be feeling, but I really don't feel anything." I said, "What you're saying to me now seems to me to be one of the first truthful things you've ever said to me." The patient said, "Yes, it feels that way to me, too." I asked, "Do you really believe that?" She said, "I don't know." The sound of the patient's voice, as she spoke those words, felt sadly true to me.

In this period of work with Ms V, there was a predominance of direct discourse ("What are you feeling?" "Anxious."). There were many ways in which the patient and I were protecting ourselves from the truth of the emptiness and despair of the situation we were in. She tried to elicit, sometimes successfully, anger-filled statements from me that helped her experience my statements as expressions of emotions she felt incapable of feeling and felt she should be feeling. For my part, I engaged in imaginary conversation with my mentor with whom I had had a real exchange of thoughts and feelings, though it was significant that this "conversation" was with a person who was dead.

Once Ms V and I became better able to talk with one another about her feeling that she was unable to feel emotion, our conversations felt more real and alive. She said at one point, "My father was a somebody, I'm a nobody." Ms V had not been aware, until the words came out of her mouth, of the double meaning of the word "nobody" in her sentence. This was one of many instances in which Ms V's way of talking became more interesting in this period of analytic work. Words carried layers of meaning, when earlier they had felt as if they carried only literal meaning or less than literal meaning (empty verbiage). Direct discourse began to be infused with life as it was spoken with a feeling that rang true ("I don't know [if I believe what I said]") and gestured towards a truth not yet known (what is it for her to be nobody?). The form of our discourse—simple declarative sentences in which there was only sparse imagery, metaphor, wit, and the like—did not change very much at this juncture in the analysis. What changed was the way we spoke these rather unadorned sentences, and the range of feelings and ideas communicated and elicited by them.

Tangential discourse

When two people are engaged in what I am calling tangential discourse, responses on the part of both participants glance off "the subject" (in both senses of the word) and allude to other subjects, other meanings, other people. Metaphor, simile, irony, wit, ambiguity, hyperbole, unexpected word choice, syntactical shifts, errors in grammar or verb tense—all these events in language, and many more, make up the sorts of language usage found in the realm of tangential discourse. This type of discourse lives in the realm of metaphor, the realm of one feeling or idea or image becoming linked with (transferred to) another, and in so doing, creating new meaning in the space that is created between the two elements being linked to one another.

The word metaphor is derived from the Greek *meta* (across or beyond) and *pherein* (to bear or transfer). In tangential discourse, we carry meanings across or beyond the border of the apparent subject of conversation to another subject. Sometimes, in literature, a neologism performs this metaphorical work. For instance, Shakespeare, in *The Tempest* (1610), invented the word sea-change (1.2.400), for which I believe there is no translation. *The New Shorter Oxford English Dictionary* (1993) tells us that sea-change means "radical change" (p. 2742), but the word sea-change and the phrase radical change are not at all the same. It is impossible to find other words to express the meaning of sea-change, a word that alludes to the sea, but the sea is so many things: it is vast and powerful, it ebbs exactly as much as it flows, it kills and gives life, and so forth. Metaphor creates a space between the two things being compared, and in that space meanings proliferate.

So, too, in the case of dreams, we cannot say what a dream "really" means. Dreams are what they are. Like the metaphor embedded in the word sea-change, dreams allude to meaning but refuse to be reduced to a meaning or even a set of meanings. This is what is difficult and wondrous about dreams and reveries. They allude to unconscious meaning, but they never define it, spell it out, or serve as translations or decodings of it. They are predominantly a visual experience for which no words suffice as an expression of that experience. Dreams and reveries are metaphors for unconscious thoughts and feelings. We are dreaming all the time, both when we are awake and asleep (Bion, 1962), and consequently we are all the time engaged in metaphor-making.

In the act of dreaming, we carry meaning "beyond" the limits of one order of experiencing (the visual experience of dreaming the dream) to another (the largely verbal experience of "understanding" the dream) (Grotstein, 2000; Sandler, 1976). But I believe that the term understanding is a misnomer for what we do with our dreaming experience. We never know or understand unconscious experience because unconscious experience is, by definition, inaccessible to consciousness. I believe it is more accurate to say that we are sometimes able to experience metaphoric renderings of the unconscious, which spew meaning (often surprising and disturbing meaning) forward and backward in time. As is the case with a poem, there are no other words with which to say it, explain it, understand it, translate it, paraphrase it, or the like. A poem is immutably itself, as is a dream.

Turning now to tangential discourse in the analytic setting, I will present a fragment of an analysis that occurred at a time in which the patient, Mr Q, and I had come to know one another quite well over the course of many years of analysis. He was a reclusive man who, when he began analysis, seemed to have relationships exclusively with figures in his internal world; his relationship with me had consisted almost entirely of projections of those figures onto me and into me, which often led me to feel taken over by them in an oppressive way. He had told me in the beginning that, ideally, he would have an analysis in the form of slipping under my door a piece of paper on which he had written something he wanted to say, and after reading it, I would slip a piece of paper back under the door to him with my response written on it.

Several years into this analysis, I met Mr Q in the waiting room and said "Hi" to him, as I always did. When I said "Hi" (not "Hello") to Mr Q one morning, I was oddly aware that in saying "Hi" in the way I did, I was as usual trying to inject life into my voice, but was feeling the flatness of my attempt and was anticipating that I would get nothing in return from Mr Q. I was aware on that particular day that I did not use the patient's name as I greeted him. I rarely address patients by their name—first name or surname—so it was a mystery to me why I would notice that absence with Mr Q on that particular day.

All of this occurred as I said the word "Hi" and as Mr Q silently rose from his chair without looking at me. As I looked at him, his rising from his chair seemed almost begrudging, and yet I could feel that I liked him, even as I was feeling locked out by him.

In his usual way, he made no verbal response to my greeting, nor did he lift his gaze from the floor as he stood and led the way into my consulting room. Halfway to the couch, he mumbled, with his back to me, "How are you?"

It struck me, as he said these words, that in using the personal pronoun "you", he was, in a sense, speaking my name for the first time. I could not remember his ever using that pronoun in that way, much less asking me how I was. I did not know what I was going to say until I heard the words come from my mouth.

I began by saying, "I'm good." But on hearing those words, I felt a need to tell the patient that I recognised all that was entailed in his response to me, so I said (again without formulating it ahead of time), "I'm very good." I thought, after I said these words, that it would have been condescending to congratulate Mr Q for saying "How are you?", but in saying "I'm very good" I was telling him (in a somewhat disguised way) that I recognised the risk he had taken in expressing his recognition of me and the beginnings of his feeling concern for me.

I think of my "two-part response" to Mr Q's question as a direct response followed by a tangential one. The second part of the response, "I'm very good", glanced off the "subjects" of his question (me and my well-being) to say something about new "subjects" (Mr Q and his question).

My questions to myself, as I said "Hi" to Mr Q in the waiting room, reflected the ways in which I was unconsciously in a state of flux in my ability to face the truth of the ways I had closed myself off to Mr Q, perhaps out of fear of feeling humiliated by his turning his back on my feelings of affection for him. I had "known" that Mr Q had experienced the humiliation of having his love ignored and rejected by his mother, and that part of him had died as a result, but I had never really known his fear of being humiliated in this way until I felt subjected to a version of it myself.

My saying "I'm very good" offered a response to the unconscious meanings of his statement (in the form of a question), which meanings had to do with his hope that I would feel the truth of the highly personal event that was occurring, and would give him an equally personal and truthful response. My two-part response, "I'm good" and then "I'm very good", opened a space of its own (though not as striking and surprising a space as Mr Q's question/statement had opened). In the second part of my response, I reached for something more personal, something that felt as if it were made specifically for Mr Q under these circumstances. The space my two-part response opened was unique to Mr Q and me, and to our joint effort to say more of the truth than we had ever said before, without saying too much, too soon. It was an open invitation (and an invitation to open ourselves) to reach for more in our efforts to speak to one another the truth of our feelings for each other.

In the years that followed that exchange, Mr Q told me several times about how important that session was to him. He said that he had said "the question" to himself many times before he was able to say it to me. (His use of the words "the question" made me think of a wedding proposal, "popping the question".) Only at that point did I recognise that Mr Q's question was not the literal "How are you?" but rather the metaphorical "Who are you?" I wished I could have sensed that, and found a way of responding to it, years earlier when he asked me how I was.

In a session much later in our work, he said, "I didn't know you then. I didn't know what to expect. If you had just given me an impersonal or canned response, I don't know that I could have ever come back." In the silence that followed his saying this, I felt an intense feeling of sorrow. I could feel, and I think he could, too, that he was, without spelling it out, referring to his sense that he had died in childhood and would never completely "come back" from that.

In subsequent years, in this long analysis, Mr Q developed, or slowly showed me—I never could be sure which it was—a wry sense of humour. We laughed deeply together. On one occasion, I could not stop myself from laughing at several points later in the session when the mood of that earlier laughter returned to me. We both could feel at these times that he was feeling real and alive, emotions that until recently he had never experienced.

Discourse of non sequiturs

In the analytic setting, discourse in the form of non sequiturs is an extreme form of tangential discourse in which the connection between the two thoughts or feelings making up the (seeming) *non sequitur* pushes the envelope of comprehensibility; and yet the *non sequitur* manages to open a space in which previously unexpressed thoughts and feelings may be communicated. I use the word *seeming* to modify the term *non sequitur* because the gap between the two statements that form the *non sequitur* is unintelligible from the point of view of the conscious mind but intelligible, to some extent, from the point of view of the unconscious mind. I will not always use the word *seeming* to modify *non sequitur*, but the modifier is always implied.

The fact that the truth communicated in the form of a *non sequitur* is unconsciously grasped by patient and analyst, at least to some degree, does not mean that the psychic truth communicated in this way is not disturbing to both patient and analyst. Quite the contrary—unrecognised truths are unrecognised because they have been too painful to bear.

Communication by means of *non sequitur* is a form of discourse in which meaning is obliquely suggested. It requires that the two people engaged in this form of discourse (which never occurs in pure form) do a good deal of unconscious psychological work as they are encompassing, as a pair, the seemingly disconnected elements of the *non sequitur*. Such conversation has a deeply intimate quality. Only the two people engaged in this kind of discourse are able to experience the full range and depth of feeling encompassed by the way they are using language. An imaginary eavesdropper on this form of conversation hears primarily the conscious level of the communication (which makes "little sense") because patient and analyst are together generating and thinking about unconscious meanings that only they are privy to.

While non sequiturs both create and traverse a divide, that divide need not announce itself in an obvious way; it may go unnoticed consciously by the two people conversing, but it never goes unnoticed by them unconsciously.

What follows is a segment of dialogue in which discourse by *non sequitur* is the dominant, but by no means the only, form of discourse taking place. I have excerpted a portion of a much longer exchange that I have previously discussed in connection with the idea of working without memory or desire (Ogden, 2015). Here I will put in brackets my thoughts concerning the nature of the discourse taking place in this portion of the session.

I had been working with Ms C for several years in a five-sessions-per-week analysis when this exchange occurred. About a year before the analysis began, Ms C, who had no other children, had had a miscarriage four and a half months into her pregnancy, which had left her severely depressed. She felt that her body was telling her that she was unfit to be a mother. In the course of our work, Ms C's depression lifted significantly, but she still held steadfastly to the belief that she was unfit to be a mother. She doubted her capacity to love or to be worthy of anyone else's love, particularly the love of her dead baby.

On meeting Ms C in the waiting room, I had the feeling that she was in the wrong place, and that I should tell her politely that the person she had come to see was located in another building on the same block as mine. This feeling was particularly puzzling because I was fond of Ms C, and I almost always looked forward to seeing her for her sessions.

When the patient lay down on the couch that day, I had the impulse to say, "I love you." [These thoughts and feelings may seem odd to the reader, as they did to me, but they also felt natural to me at the time. There was not time to try to grasp in the moment what it meant that I was feeling that the patient was in the wrong place and should be seeing a therapist down the block, or to try to understand why I felt the impulse to tell her I loved her. I felt that I was in the grip of something I did not understand, but at the same time, I felt open to allowing these thoughts and feelings to take what course they would.]

In response to Ms C's telling me a dream in which she had lost something, but did not know what she had lost, I said, "Is loving me such a terrible thing that you have to leave it somewhere else when you come to see me?" [I had not planned to say this to the patient, but it felt true as I said it. Ms C and I were now talking with one another in a discourse of (seeming) non sequiturs in which unconscious truth linked what was left out of the manifest level of what we were saying to one another.]

Without pause, Ms C responded by saying, "You've never told me that you love me before." [Of course, I had not told her I loved her, but I had in fact imagined saying it to her. What I had actually told her in the sentence just cited was that I thought she felt that "loving me" was a "terrible thing" for her to bring into the room with me, so she left it somewhere else before coming to see me. This comment was a spontaneous (*non sequitur*) response to the patient's dream in which she lost something but did not know what it was; my comment was also informed by the feeling I had had in the waiting room that Ms C (her love) was in the wrong place and should be "down the street" with someone else.]

I said, "Would my love be in the wrong place if I were to love you?" [This *non sequitur* was my way of saying to Ms C (in the form of a semi-rhetorical question) that, despite her feelings to the contrary, it might be that she was worthy of my love, which in this moment was inseparable from being worthy of the love of her dead baby.]

The patient said, "Yes, I think it would, but I would feel empty if I were to give it back." [Here the patient was saying that my love (and her dead baby's love) would be misplaced if it were directed at her. But she was saying more than that. She was adding something very complex and ambiguous. Ms C was saying that she would feel empty if she could not accept my love (that is, if she were to "give it back" to me unreciprocated); and she would feel empty if she were able to reciprocate ("give back") my love. Why she would feel empty if she were to reciprocate my love and her baby's love was still a mystery.]

Because my commentary disrupts the flow of (seeming) non sequiturs, I will provide the uninterrupted dialogue in order to recreate something closer to my experience in the session:

In response to Ms C's telling me a dream in which she had lost something, but did not know what she had lost, I said, "Is loving me such a terrible thing that you have to leave it somewhere else when you come to see me?"

Without pause, Ms C responded by saying, "You've never told me that you love me before."

I said, "Would my love be in the wrong place if I were to love you?"

Ms C said, "Yes, I think it would, but I would feel empty if I were to give it back."

Without the unconscious linkages underlying this series of non sequiturs, the exchange is baffling. But even when I add to the sentences that the patient and I actually spoke—add my own unspoken thoughts and feelings, and my very tentative grasp of what was happening at an unconscious level in this dialogue—there remains much that is "unexplained". This is so because unconscious thoughts and feelings are "inexplicable"—untranslatable into conscious, secondary-process narratives. Discourse in the form of *non sequitur*, I believe, closely reflects unconscious experience because, in a discourse of non sequiturs, there are far fewer linkages between lived experience and verbally symbolic meaning than in direct discourse, or even in tangential discourse. So much more is left to the imagination in this form of discourse. The "commentary" I have offered in my discussion of the very brief exchange between Ms C and me reads like a poor translation of an ancient language no longer spoken, but which is nonetheless the foundation of the language we are currently speaking.

Concluding comments

The way in which patient and analyst talk to one another (the form of discourse in which they engage) is not simply a way of conveying the truth of what is happening at a given moment in the session; the experience of talking together in a particular way (the experience of a particular form of discourse) is itself an integral part of the truth of what is occurring at that moment in the session. I have discussed three forms of discourse in the analytic setting—direct discourse, tangential discourse, and discourse in the form of *non sequitur*. Each of these forms of discourse involves a different form of closeness between patient and analyst, none necessarily involving greater intimacy than the others, but each involving a different type of intimacy.

The truth in the analytic setting is extremely difficult and painful to experience and express, for the truth that the patient seeks when asking an analyst for help is the truth of experiences that were unbearable when they occurred and remain unbearable. Every analytic pair is engaged from the outset in the task of creating a way of talking together that is adequate to give expression both to the patient's fear of the truth and to the patient's need to know the truth of his or her experience.

References

Bion, W. R. (1962). *Learning from Experience*. London: Tavistock.
Grotstein, J. S. (2000). *Who Is the Dreamer Who Dreams the Dream? A Study of Psychic Presences*. Hillsdale, NJ: Analytic Press.
Ogden, T. H. (1997). Reverie and interpretation. *Psychoanalytic Quarterly*, *66*: 567–595.
Ogden, T. H. (2004). This art of psychoanalysis: Dreaming undreamt dreams and interrupted cries. *International Journal of Psychoanalysis*, *85*: 857–878.
Ogden, T. H. (2007). On talking-as-dreaming. *International Journal of Psychoanalysis*, *88*: 575–589.
Ogden, T. H. (2014). Fear of breakdown and the unlived life. *International Journal of Psychoanalysis*, *95*: 205–224.
Ogden, T. H. (2015). Intuiting the truth of what's happening: On Bion's "Notes on memory and desire". *Psychoanalytic Quarterly*, *84*: 285–306.
Sandler, J. (1976). Dreams, unconscious fantasies and "identity of perception". *International Review of Psycho-Analysis*, *3*: 33–42.
Shakespeare, W. (1610). *The Tempest*. In: *The Comedies of William Shakespeare*. New York: Modern Library, 1994.
The New Shorter Oxford English Dictionary (1993). Oxford: Clarendon.
Winnicott, D. W. (1974). Fear of breakdown. *International Review of Psycho-Analysis*, *1*: 103–107.

CHAPTER 2

Belief and psychic reality*

Ronald Britton

We call a belief an illusion when a wish-fulfilment is a prominent factor in its motivation.
—Freud (1927c, p. 31)

After writing this paper several people have pointed out to me that surprisingly little exists in the psychoanalytic literature on the subject of belief. It is surprising because the daily work of psychoanalysts includes the exploration of their patients' conscious and unconscious beliefs. It is also a continuous task for practising analysts to examine, as best they can, their own. It seems to be the case that not only the exploration of beliefs in daily psychoanalytic practice is taken for granted, but also the role of belief in everyday life. Our moment-to-moment sense of security depends on our belief in the well-being of ourselves, our loved ones and our valued objects. Belief rests on probability, not certainty, and yet it produces the emotional state that goes with certainty. The state of mind consequent on losing the security of

* This chapter was originally published as Britton, R. (1998). Belief and psychic reality. In: *Belief and Imagination: Explorations in Psychoanalysis* (pp. 8–18). Hove, UK: Routledge.

belief is one in which anyone might find themselves; some unfortunate individuals live constantly in doubt of everyday beliefs. They are often the same people who are afflicted with beliefs of which they cannot rid themselves with the aid of reality. One so afflicted I will describe later in this chapter, who believed she would go blind if she did not see her mother, who in fact was dead.

A belief in a specific impending calamity may be unconscious, so that we are anxious without knowing why. If we have an unconscious belief that someone has betrayed us, we hate them without apparent cause; if we believe unconsciously that we have done them an injury we feel guilt towards them for no obvious reason. Psychopathology can, in this way, be a result of the nature of unconscious beliefs and we might describe this as neurosis. There can also be, I think, disorders of the belief function itself. It is the latter that I will concentrate on mainly in this chapter, but first I need to make clear my ideas on the role and place of belief in mental life, and to explain what I mean by psychic reality.

I will itemise the description of the steps in the development and testing of beliefs for the reader to use as a guide to the rest of this chapter:

- Phantasies are generated and persist unconsciously from infancy onwards.
- The status of belief is conferred on some pre-existing phantasies, which then have emotional and behavioural consequences which otherwise they do not. Beliefs may be unconscious and yet exert effects.
- When belief is attached to a phantasy or idea, initially it is treated as a fact. The realisation that it is a belief is a secondary process which depends on viewing the belief from outside the system of the belief itself. This depends on internal objectivity, which in turn depends on the individual finding a third position from which to view his or her subjective belief about the object concerned. This, I think, depends on the internalisation and tolerance of the early Oedipus situation.
- Once it is conscious and recognised to be a belief it can be tested against perception, memory, known facts, and other existing beliefs.
- When a belief fails the test of reality it has to be relinquished, in the same sense that an object has to be relinquished when it ceases to exist. As a lost object has to be mourned by the repeated discovery of its disappearance, so a lost belief has to be mourned by the

repeated discovery of its invalidity. This, in analysis, constitutes part of working through.

- The repression of a belief renders the particular belief unconscious but does not abolish some of its effects. Other measures that are taken to deal with threatening beliefs are directed at the belief function itself. Counter-beliefs may usurp the place of disturbing beliefs, creating an alternative to psychic reality, as in mania. The function of belief may be suspended, producing a pervading sense of evenly distributed psychic unreality, as in the "as-if" syndrome; or the apparatus of belief may be destroyed or dismantled, as may be found in some psychotic states.
- What is perceived requires belief to become knowledge. Disbelief can therefore be used as a defence against either phantasies or perceptions.

Psychic reality

In 1897 Freud wrote: "Belief (and doubt) is a phenomenon that belongs wholly to the system of the ego (the Cs. [the conscious]) and has no counterpart in the Ucs. [the unconscious]" (Freud, 1897, pp. 255–256). He equated belief with "a judgement of reality" (Freud, 1895d, p. 333). "If after the conclusion of the act of thought the indication of reality reaches the perception, then a judgement of reality, belief has been achieved" (ibid., p. 313). In addition to the physical senses, "indications of reality" could be achieved through speech, but this would apply only to "thought reality", which was different from "external reality" (ibid., p. 373).

This difference between thought reality and external reality is his first formulation of this crucial distinction: "Psychical reality is a particular form of existence not to be confused with material reality" (Freud, 1900a, p. 620). He did not subsequently describe belief as a process in his writing, leaving it in place in his theoretical account of psychic function as something accomplished by conferring the status of reality on perceptions and thoughts. He was convinced that this function was located in the "system of the ego" (Freud, 1897, p. 255); he never changed that opinion and was adamant that the system *Ucs*, later called the id, knew nothing of belief, reality, contradiction, space, or time (Freud, 1933a, p. 74). Unlike the id, he thought the "Ego has the character of *Pcpt.-Cs.* [perception]", which places all its material in space and time (ibid., p. 75).

Freud returned repeatedly to Kant's philosophical assertion that space and time are necessary forms of the human mind, claiming that the system unconscious did not conform to the philosopher's theorem, but that the ego, because of its roots in the conscious perceptual apparatus, necessarily disposed itself in conformity with that system's construction of space and time. I suggest that our beliefs necessarily conform to this construction of space/time, as does what we describe as our "imagination", in which we locate some phantasies.

When he wrote about belief in 1897, Freud equated the ego with consciousness. By the time he wrote *The Ego and the Id* he was quite clear that "A part of the ego ... undoubtedly is Ucs" (Freud, 1923b, p. 18), and he regarded mental processes as themselves unconscious (Freud, 1915e, p. 171). I take believing to be such a process, and therefore unconscious, and I think that the resulting beliefs may become conscious, remain unconscious, or become unconscious.

Freud, having established the term psychic reality, somewhat confuses the issue by the way he uses it in two senses. He does the same with "internal reality" as he does with "external reality". Following Kant, he regards the thing in itself as unknowable, the noumenon, and the reality experienced, that is, created by perception (ibid., p. 171). Sometimes when he refers to reality he means the thing in itself and sometimes he means perceptual reality. In the same way, sometimes he equates psychic reality with an unknowable unconscious system: "The unconscious", he wrote, "is the true psychical reality; in its innermost nature it is as much unknown to us as the reality of the external world" (Freud, 1900a, p. 613).

At other times he means psychic reality to be something created by the "judgement of reality, belief" (Freud, 1895d, p. 333). It is in this latter sense that I am using psychic reality—that is, as that which is created by belief—and I regard belief as the function that confers the status of reality on to phantasies and ideas. I suggest that belief is to psychic reality what perception is to material reality. Belief gives the force of reality to that which is psychic, just as perception does to that which is physical. Like perception, belief is an active process, and, like perception, it is influenced by desire, fear, and expectation—and, just as perceptions can be denied, so beliefs can be disavowed. Freud thought that in neurosis belief was "refused to repressed material" and displaced "on to the defending material" (Freud, 1897, pp. 255–256). I am modifying this by making use of his later notion of an unconscious ego to suggest that there are repressed beliefs which may produce neurotic symptoms.

Beliefs have consequences: they arouse feelings, influence perceptions, and promote actions. Phantasies, conscious or unconscious, which are not the object of belief do not have consequences: disavowal therefore can be used to evade these consequences. Unconscious beliefs have consequences, so we feel and act quite often for no apparent reason and may find a spurious reason to explain our feelings and actions. Rationalisation is the artefact of a constructed logical justification for a strongly held conviction that is really based on an unconscious belief.

The role and place of belief

I regard the epistemophilic instinct (*Wissentrieb*) to be on a par with and independent of the other instincts; in other words, I think that the desire for knowledge exists alongside love and hate. Human beings have an urge to love, to hate, to know, and a desire to be loved, a fear of being hated, and a wish to be understood. Unlike Freud and Klein, I do not think of *Wissentrieb* as a component instinct, but as an instinct with components. Exploration, recognition, and belief are among such components. They can be thought of as mental counterparts of basic biological functions such as molecular recognition and binding.

We need to believe in order to act and react, and a good deal of the time we have to do so without knowledge. I think that we believe in ideas in a similar way to that in which we "cathect" objects. A belief is a phantasy invested with the qualities of a psychic object and believing is a form of object relating. I think belief, as an act, is in the realm of knowledge, what attachment is in the realm of love. The language of belief is clearly cast in the language of a relationship. We embrace beliefs or surrender to them; we hold beliefs and we abandon them; sometimes we feel that we betray them. There are times when we are in the grip of a belief, held captive by it, feel persecuted by it, or are possessed by it. We relinquish our most deeply held beliefs, as we relinquish our deepest personal relationships, only through a process of mourning. It is my observation that those people who have difficulty relinquishing objects have difficulty relinquishing beliefs.

Belief and knowledge

To believe something is not the same as to know it. The following philosophical distinction is helpful and relevant, not only in theory, but also in analytic practice. Belief is defined as:

> The epistemic attitude of holding a proposition p to be true where there is some degree of evidence, though not conclusive evidence, for the truth of p ... while knowing p would generally be considered to entail ... that p is true, believing p is consistent with the actual falsity of p. (Flew, 1979, p. 38)

My purpose in offering a philosophical dictionary definition of the term "belief" is not to enter into a philosophical discussion of the concepts of belief and knowledge, but to provide an acceptable description of the word "belief". In ordinary usage we happily describe someone as believing something even if we are aware that what they believe is not the case. We would not describe them as knowing something if we were aware that what they believed was untrue; in both philosophy and common speech the use of the two words differs. My reason for emphasising this point is that claiming to know something means that one asserts that it is incontrovertibly true, whereas stating that one believes something is saying that one takes it to be true but accepts the possibility that it may not be true. However, our emotional reactions and often also our actions do not wait for knowledge but are based on belief. In other words, we are apt initially to treat believing as knowing and beliefs as facts. We are captives of our beliefs while we regard them as knowledge, never more so than when they are unconscious; the realisation that they are only beliefs is an act of emancipation. I think that such psychic emancipation is a function of psychoanalysis. Only through psychic development do we recognise that we actively believe something and that we are not simply in the presence of facts. This recognition is a first stage in the relinquishment of a redundant belief as it admits the possibility of doubt. Cognitive, scientific, and cultural development is not simply the acquisition of new ideas but an act of emancipation from pre-existing beliefs. I suggest that this involves the bringing together of subjective experience with objective self-awareness so that one sees oneself in the act of believing something. This depends on internal triangulation, and that in turn requires the toleration of an internal version of the oedipal situation. I suggest that the recognition that one has a belief rather than that one is in possession of a fact requires what I describe as triangular psychic space—a third position in mental space is needed from which the subjective self can be observed having a relationship with an idea.

In the model I am proposing subjective belief comes first before objective evaluation or reality testing. Objective evaluation may use external perception, in reality testing, or it may simply involve correlation internally with known facts or related beliefs. The internal objective evaluation of a subjective belief is particularly crucial in situations where direct perceptual confirmation is not possible. It depends on two processes, both of which provoke resistance. One is the correlation of subjective and objective points of view, and the other is the relinquishment of an existing belief. The former involves the oedipal triangle and the latter mourning.

Just as beliefs require sensory confirmation (reality testing) in order to become knowledge, so what is perceived requires belief to be regarded as knowledge. Seeing is not necessarily believing. Disbelief can be used, therefore, as a defence against both phantasies and perceptions, and it plays a familiar role in neurosis and everyday life, where it is usually called denial. It can also be a manifestation of aversion towards otherness. If any cognitive tie outside the existing belief system of the self is treated as a dangerous link to something alien, then all such mental links may be destroyed, as Bion described in his paper "Attacks on linking" (1959). This may eliminate the capacity for belief in anything.

A state in which belief is treated as knowledge is usually described as omniscience, and the resultant beliefs as delusions. However, initially in my scheme of mental events beliefs are taken to be facts, and I would not describe this as delusional, but as naive, just as I would not call infantile mentation psychotic just because adults who use it are psychotic. It would be more useful to describe delusion belief which is treated axiomatically as knowledge even though it runs counter to perceived reality. My starting point in this business of considering belief was, like Descartes', the realisation that I had held in the course of my life, without question, fallacious beliefs. Descartes wrote in his *First Meditation*:

"Some years ago I was struck by the large number of falsehoods that I had accepted as true in my childhood, and by the doubtful nature of the whole edifice that I had subsequently based on them" (quoted in Ayer & O'Grady, 1992, p. 111).

For me, the doubtful edifice I accepted without question as a young child included the existence of God. As a child I did not realise until I first encountered the word "atheist" that I believed in God; until that moment I thought God was a fact. There was an unnerving precedent for this discovery, which was that at a much earlier age I met a child sceptic, and it was only then I realised that Father Christmas was not a fact but a belief of mine. This transition from assumed knowledge to belief was to be followed eventually by disbelief. I can remember thinking when my friend shocked me by telling me what an atheist was, "I hope this doesn't turn out to be like Father Christmas." It needed the discovery that it was possible not to believe to discover that I had a belief and did not know a fact. It is the shift from thinking one knows a fact to realising that one has a belief which is linked to self-awareness.

Before discussing the psychopathology of belief, I will summarise the sequence I have been describing. The unconscious that is there all along, as Freud thought of it, is unknowable, and contains phantasies which are unreconciled with each other and uncontaminated by beliefs about the outside world. From this source arise ideas that may become the objects of belief. Once ideas become beliefs they have consequences. Beliefs may be conscious or unconscious, but they cannot be tested or relinquished without becoming conscious. Beliefs require reality testing to become knowledge. Reality testing occurs through perception of the external world or through internal correlation with already known facts and other beliefs. If subsequent experience and knowledge discredit a belief it needs to be relinquished; this requires a process of mourning if it is an important or precious belief.

Disorders of the belief function

In addition to disorders arising from the content or denial of particular beliefs, there are disorders of the belief function itself that give rise to psychic impairments.

The annihilation of the function of belief

This is a drastic measure. It can be found in severe psychoses, in which ordinary belief systems are lost and normal thinking unavailable. Belief, conscious and unconscious, is necessary for a sense of psychic reality. If this function is annihilated the ordinary unthought sense of certainty of self-continuity and the everydayness of the perceived world is lost. The individual is then detached, not simply from external reality, but also from psychic reality. Everything is possible and nothing is probable. Delusional certainty may be substituted to fill the void in some cases, as Freud suggested in the Schreber case (Freud, 1911c). In such cases belief is asserted to be knowledge and it may also be imposed on perception, resulting in hallucination. In other psychotic states an arbitrary—sometimes capricious—kaleidoscope of ideas floats freely, untethered by belief, giving a facile, often foolish quality to thinking.

Presumably the belief function may be undeveloped or impaired because its basis in brain function is not intact; in other words, the "hardware" may be defective. In other instances, the "software" may have been deleted; that is, the mental apparatus of belief may have been dismantled or destroyed to abolish any attachment to ideas. I think this dismantling is analogous to abolishing emotional ties to all objects, thereby producing a loss of a sense of reality; similarly, abolition of the capacity to believe produces a loss of a sense of psychic reality.

The suspension of belief

In a footnote to *Studies on Hysteria* Freud drew attention to a state of mind which he described as the "blindness of the seeing eye", in which "one knows and does not know a thing at the same time" (Freud, 1895d, p. 117). Later he was to use the noun *Verleugnung* to describe this non-psychotic form of denial, which Strachey translated as "disavowal" (Freud, 1924e, 1927c, 1940e). I am suggesting that the suspension of belief is a non-psychotic form of disavowal in which one believes and does not believe a thing at the same time. Coleridge suggested that in order to be enthralled by drama we willingly suspend disbelief, thus conferring a sense of reality on what we know to be unreal (Coleridge, 1968, p. 6). I suggest that in certain psychic states of everyday life and analysis the reverse takes place. Belief is willingly suspended to avoid the emotional consequences, and the resultant state is one of psychic unreality. This may be an intermittent phenomenon temporarily arising in analysis to deal with emerging beliefs, or it may be persistent and pervasive.

If disavowal is all-pervasive, it manifests itself in the state of inconsequentiality that is found clinically in the as-if personality. In this state all beliefs are treated as is recommended for religious beliefs in the as-if philosophy. Vaihinger suggested that although religious beliefs were now untenable in a scientific age they could be maintained on an as-if basis—that is, "they perish only as theoretical truths; as practical fictions we leave them all intact" (Vaihinger, 1911, quoted in Freud, 1927c, p. 29, fn.). Therefore, in the analysis of a patient in such a state, interpretation (the analyst's belief) or insight (the patient's belief) can be treated as only practical fictions, useful but not truthful. Belief as a function is thereby suspended along with disbelief, and phantasies are treated as neither true nor untrue—or, more accurately, true and untrue. It is the either/and state of mind evading either/or. Not only is belief suspended, but so are its emotional consequences, and calmness is purchased at the price of a prevailing sense of unreality. Ambiguity is used as a defence against ambivalence. The place in the mind sought or created by this suspension of belief is, I think, related to Winnicott's notion of transitional space, which he described as "an intermediate area of experience which is not challenged (arts, religion, etc.)" (Winnicott, 1951, p. 240).

It is not challenged with a question as to whether its contents were conceived or found. This, I think, is a space where the question "Do you believe it?" is not to be asked. An individual who spends his life in such an area could be described as an as-if personality.

Counter-belief

Counter-beliefs may be produced as a defence against the unconscious beliefs that constitute the individual's psychic reality. As Winnicott said in his paper on the "manic defence", "Omnipotent fantasies are not so much the inner reality itself as a defence against the acceptance of it" (Winnicott, 1935, p. 130). If wish-fulfilling beliefs are used to serve the defensive purpose of denying psychic reality, anxiety increases the tenacity with which they are held. Considerable violence may be used to enforce such beliefs and to prevent their being challenged and discredited. Many political and religious beliefs fall into this category. Such counter-beliefs are at the heart of pathological organisations. I find very convincing Freud's definition from *The Future of an Illusion*, quoted at the head of this chapter: "Thus we call a belief an illusion when a wish-fulfilment is a prominent factor in its motivation, and in doing so we disregard its relations to reality, just as the illusion itself sets no store by verification" (Freud, 1927c, p. 31). To this I would add that an illusional belief sets no store by psychic reality and thus creates psychic unreality.

The conclusion I come to differs in one regard from that of Freud on the subject of religion. Some religious beliefs are illusional in the sense that they are the products of wish-fulfilling beliefs running counter to psychic reality, but others, even though based on psychic and not external reality, still seek the truth. This is also the case with fiction; some fiction is true, and some is false.

Some counter-beliefs form the basis of transference illusions, which defend the patient from the psychic reality of transference fears, conflicts, or pain. For example, the following typical counter-belief was found in the analysis of a young woman patient. The patient believed that she (as daughter) shared a special analytic understanding (secret relationship) with her analyst (as father) which his wife (as mother) and other patients (as her siblings) did not possess. This wish-fulfilling counter-belief defended the patient from believing her existing phantasies associated with exclusion from the parental relationship. It produced complacency and stasis; her relinquishment of this counter-belief was followed by the emotional flux one hopes to meet in analysis.

The failure to relinquish belief

Relinquishing beliefs involves mourning; I have found that those who are unable to relinquish their discredited beliefs are the same people who cannot relinquish their lost objects. The relinquishment of the lost object is linked with realising and tolerating the distinction between what is mental and what is material. The maintenance of the differentiation between belief and knowledge is also linked with realising and tolerating this distinction. Thus, the person who cannot make a distinction between belief and knowledge is unable to give up beliefs. To conclude, therefore, I will briefly describe a patient who could have been said to suffer from a surfeit of beliefs that were immune to the experience of reality.

The patient, Miss A, could not hold to the distinction between belief and knowledge. She could not derive any security from belief unless she regarded it as knowledge; probability did not exist for her, only possibility or certainty. Unless, therefore, she believed she knew her object's exact whereabouts she was in a panic. For this reason, she developed elaborate strategies to avoid any occasion that would prompt her to doubt for a moment that she knew the whereabouts of her primary object. This meant manipulating not only her environment but also her mind. Her ultimate weapon against uncertainty was a system of counter-beliefs which she treated as knowledge. These counter-beliefs, in turn, plagued her as they had dire consequences. One such counter-belief was that she would go blind. From childhood her greatest fear was the fate of her mother if she was "out of sight". Her mother's continuing existence "out of sight" meant she was "in the other room". The "other room" was her parents' room, the setting of the primal scene, which for this patient was a murderous scenario.

The counter-belief she mounted as protection from her own phantasy was that her mother was not out of sight but that she herself was blind. This then became the belief that unless she saw her mother she would go blind. Finally, it took the form "if my mother dies I will go blind". This was the form in which it emerged in the transference, when she believed that my disappearance would cause her blindness. The only means of ridding herself of this belief was to take a number of physical actions representing evacuation of her mind symbolically, such as flushing the toilet repeatedly.

There was compelling evidence that this inability to relinquish a belief was parallel with an inability to relinquish her object. Following the death of her mother, while she accepted the external reality of this event, she could not accept it psychically. She perceived her mother's absence, she knew of her death, but she did not believe it. Her fearful delusion soon returned; once more she believed that if she did not see her mother she would go blind. This counter-belief was now a means of denying the reality of her mother's death.

My patient's pathological mourning resembled a situation described by Hanna Segal (1994, p. 397); her idea of her mother was like a dead concrete object inside her, not a symbolic presence, and therefore could only be revived in the flesh and not in spirit. Freud wrote: "The distinction between imagination and reality is effaced … when the symbol takes over the full functions of the thing it symbolises" (Freud, 1919h, p. 244). He went on to link this with "the over-accentuation of psychical reality in comparison with material reality—a feature closely allied to the belief in the omnipotence of thoughts" (ibid.). Hanna Segal's (1957) work on the failure of symbolisation clarified this phenomenon when she linked it to a failure to work through the depressive position, and hence an inability to achieve normal mourning.

I think there are complex reasons why particular individuals have problems distinguishing material from psychic reality, symbol from object, and belief from knowledge. By relinquishing objects, I do not mean simply accepting the fact of their loss but, rather, accepting all the necessary changes in beliefs about the world that follow from that loss. One such belief which has to be relinquished is that the lost object is indispensable to life. In that sense, some people have the same difficulty with beliefs as they do with objects: they cannot accept that their beliefs are not indispensable to them.

References

Ayer, A. J., & O'Grady, J. (1992). *Dictionary of Philosophical Quotations*. Oxford: Blackwell.

Bion, W. R. (1959). Attacks on linking. *International Journal of Psychoanalysis*, *40*: 308–315.

Coleridge, S. T. (1968). *The Notebooks of Samuel Taylor Coleridge (Vol. II)*. K. Coburn (Shawcross) (Ed.). London: Routledge & Kegan Paul.

Flew, A. (1979). *Dictionary of Philosophy*. London: Pan.

Freud, S., with Breuer, J. (1895d). *Studies on Hysteria*. *S. E.*, *2*: 313–373. London: Hogarth.

Freud, S. (1897). Letter to Wilhelm Fliess. *The Complete Letters of Sigmund Freud to Wilhelm Fliess, 1887–1904*. Cambridge, MA: Harvard University Press.

Freud, S. (1900a). *The Interpretation of Dreams*. *S. E.*, *4–5*. London: Hogarth.

Freud, S. (1911c). Psycho-analytic notes on an autobiographical account of a case of paranoia (dementia paranoides). *S. E.*, *12*: 82. London: Hogarth.

Freud, S. (1915e). The unconscious. *S. E., 14*: 159–215. London: Hogarth.
Freud, S. (1919h). The "uncanny". *S. E., 17*: 217–256. London: Hogarth.
Freud, S. (1923b). *The Ego and the Id. S. E., 19.* London: Hogarth.
Freud, S. (1924e). The loss of reality in neurosis and psychosis. *S. E., 19*: 183–187. London: Hogarth.
Freud, S. (1927c). *The Future of an Illusion. S. E., 21.* London: Hogarth.
Freud, S. (1933a). *New Introductory Lectures on Psycho-Analysis. S. E., 22.* London: Hogarth.
Freud, S. (1940e). Splitting of the ego in the process of defence. *S. E., 23*: 271–278. London: Hogarth.
Segal, H. (1957). Notes on symbol formation. *International Journal of Psychoanalysis, 38*: 391–397.
Segal, H. (1994). On symbolism. *International Journal of Psychoanalysis, 75*: 397–406.
Vaihinger, H. (1911). *The Philosophy of "As If": A System of the Theoretical, Practical and Religious Fictions of Mankind.* C. K. Ogden (Trans.). London: Kegan Paul, 1924.
Winnicott, D. W. (1935). The manic defence. *Collected Papers: Through Paediatrics to Psycho-Analysis.* London: Tavistock.
Winnicott, D. W. (1951). Transitional objects and transitional phenomena. *International Journal of Psychoanalysis, 34*: 89–97.

CHAPTER 3

Do unconscious phantasies really exist?*

Mark Solms

In psychoanalysis today, different analysts use the term "unconscious phantasy" to refer to different things. This is bound to lead to confusion. In this paper I will use the term in the sense that Melanie Klein and her followers used it with the aim of clarifying from a Freudian point of view what this thing that they call "unconscious phantasy" actually is, and whether it really exists.

Do unconscious phantasies really exist? This is not an idle question. When we use the word "phantasy", we do so in order to contrast it with something that we call "reality". That is the conventional meaning of the word "phantasy". We say: that thing is not real, it is only a phantasy. But unconscious phantasy is also supposed to be the basic stuff of what psychoanalysis is about. Unconscious phantasies (in the Kleinian sense of the term) are the essential object of study of psychoanalytic research; and a principal aim of psychoanalytic therapy is to make our patients aware of the unconscious phantasies that lead them to do and feel the things that bring them into treatment in the first place.

---

* This chapter was originally published as Solms, M. (2003). Do unconscious phantasies really exist? In: R. Steiner (Ed.), *Unconscious Phantasy* (pp. 89–106). London: Karnac.

Clearly, if phantasies are not real things, then everything that we do in this field makes little sense. But what do we mean when we say that something is not real? How exactly do we decide whether something is real or not?

To begin with, when we say that phantasies are not real, we mean that they don't have a physical existence in the world around us. In other words, we mean that we can't see them or hear them or touch them. If we can see or hear or touch something and, better still, smell it and taste it, too, then we have little doubt about its reality; if not, its reality is brought into question. So, one criterion for deciding whether something is real or not is: if we can perceive it through one or more of our external sensory modalities, then it really exists. I will call this our first criterion of reality.

This simple, conventional criterion is complicated by the fact that some people see and hear things that nobody else can see or hear. In these cases, we say that there is something wrong with their sense of reality. We don't call their perceptions "perceptions", we call them "hallucinations". Accordingly, hallucinations, being something "not real", are included under the heading of phantasy. The first criterion of reality therefore stands; we can still maintain that only things that we actually perceive really exist. But we need to add a second, qualifying criterion: we must say that something is real if, first of all, you can actually perceive it, and, in addition, everyone else can perceive it, too.

But what about introspective perceptions? What about emotions, for example—the purest form of internal perception. Aren't they real? If you learn that you have won the National Lottery, and you feel an exquisite sense of joy, is that not something real? Nobody can seriously deny that things like "joy" really exist, even if a feeling of joy is not accessible to public scrutiny. You may be the only one who can actually feel your own sense of joy, but that doesn't make it a hallucination. Clearly, we must concede that emotional feelings, too, are perceptions. They, too, refer to something real notwithstanding the fact that they are introspective perceptions—that is to say, conscious perceptions of a type that other people around us cannot share. And the same applies to memories.

This obviously undermines my second criterion of reality. I wrote that things that you can perceive and everybody around you can also perceive deserve to be described as real. We therefore need to modify further the criteria of reality, in order to take account of the phenomenological reality of internal perceptions. In doing so we immediately come to the nub of some of the most difficult theoretical problems that we confront in psychoanalysis. We have to draw a distinction between two kinds of reality. We have to say that there are things that we perceive in the external world around us, through our external sensory modalities (such as vision and hearing), and, in addition, we have to say that there are other things that we perceive within our own selves, through our internal sensory modalities (such as our emotions and memories). These things are equally real, even though only the externally perceived ones are reliably available to public scrutiny. We distinguish between these two things by speaking of external as opposed to internal reality.

Freud found a place for this basic distinction in the way that we perceive the world in his theoretical model of the mind by saying that consciousness registers perceptions on two sensory surfaces. One perceptual surface of consciousness is externally directed and registers reality in the form of material objects (through our external sensory modalities), whereas the other perceptual surface is internally directed and registers reality in a psychical form (through internal sensory modalities). This is the basis of Freud's fundamental theoretical distinction between what he called "material reality" on the one hand and "psychical reality" on the other. This theoretical distinction runs through every subsequent psychoanalytic model of the mind, right up to the present day, notwithstanding all of the disagreements in regard to other matters that have sprung up along the way. For example, Wilfred Bion, who in some respects is far removed theoretically from Freud, reserved a central place in his model of the mind for the distinction between what he called "reality sensual" and "reality psychic".

In accordance with this fundamental theoretical distinction, which does little more than formalise our ordinary, everyday experience, we need to specify the origin of a perception before we know what we really mean when we say that it is real. If a perception is stimulated from the outside and therefore is registered on the external sensory surface of consciousness, we say that it is materially real; whereas if the perception is stimulated from inside and therefore is registered on the internal surface of consciousness, we say that it is psychically real. This matter of the origin of a perception clarifies the earlier complication that was raised by the problem of hallucinations. Although they appear subjectively to have their origin in the outside world, hallucinations actually have their origin within us. They are only psychically real. This is where the mechanism that we call "reality testing" comes in; it determines the origin of a perception, and—all being well—thereby classifies it as internal or external.

So, the fundamental psychoanalytic concept of a "psychical reality" is completely synonymous with the concept of "inner reality" or an "internal world". The term "psychical reality" simply refers to the portion of reality that exists within us, the portion that we perceive by looking inwards, as opposed to the "material reality" that we perceive by looking outwards. The term "psychical reality" is therefore also synonymous with subjective as opposed to objective reality. Psychical reality exists within the subject and is perceived in the intangible form of thoughts and feelings, whereas material reality exists outside the subject, and is perceived in the tangible form of physical things (objects).

This distinction makes an enormous difference. Consider, for example, the difference between an external perception such as the objective perception of an alarm clock, and an internal perception such as the subjective feeling of depression. Because, as I wrote earlier, our external perceptions are shared by the people around us, we can all agree that something out there in the world at this point in time is indeed an alarm clock. In other words, we can all agree that it is not an hallucination. But who is to decide whether a feeling of depression that you perceive when you wake up one morning is an accurate perception of the things that are currently going on inside you? It is problematical to say that one person's feeling of depression is real whereas another person's depression is an hallucination.

With some modifications, the same applies to memories. If the two sole witnesses to an event recall that event completely differently, how do we decide whose memory is real? Here we have the essence of the current controversy about so-called "false memories". That controversy revolves around precisely the distinction that I am drawing here, between material (or objective) reality and psychical (or subjective) reality; that is, it revolves around the distinction between things that we believe to be real because we see them in front of us, and things that we believe to be real because we feel them inside ourselves. That is why I am saying that this distinction brings us to the nub of some of the most difficult theoretical problems that we confront in psychoanalysis.

Rather than deny the reality of things such as depression, we in psychoanalysis have attempted to incorporate them into our picture of the natural world. As I have said, we have done so by proposing (with Freud) that consciousness has two perceptual surfaces, one of which is directed outward and registers the world around us in the form of material objects, while the other is directed inward and registers the world within us in a psychical form. Just as physical scientists study the things that are perceived on the outer surface of consciousness, psychoanalysts study the things that are perceived on the inner surface of consciousness. On this basis, we proceed in the same way as any other science would in relation to any other object of study. We attempt to formulate a coherent understanding of the law—governed processes that organise our introspective perceptions, using appropriate methods. In so doing, we attempt to lay bare the natural processes that lie behind our internal perceptions, ultimately in order to be able to intervene in those processes and thereby alter the quality of life (that is, the subjective experiences) of people who are troubled by them.

Although at first sight this seems to be an obvious and straightforward way to proceed, in fact it gives rise to some extremely difficult problems. The most important of them is this: when I say that the reality around us is represented on the external perceptual surface of consciousness, whereas the reality within us is represented on its internal perceptual surface, what do I actually mean by "the reality within us"? I have indicated that I mean by this phrase the internal processes that generate our thoughts and feelings. But isn't it bodily processes, and specifically brain processes, that generate our internal perceptions? And doesn't that imply that the "reality within us" is, in fact, the physical reality of the body and the brain? And if it is true that the reality within us is the physical reality of the brain—which is a reality that can be seen and touched just like any other physical object—then why did Freud find it necessary to postulate the spooky thing called "psychical reality", and make it the fundamental object of study of a whole new branch of science? This attitude to the reality within us (namely, that it is a part of the physical world) is held by a good many serious and thoughtful medical and scientific colleagues, who choose to study and treat things like emotions and hallucinations by way of physical entities like neurotransmitters.

In order to understand why psychoanalysts have chosen instead to postulate a "psychical reality", we must return to the observations that led us to postulate its existence in the first place. We started from the observation that our perceptions of the world included things like joy and depression, which have particular perceptual qualities. We observed, in addition, that perceptions of this type can only arise from within our own selves. We cannot hear or touch depression, we can only feel it within ourselves. Other things, such as alarm clocks, the sounds they make, and the colours they assume, also have particular perceptual qualities—which we can only perceive through our external sensory organs. The sound of an alarm clock is quite unlike an emotion, and we can never feel the colour green arising from within us. These self-evident observations reflect a basic fact about reality and the way that we perceive it. We can only perceive the world in a limited variety of ways, which correspond to the limited properties of our different sensory modalities, the sense of vision and touch and so on. Each of those modalities arises from a sensory apparatus which occupies a fixed position in space. For this reason, it is in the nature of the modality called vision, for example, that it can only perceive processes that are external to the subject; and it is in the nature of the modality called emotion that it can only perceive processes that are internal to the subject.

Moreover, it is in the nature of the modality called vision that it can only represent the things it perceives in a particular way, that is, within the qualitative range that is appropriate to the visual sensory apparatus. In other words, it can only represent things in the form of light, colour, orientation, and so on. No matter what the actual properties might be of the thing that exists out there in the world, the visual modality can only represent that thing in a visual form, in the form of visual images. Similarly, it is in the nature of the modality called emotion that it can only represent the things that it perceives in a particular way, that is, within the qualitative range that is appropriate to the emotional apparatus. In other words, it can only represent things in the form of pleasure and unpleasure and so on. No matter what the actual properties might be of the things that exist deep within us, the emotional modality can only represent them in an emotional form, in the form of emotional states.

Let me illustrate these principles by way of a simple example. If you place an alarm clock in front of somebody, he can see, hear, and touch it, and, if he wants to, he can smell and taste it, too. Each of his external sensory modalities registers a different aspect of the alarm clock and represents it in its own particular way. As a result, the person doing the perceiving has five different representations of the thing that he calls an alarm clock. In accordance with convention, he would think of the alarm clock itself as being a combination of these five representations of it. But this is not strictly correct. Strictly speaking, it would be more correct for him to say that the alarm clock itself can never be perceived directly. The alarm clock itself is the origin of his five perceptual images of it; but it is not the images themselves. All that we can ever know about the alarm clock is the different perceptual representations of it that are generated by our five senses. If we had additional senses, we might be able to perceptually represent other properties of the alarm clock itself, and our image of what an alarm clock actually is might be completely different.

But we have to make do with what we have got; and on this basis we piece together our picture of the natural world by making inferences from our incomplete and untrustworthy perceptual representations of it; we attempt to know its real underlying properties. Of course, since we all do this all the time, we do it without even realising it. But when it comes to scientific observations we have to be more precise about what we really can and cannot know. That is why when a physicist, for example, looks at an alarm clock, or at one of its components, such as the quartz crystal that drives it, he is not content with a phenomenological description of its superficial, perceptual properties. Instead, he wants to know what lies behind the perceptual attributes of the object under examination. To this end, he makes use of artificial aids, such as electron microscopes, which extend the efficiency of his sense organs to the farthest possible extent, and he concludes that what appears to be a solid body of quartz is in fact made up of invisible entities, such as waves and energies, which possess certain fundamental properties and occupy certain relative positions.

Consider for a moment what all of this means for our attempts to define reality. I wrote previously that the first criterion for determining the reality of something depended upon whether or not we can actually perceive it. Now we have to significantly revise that criterion once again. We have to admit that it is not the things we perceive that are ultimately real, but rather the things that lie at the origin of our perceptions, the things that lie behind the perceptions. Moreover, the fundamental properties of those things can never be perceived directly, since we can never free ourselves from the decisive influence of the apparatus which is interposed between them and our perceptions of what we finally perceive. We can, therefore, only ever infer the fundamental properties of reality. We can never actually perceive them.

Not surprisingly, all of this applies to internal perceptions just as much as it does to external ones. We are capable of representing the things that occur inside us in different ways, depending on the sensory channels that are used for that purpose. Something that is going on in the depths of our selves can be represented visually if we look at it, or it can be represented emotionally if we feel it. Whether we see or feel the thing that is occurring inside us simply depends on which perceptual modality we use to represent it. Thus, one and the same thing—depression, for example—can be perceived as a subjective emotional state from one point of view and an objective chemical imbalance from another. If it is perceived through an internally directed perceptual modality (and registered on the inner surface of consciousness) it is a feeling state, whereas if it is perceived through an externally directed modality (and registered on the outer surface of consciousness) it is a material process.

In this respect the difference between our inner and outer perceptions is just the same as the differences between the various external sensory modalities. If one listens to something, one obtains one type of image of it, and if one looks at the same thing, one obtains a different type of image of it. Both images are perceptions of something real, although neither image is the underlying reality itself. However, given the fixed spatial orientation of the different sensory modalities, it so happens that one can only perceive one's own feeling states as feeling states, whereas the visual equivalent of those feelings, which take the form of neurochemical processes, can be scrutinised publicly. That is, the internal representation of your current inner state (your feelings) can be perceived by you alone, whereas the external representation of that same state (your neurochemistry) can be perceived by others around you. That is why we classify psychical perceptions (like memories and feelings) under the heading of internal reality, and material perceptions (like brains and chemicals) under the heading of external reality.

I will not delve into the complication introduced by the fact that we can indirectly perceive the feelings of another person as feelings in ourselves, by means of an intriguing process called "empathy". This process forms the basis of the modem concept of countertransference and suggests a surprisingly literal basis for the notion of a "sixth sense". We become aware of aspects of our patients' experience by directing our attention inwards. This underlines the fact that the internal perspective on reality occupies a fixed position in space; feelings (including those belonging to other people) can only be felt internally.

Two important implications flow from all this. One is that the feeling of depression and the neurochemical process that corresponds to it are in fact two different perceptual representations of the same underlying thing. The other is that the unitary underlying thing that generates both of these perceptual realisations is in fact neither an emotional feeling nor a visual image. Behind both the emotional feeling of depression and the visual image of the chemical process that corresponds to it, there lies something else, something which is independent of our perceptual modalities, and which can, in itself, never be perceived directly. Our conscious perceptions of this underlying reality are, and can only be, indirect representations of it. In other words, behind the different varieties of conscious perception there lies the actual stuff of reality, which is in itself non-perceptual, and therefore unconscious.

This has significant implications for psychoanalysis. It implies that the things that we study in psychoanalysis are in fact the very same things that are studied by our colleagues in the neurological sciences. The differences between these disciplines arise only from the fact that they use different perceptual channels to study that unitary underlying thing. Psychoanalysts study the workings of the mind through internally directed perceptual channels, whereas our colleagues in the neurological sciences study it through externally directed channels. Each of these two approaches to the underlying reality of the mind has strengths and weaknesses of its own, and these derive directly from the functional properties and spatial orientations of the perceptual channels upon which they depend. In relation to the problem that we are considering it is essential for us to recognise the inescapable conclusion that the things that we study in psychoanalysis are no less real in themselves than the things that are studied by neuroscientists. It is only our perceptual vantage points that are different. The underlying reality is the same. And this is the reality that we study in psychoanalysis.

The following short passage is from Freud's posthumously published essay entitled *An Outline of Psycho-Analysis*, in which he rather beautifully summarises the points that I have just been making:

> In our science as in the others the problem is the same: behind the attributes (qualities) of the object under examination which are presented directly to our perception, we have to discover something else which is more independent of the particular receptive capacity of our sense-organs and which approximates more closely to what may be supposed to be the real state of affairs. We have no hope of being able to reach the latter itself, since it is evident that everything new that we have inferred must nevertheless be translated back into the language of our perceptions, from which it is simply impossible to free ourselves. But herein lies the very nature and limitation of our science. It is as though we were to say in physics: "If we could see clearly enough we should find that what appears to be a solid body is made up of particles of such and such a shape and size occupying such and such relative positions." In the meantime, we try to increase the efficiency of our sense-organs to the farthest possible extent by artificial aids; but it may be expected that all such efforts will fail to affect the ultimate outcome. Reality in itself will always remain "unknowable". (Freud, 1940a, p. 196)

So that is the psychoanalytic method. It is an artificial aid which increases the efficiency of our internally directed perceptions to the farthest possible extent—just like the microscope does for the externally directed modality of vision—and it thereby enables us to perceive as clearly and accurately as possible the actual things that exist within us. But still the picture that we are left with is incomplete and untrustworthy, and still it is limited by the fundamental parameters of internal perception, from which it is simply impossible to free ourselves.

Before I pull the strands of my argument together, in order to clarify its implications for the problem of unconscious phantasy, I would like to take stock of the picture that has emerged so far. One way of studying the internal workings of the human mind is to examine it in the form in which it is represented materially, through our external perceptual apparatus—that is, as an anatomical phenomenon. Another way of studying the internal workings of the human mind is to examine it as it is represented psychically, through our internal perceptual apparatus, in the form of our subjective awareness. Either way, the thing that we are studying is entirely real. The scientific limitations that we face arise from the fact that we can only study that real thing indirectly, by way of the incomplete and untrustworthy images of which our perceptual modalities are capable. We in psychoanalysis study the human mind from the vantage point of subjective perception. We do this because that is where our patients locate their suffering, and because that is the perceptual window on the reality of the human being that science has hitherto neglected. If you think about the relationship between our perceptions of reality and reality itself and liken this situation to the tale about the blind men and the elephant (each palpated a different part of the elephant—long trunk, flat ear, rotund belly, skinny tail—and mistook its properties for those of the animal as a whole) then I am sure you will agree that there are significant advantages to be gained from studying the underlying reality within us from as many different vantage points as possible.

When Freud first began to study this portion of reality from the vantage point of introspective awareness, around 100 years ago, we obtained our initial bearings by relying on a simple map of our subject matter—which did little more than formalise the starting points of our investigation and attach scientific names to them. We pictured the mind as a compound apparatus, the most superficial portion of which was the inner surface of consciousness, which registered the processes going on within the mind in the form of subjective perceptions. Freud called this superficial surface the "system Conscious", and he called the hidden interior the "system Unconscious". These names signify the fundamental difference between the two systems—namely, that one of them cannot be perceived. With this simple map, he set about the arduous task of trying to infer what the properties of the hidden, unconscious reality of the mind must be in order for it to generate the manifest, conscious perceptions that it does. One of the first things that struck him in this regard was the fact that our subjective conscious perceptions—unlike our visual perceptions, for example—formed incomplete sequences, which were causally discontinuous. He therefore decided to study these breaks in the causal sequence, in order to isolate their typical antecedents and consequences. On this basis, he attempted to reconstruct the missing links in the psychical chain. His aim was to gain some impression of the complete sequence of underlying mental events.

In doing so, he was driven to conclude that the breaks in the sequence of perception did not occur randomly: he observed, for example, that the missing bits tended to be unpleasant, from the viewpoint of the perceiving subject. He also observed that whenever he tried to fill in the gaps by communicating the missing bits to the perceiving subject, the thoughts and feelings in question were immediately ejected once more from perceptual awareness. Freud called this clinical phenomenon "resistance". On this basis, he began to construct a theoretical picture of what the functional properties of the underlying processes must be. He observed, for example, that the underlying processes functioned according to a basic principle whereby all psychical material that was likely to arouse unpleasurable thoughts and feelings was kept away from consciousness. Freud called this the "pleasure principle". Next, he inferred that there must be a mechanism whereby this process of selective exclusion is achieved. He called this mechanism "repression". Then Freud looked at the exceptions to the rule that he had established; that is, he looked at the unpleasurable thoughts that did manage to enter perceptual awareness. This led him to distinguish between what he called the "primary and secondary processes" of the underlying apparatus (only the primary process obeys the pleasure principle exclusively). Proceeding in this way, piece by piece, and by continually revising his map, Freud gradually built up an extremely elaborate picture of how the underlying mental apparatus functioned. That is to say, he constructed a theoretical picture of what the perceptually unknowable reality must be that generates our subjective awareness.

According to that picture, the ultimate origins of the processes that end in subjective awareness are two fundamental biological forces, which ultimately cause the organism to react in all the different ways that it does in relation to the stimuli that impinge upon it. Freud called these the Life and Death "drives". These drives can never be perceived directly; they are theoretical entities, which we assume to be the fundamental properties of the unconscious—that is, of the unperceivable, underlying reality within us.

Between these fundamental drives and the superficial awareness of our thoughts and feelings lie a great many complex mechanisms, some of which I have already mentioned, such as reality-testing, repression, the pleasure principle, and the primary and secondary processes. Mechanisms such as these, which mediate between the innermost drives of the subject and the myriad stimuli that impinge upon it, are responsible for the great complexity of mental life.

I have said that the basic mechanisms of the mental apparatus which Freud inferred from the data of subjective awareness, such as those that I have just mentioned, are assumed to be the fundamental properties of the portion of reality that exists within us. These mechanisms can also be studied from an anatomical or a physiological viewpoint; that is to say, they can also be studied via external perceptual channels, as physical things. But we in psychoanalysis do not do that; rather, we study them from the vantage point of the introspective portion of the perceptual apparatus. The important point is that even though all of these underlying processes are—in themselves—no less unconscious and unperceivable than the drives are, and can therefore never be known directly, they are, nevertheless, the fundamental reality within us.

That is to say, they are the ultimate origin of all our introspective perceptions. In this respect, they have the same status in psychoanalysis as things like waves and energies have in physics. Our knowledge of the internal reality within us ultimately consists of these theoretical things. And nothing could be more real than these things, even though our knowledge of them is far from secure.

We are approaching the heart of the matter. In recognition of the fact that we can never directly perceive those things that generate our internal perceptions, we in (Freudian) psychoanalysis have traditionally described them in abstract, non-experiential terms. When Freud invented his abstract, mechanistic language, known as metapsychology, he was attempting to describe the unknowable depths of the mind in a language that was—in the words of the quotation given a few pages above—as far as possible "independent of the particular receptive capacity of our sense organs". The aim of doing this was, to quote Freud again, to "approximate more closely to what may be supposed to be the real state of affairs". In other words, Freud used an abstract, non-experiential language in his descriptions of the hidden depths of the mind, in an admittedly futile attempt to escape what he called "the language of perception".

I say, "admittedly futile", because it is in fact impossible to free ourselves from the language of perception. In other words, Freud's metapsychological language, too, inevitably relied upon perceptual images; that is why he so frequently had recourse to figurative analogies. As a result, we, the readers of these abstract, mechanical descriptions of the mind's internal workings, inevitably form images in our minds of the apparatus that Freud was describing. This was the origin of the all-too-common tendency of classical psychoanalysts to reify their concepts. There has been a pernicious tendency to think of the human mental apparatus as though it really were a machine. But the mind is not a machine; it is in itself—that is to say, in reality—something of which we are totally unable to form a picture. It is, in its essence, unperceivable. For that reason, we can describe it in many different ways. Some post-Freudian analysts, like Bion and Ignacio Matte-Blanco, for example, have endeavoured to render the mind in an even more abstract language than Freud did, and have relied upon quasi-mathematical descriptions. Other analysts, like Melanie Klein and after her Herbert Rosenfeld, and Hanna Segal, in particular, have taken a different tack. I am not sure to what extent she did so deliberately, but starting in the 1920s and 1930s, Melanie Klein gradually began to describe the inner workings of the mental apparatus as if they were subjective experiences.

This is what unconscious phantasy (in the sense that Melanie Klein used that term) actually is. It is an attempt to describe the very same processes that Freud attempted to describe (in abstract, mechanistic terms), in the language of personal experience. The living theatre of unconscious phantasy is nothing more and nothing less than a different way of depicting the unperceivable events that occur within the portion of reality that ultimately generates our subjective states of awareness.

This new way of depicting the mental apparatus has some advantages over the classical approach. There was an uncomfortable hiatus between

Freud's descriptions of his clinical observations and his metapsychological explanations of them. In order to move from the one level of analysis to the other, it was necessary for the analyst to affect a translation from the language of personal experience into the language of scientific abstraction. I have already mentioned why Freud considered this translation to be necessary: he wanted to "discover something else which is more independent of the particular receptive capacity of our sense-organs and which approximates more closely to what may be supposed to be the real state of affairs". But Melanie Klein's approach had the advantage of being able to explain the patient's subjective experiences in a language that did not differ fundamentally from the language of the experiences themselves. This was a language that the patient himself could immediately identify with. As a result, the analyst could put his metapsychological inferences about what the patient was saying and doing directly to the patient, in the same language that the patient himself was using to depict his lived experiences. And, moreover, the analyst could later communicate exactly the same inferential descriptions to his colleagues, and in this way assimilate them directly into theory, without having to affect the unwelcome translations that I mentioned a moment ago. The effect was instantaneous; it was as if, suddenly, the unconscious had come to life. Where previously there were energies and forces and structures and the like, now there were simply experiences (extraordinary as those experiences might be). There were of course other advantages, and disadvantages, too, of proceeding in this way. But I believe that the direct, experiential quality of the language of unconscious phantasy has played no small part in it gaining such popularity among modern psychoanalytic clinicians.

We must not forget, though, that the language of unconscious phantasy is just another figurative language. Unconscious phantasies can still never be perceived directly; they can still only ever be inferred from the data of conscious perception. As a result, some unconscious phantasies are bound to sound strange to the uninitiated. Any attempt to describe the deepest processes of the mind, which correspond in classical metapsychology to the seething cauldron of the drives, in the language of subjective awareness, will inevitably bear very little resemblance to the ordinary subjective experiences with which we are familiar, and which we are actually capable of perceiving. Likewise, the mental processes of the small infant, which in classical theory were almost devoid of secondary processes, are bound to sound strange when they are translated into the reflective language of adult experience. This was the cause of much of the controversy that occurred in the British Psychoanalytical Society in the 1940s, when Anna Freud and her supporters found it so hard to believe that small infants could actually have the thoughts and feelings that the Kleinians said they were having "in phantasy". The point is, though, as I hope I have made clear: they don't actually have them—or rather, I should say they can't actually have them; their unconscious mental processes themselves exist in some form of which they (and we) are by definition totally unable to form a direct perceptual image.

What Melanie Klein and her supporters were describing were inferences, framed in a figurative language that they believed provided the most appropriate analogies, the closest possible approximations, of "the real state of affairs".

Even in the happiest of clinical circumstances, where an analysis facilitates explicit awareness of a previously unconscious phantasy, what the patient becomes aware of is not the unconscious phantasy itself. Rather, it is a conscious representation (or re-transcription) of the phantasy itself. Unconscious phantasies remain forever unconscious, no matter what we call them and how we describe them. And this applies even if their modes of perceptual transformation into consciousness (and even the phantasies themselves) are altered by the process of analysis.

This is not to deny that some descriptions are more plausible than others, more commensurate with the perceivable data. But before one description can be compared with another, we need to distinguish between the figurative language and the inferential content of each description. The alternative is Babel.

So, as you can see, we have finally answered the question that the title of my paper posed for us. Do unconscious phantasies really exist? Well, yes and no. Yes, they do really exist in the sense that they are (more or less plausible) descriptions of the things that actually do make up the inner workings of our minds, and which really do cause us to think and feel our conscious thoughts and feelings. In this sense they are just as real as the waves and energies that physicists tell us cause matter to behave in the ways that it does, when we kick it or boil it or send it hurtling into outer space. But unconscious phantasies also do not really exist, because we can never perceive them directly. They are not phenomenologically real. They are and can only ever be inferences about what it is that really lies beyond the envelope of conscious awareness.

Significantly, in this respect, too, unconscious phantasies are no different from the waves and energies of the physicists. The only essential difference between them is the difference that I mentioned at the outset. I am referring to the fact that even the conscious perceptions that are derived from unconscious phantasies cannot be publicly verified. That is simply due to the spatial arrangement of the different perceptual modalities, as a result of which our personal, subjective experiences will always be personal and subjective. In this respect our scientific attempts to describe the inner workings of the mind from a subjective, psychical point of view will always fall short of our descriptions of its objective, material realisation in the tissues of the brain. But then, again, the introspective approach has the significant virtue of looking at the things that go on inside us from the same point of view as our patients. And it is, as I have said, in their subjective experiences that our patients locate their suffering. And that, as I have also said already, is the greatest virtue of the concept of unconscious phantasy: it lays bare the causes of our patients' suffering in a language that the patients themselves can identify with, and it thereby renders the unthinkable thinkable.

Reference

Freud, S. (1940a). *An Outline of Psycho-Analysis. S. E., 23*: 141–207.

CHAPTER 4

The expansion of the notion of truth in psychoanalytic inquiry

Jorge L. Ahumada

Issues of truth pose elusive problems. In daily life we must, and do, discern true and false in a multitude of matters. The notion of Truth though, frequently appearing in capitalised form, takes pride of place in philosophical and scientific discussions, not exempt from religious overtones.

Pure reason at the origin of science

As elsewhere detailed (Ahumada, 2011) Western science started with Pythagoras' geometry, devised upon practical procedures for construction, accounting, and irrigation as used in the Middle East where he studied for two decades. He founded in Sicily a monastic community at once religious, scientific, and political. For the Pythagoreans valid knowledge resulted from strict deduction out of indubitable simple premises: *the idea of change was incompatible with valid knowledge*, while the changes obvious to our perception were proof of the unreliability of the senses. The rigid causality of astral dynamics modelled all empirical knowledge: "Everything is Number" was the ultimate, sacred Truth nearing man to the gods. Entire numbers and their fractions and the holy simplicity of geometrical forms held together the veritable, eternal structure of the universe. The simplest motion representing ultimate order, uniform circular motion, ruled their attempts to grasp the complex planetary movement, the "errant" or "vagabond" bodies. This *formalistic, absolutistic tradition of truth* extant in the mathematical sciences—the so-called exact sciences—relying on strict deduction and only on it, was pursued by Democritus, by Eudoxus, by Euclid in his *Elements*, and by Ptolemy whose magisterial mathematical work, the summit of ancient Greek astronomy unchallenged for fifteen centuries, was adopted in modernity by Copernicus, by Galileo who hailed the primacy of the circle as a cosmological certainty (Lindberg, 2007, p. 102), and by Descartes, who flatly dismissed Galileo's laws of the fall of bodies as well as the notions of vacuum and gravity because of their being obtained by experiment, not by strict deduction from premises. Kepler, and decades later Newton, brought a fresh breeze of empiricism to these sacred formal precincts: however, Truth as Absolute Knowledge backing a *mechanical theory of the universe* upholding rigid overall causality is stoutly held today by positivisms and by logicisms for all science, human affairs included. Such mechanical-deductivistic theory is driven, as Freud (1926e, p. 191) aptly notes, by our longing for definiteness, immutability, and infallibility, and is loosely applied to immaterial facts as well as to material ones.

Process and change in observational-descriptive sciences

Centuries after Pythagoras, Aristotle, son of the physician of the Macedonia court and a physician himself, introduced *the ideas of process and change*, which were anathema to the Pythagoreans.

Neither mathematician nor astronomer, Aristotle pioneered mineralogy, botany, zoology, and psychology, as well as politics, poetics, rhetoric, and the rise and decay of the Greek *polis*. Besides, he authored syllogistic logic which remained unchallenged until the late nineteenth century. Immanuel Kant was convinced it was the definitive version of logic. His outlook on the dissimilar nature of truth in different empirical fields was mostly influenced by his biological studies, a sizeable part of his known work, built not upon deduction but on precise, systematic observation, and description of singular instances, and discerning similitudes and differences (*genus et differentia*). Being a scrupulous researcher, aware that the ways of analysing phenomena in the domains of physics did not apply to the biological realm, he kept away from seeking a unified system, as is standard fare for philosophers.

Of the five classic Aristotelian questions, "what", "how", "where", "when", and "why", enquiry along the first four questions sets the ground for addressing the fifth, "why", which conjecturally attempts to tie together the findings along the first four questions, which are the steps of the basic epistemic structure in *observational-descriptive sciences*, of which Aristotle was the undisputed pioneer, as acknowledged by Charles Darwin, and by Richard Owen, the founding father of comparative anatomy.

To Aristotle biology was not an "exact" science; its causality's *conditional necessity* gave place to the variability and spontaneity of phenomena, quite distinctly from the rigid, mechanistic *absolute necessity* of the Pythagorean cosmogony: he was well aware that what depends on the cases and circumstances cannot be defined *a priori*. He classified more than 500 animal species and introduced systematic observation, dissecting fertilised eggs in controlled intervals to observe the genesis of organs, arriving to an epigenetic theory where organs emerged in a predetermined hierarchical sequence.

Soul (*psyche*) and body were to Aristotle a unity of form and function, holding that dreams were natural, not godly phenomena, and that men created gods of their own image. While Plato split apart the mortal body and the immortal soul, the soul being purely ideational, eternal, and thereby real while the body, being material, transitory, and corruptible, was unreal, to Aristotle wishes and perceptions are genuine entities endowed with causal powers, shunning the reductionisms Pythagoreans aimed at. The notions of change and process guided his approach to the study of human societies.

To Aristotle truth is plural, subject to the qualities of each domain of inquiry. As he puts it: "As is the science so is its truth; for each science takes cognisance of its peculiar truths" (Aristotle, c. 350 BC, p. 49). What observational inquiry discloses in each field acquires primacy over formal schemes and over preconceptions on truth, right against the rigid formalistic concepts modelled on astronomy and physics.

Truth in philosophy and truth in the sciences

To the philosopher Donald Davidson a deep confusion, a veritable category mistake, flourishes along the history of philosophy upon the spell of the Socratic idea that we must keep asking for the *essence* of an idea:

this leads to the "freshman fallacy", demanding that we *define* our terms as a prelude to say anything further with or about them (Davidson, 1999, p. 320). But excepting a given empirical connection, the concept of truth has no content at all (p. 321). *Truth*, he says, *is not an object, it is a concept* and is intelligibly attributed to things like sentences, utterances, beliefs, and propositions, entities which have a propositional content. The mistake percolates down to the idea that a theory of truth must somehow tell us what, in general, is true, or at least how to discover truths (Davidson, 2004, p. 1225).

However, the pretence of philosophy to be an overriding knowledge set above the sciences will likely never be overcome. Thus, for the influential US philosopher Richard Rorty, given that it can no longer aspire to be *regina scientiarum*, the queen of the sciences, as enjoyed until modern times, philosophy must become *dominatrix scientiarum* (Rorty, 1978), the domineer of the sciences: the philosopher's discourse thus places itself above the level of the findings of sciences he is not part of and has not worked in. But as he later on tellingly admits, such deigning no contact with the evidence of this world amounts to a death of evidences bolstering philosophy into a super science, into a sacred precinct just a step away from immediately accessible ultimate truths, whereby the philosopher's superior mind becomes its own Archimedian *point d'appui* (Rorty, 1983).

It must be highlighted, though, that while Truth as Absolute Knowledge along mechanistic-deductive lines is overridingly held as a given by the lay public as well as by positivists and logicians, this is not the case in "hard" sciences themselves. Over seven decades ago, introducing a Festschrift he called "my own obituary", Albert Einstein stated:

> For me it is not dubious that our thinking goes on for the most part without the use of signs (words) and beyond that to a considerable degree unconsciously. For how, otherwise, should it happen that sometimes we "wonder" quite spontaneously about some experience? This "wondering" seems to occur when an experience comes into conflict with a world of concepts which is already sufficiently fixed in us. Whenever such a conflict is experienced hard and intensively it reacts back upon our thought world in a decisive way. The development of this thought world is in a certain sense a continuous flight from "wonder". (Einstein, 1949a, p. 9)

In his maturity he thought Hume saw clearly that concepts such as causality cannot be deduced from the material of experience by logical methods and, against Kant, that all concepts, even those closer to experience, are from the point of view of logic freely chosen conventions. He therefore reproaches the physicists of the previous century for their futile efforts to fit physics, and in fact all natural science under the mantle of mechanics (ibid., p. 21).

He also remarks that as soon as the epistemologist attains a clear system, he tends to interpret the thought-content of science in terms of his system, accepting what fits it and rejecting what does not. The scientist's conceptual world, bound by the facts of experience, appears to the systematic epistemologist as a type of unscrupulous opportunist (Einstein, 1949b, p. 684). Years before he had stated that the words or the language did not seem to play any role in his processes of thought, which are of visual and some muscular type, images which can be "voluntarily" reproduced and combined. Conventional words or other signs are sought laboriously only secondarily, when the associative play is sufficiently established and can be reproduced at will (Einstein, 1945, p. 25).

These final statements by that most eminent of physicists, Albert Einstein, far depart from the formal-mechanistic stance pursuing Truth as Absolute Knowledge valid for all fields. Long before and as spelt out elsewhere (Ahumada, 2011) Henri Poincaré, to whom Einstein offers thanks for mathematical work helping him attain the theory of relativity, ironised at the notions of univocity, deductivity, and certainty of "pure" scientific "facts", arguing that for the superficial observer scientific truth is beyond doubt and mathematical truths derive from a small number of evident propositions by means of a series of impeccable reasonings. They impose on us, and also on nature: they chain the Creator, so to say, being for many, and for high-school students in their first physics lessons, the origin of certainty in science (Poincaré, 1902, p. 23). Far from strict deduction in the Pythagorean–Euclidean mode, mathematical discovery achieving genuine new theories depends on intuition preceded by long unconscious labour; it rests upon unconscious ideational work and does not follow explicit rules: the subliminal ego, he notes, guesses better than the conscious ego and is successful when this last fails (Poincaré, 1908, pp. 55–57). On his side a founding father of mathematical logic, Bertrand Russell (1903), advancing a wide posture of methodological fallibilism as facts are concerned, warned that empirical statements can be refuted but never proven, and that absence of contradictions and counterexamples never amounts to proof.

Back to truth in philosophy. From the standpoint of US analytic philosophy, "Philosophy deals with abstractions. It is concerned with highly general categories, such as mind, matter, consciousness, causation, time, values and so on," the question being: "What do all true propositions share that is lacking by all false ones?" (Blackburn & Simmons, 1999, p. 1). Thus stated, the issues of truth are restricted, and subordinated, to stated propositions. An akin response comes from hermeneutic quarters, in which language delimits the realm of knowledge to the detriment of pragmatic issues. Already Descartes (1637) had set language as marking an ontic barrier between the mechanical nature of animals and what pertains to the body on the one hand, and the cogitative self-transparency of the human spirit on the other hand. Truth, though, needs being explored in a wide light in the psychoanalyst's enquiry in mind, where it becomes obvious that meaning and communication extend far beyond language.

The issues of truth in psychoanalysis

Freud's comment in a private letter to Albert Einstein on March 26, 1929, which he asked Einstein to destroy, forcefully posits the elusive hardships in studying the unconscious psyche:

> All our attention is directed to the outside, whence dangers threaten and satisfactions beckon. From the inside, we want only to be left in peace. So, if someone tries to turn our awareness inward, in effect twisting its neck round, then our whole organisation resists—just as, for example, the oesophagus and the urethra resist any attempt to reverse their normal direction of passage. (Quoted by Grubrich-Simitis, 1995)

There is deep insight in this offhand comment, coinciding with what, unknown in Freud's time, we currently know about the ethology of mind along the protracted evolution of our species, self-awareness being an extremely late acquisition (see Ahumada, 2021, 2022). As concerns the philosophies of mind, holding that the attempt to turn our awareness to our own psyche amounts to turning the neck round strictly opposes the Cartesian postulate of self-transparency of consciousness upon which terms philosophies usually define the psychic. Similarly, the Freudian aphorism "the ego is first and foremost a bodily ego" (Freud, 1923b, p. 26) goes right across the Platonic–Cartesian dichotomy of the psychic and the bodily.

Thus, psychoanalysis must gain its knowledge mostly at counter-current, clinically as well as in building its conceptual world. Moreover, as Freud astutely notes in *The Question of Lay Analysis*, "Every philosopher, every imaginative writer, every historian and every biographer makes up his own psychology for himself, brings forward his own particular hypotheses concerning the interconnection and aims of mental acts—all more or less plausible and all equally untrustworthy": as in the field of psychology there is no authority, "everyone can 'run wild' as he chooses" (Freud, 1926e, p. 102)—a hot issue amid the current postmodern literary-philosophical vogue of the "death of evidences".

In his papers on technique, he declares: "Psychoanalytic treatment is founded on truthfulness" (Freud, 1915a, p. 164). Mind being intrinsically directed to the outside, the effort for truthfulness by analyst and patient is the lever for turning mind's neck round to an untoward task: moving from the pleasure principle to the reality principle, which he closely links to renouncement of omnipotence opening the road to mental growth. This is why the German term *Arbeit* (work) comes recurrently to his texts: *Deutungsarbeit*, the analyst's work in arriving at interpretation, *Durcharbeitung*, working-through upon his own up-to-then unknown aspects on the side of the patient, to Freud the most critical aspect of the therapeutic process.

On the quite different levels at the origins of human mind

Concerning the initial stages of mind Balint (1968) discriminates three schemes of origins in Freud's conceptual universe: primary autoerotism, primary narcissism, and primary object relation. Current evidence is conclusive: in the last months of pregnancy the baby recognises mother's voice and reacts uniquely to it; after birth, when put in twilight upon mother's belly the infant will after some minutes start slowly creeping towards the breast, and upon hearing mother's voice will look up at her eyes. That the newborn seeks a link shows the mother has for the neonate a unique "*Truth-value*" at a pragmatic level, on from the very start: I here capitalise the term because as we know from René Spitz's (1945) work on "hospitalism" the affectionate tie to the mother is crucial not only for the baby's healthy emotional growth but often for survival.

Now, what to think of this primary relation to the maternal object? Let me summarise everyday examples from healthy lively infants, amplified in our book *Contacting the Autistic Child: Five Successful Early Psychoanalytic Interventions* (Busch de Ahumada & Ahumada, 2017), in order to differentiate perceptual awareness on the one hand, and achievement of otherness, that is, self–object affective discernment on the other hand; such issues pertain to quite different levels of mind and run quite different courses, in infancy and indeed throughout life. The fusional baby–mother omnipotent level of psychic reality was hinted at early on by Ferenczi in "Stages in the development of the sense of reality" (1913): while it is a commonplace to refer to these levels as "psychotic", I must consider them as primordial.

A lively baby engaged in gleeful interchanges, smiling, crackling with laughter, "verbalising" gurgling sounds with his mother and the immediate family, his gaze firmly locked onto his interlocutor's gaze. By that time, he has once and again visually contemplated his hands, played with these and explored sucking them in various ways.

Our First Scene in the five interventions, shortly before three months of age, concerns a little boy's "discovery" of his right foot: calmly bending his trunk he pushed both hands forward until he found the foot, which brought an upsurge of joy, an act repeated again and again; at these times he was, so to say, very much with himself, though readily available to connect with those around. Such discovery with its accompanying glee evidences a capacity for, and his joy at, attaining *perceptual* bodily distinctions at a quite early age (discovering his left foot took weeks longer). We cannot know what role had mother at those moments in the baby's mind, though we might surmise that she was present in the background as "mother-as-environment"; during these enterprises of joyful corporeal "eureka" discovery he evinced no sign of the anguishes of "spilling over" or "falling into a void" that Esther Bick assumed happened in a hypothetical early fluctuating stage of the ego limits: his enterprise of bodily self-discovery—his gleeful expansion of his bodily ego limits—was an enjoyable part of his going-on-being. We might here witness, at three months of age, the inklings of a context of play.

Our Second Scene took place the following week, after he turned three months. Sitting in his pushchair he was immersed in an intensely joyful smiling and laughing and kicking orgy with his maternal grandmother, his gleaming gaze firmly anchored to hers: then, calamitously, Grandma's cell phone rang and for some five minutes she took the call, disconnecting herself. On turning again to the baby, things had changed drastically: angry and despondent he avoided her gaze, turning his head away whenever she tried to approach and to reconnect visually; he kept up, though, a lively connection with other family members, his mother included. It took a half day for the baby to "pardon" the grandmother for her withdrawal of attention, after which she was readmitted to his affect. Again, we here find, observationally, evidence of separateness, in this instance not just perceptual on the baby's side as it included a violent emotive enacted response, apparent in his withdrawing again and again from the inattentive grandmother's efforts to contact him. The peak of ecstatic emotional "fusion" with the love-object, his euphoric merging, his joyful "flowing over at one-ness" (Tustin's terms) to his [grand] mother exposed him to the hardships of rupture. Nothing akin took place when attention was withdrawn from the baby in usual, calmer circumstances, by the mother or by others. Ecstatic merging states, which we regard as sexual inasmuch as they are blatantly erotic (I used the term "orgy" advisedly, highlighting its sexual character) involve risky contacts, potentially leading to mini remakes of a ruptural trauma. If we follow Tustin in that "Autistic reactions are an exaggeration of an inbuilt repertoire of elemental reactions which are part of the lot of all human beings" (1988, p. 44), this scene likely provides a mini model of the sort of elemental threat of ruptural loss of a sense of existence which, if reiterated often enough, could eventually lead to autistic spectrum disorders. Our book (Busch de Ahumada & Ahumada, 2017) presents detailed clinical evidence of the eventual reversibility of autistic ruptures when treatment starts early enough.

We join Salomonsson (2012) in that sexuality is undervalued and mostly forsaken in present-day psychoanalytic infant theorisation, being displaced by attachment theory. As illustrated by the scene just described, baby–mother sexuality does not necessarily involve organ contact: in fact, nothing akin happened when our baby fed at the breast. That in this scene the love-object was the grandmother rather than the mother should not surprise those acquainted with Matte-Blanco's (1988) overall dictum that the unconscious does not recognise individuals.

A Third Scene came up days later: the baby, who up to then had been breastfed except for occasional bottle feedings of mother's milk in short absences, was suddenly withdrawn from the breast due to his mother's ingestion of a toxic antibiotic. For the first time the mother fed him formula for a week and then resumed breastfeeding. Relevantly for the discussion the baby showed disgust, mildly protesting when bottle-fed the formula, but such abrupt withholding of the nipple/breast and of maternal milk did not evince an adverse withdrawal from his mother akin to the rupture shown upon Grandma's brusque inattention during their ecstatic glee.

The issue, then, of what the psychoanalytic literature conveniently refers to in organ language as "the breast" consists, admits no simple answer. Somewhere Bion wryly commented that were he asked what he meant by the breast, he would respond that he means what he assumes the baby means by the breast! As to Winnicott, in a 1954 letter to Betty Joseph he states, "I find it very difficult to get people to leave for a moment the infant's fantasy of a bad breast and to go to a stage further back to the effect of a bad mothering technique, such as for instance rigidity [mother's defence against hate] or muddle [expression of mother's chaotic state]" (Winnicott, 1987, p. 59): for better *and* for worse, the baby is in direct contact with mother's affective states.

Some time later, when the baby was six months of age, he was weaned from the breast and put to the bottle with no untoward reaction. But, whenever his mother took a phone call while bottle-feeding him, withdrawing her gaze and her attention, the baby evinced an angry adversative withdrawal, a rupture akin to that displayed with his grandmother at the age of three months. As illustrated by Salomonsson's (2012) work with nursing baby–mother duets, these ruptural experiences are, in Winnicott's remarkable phrase, "the (lost) memory of unthinkable anxiety" (1967, p. 221).

From these examples it might be surmised that what our three-month-old baby meant by "the breast" relates as much to the emotional psychic link to mother's mind (eventually to grandmother located in the maternal emotional place), as to the breast (or its milk) as a feeding organ. Already close to the beginnings, and presumably from the beginnings on, *instinct is inter-psychical* and centrally involves cognitive dimensions.

Perceptual awareness might conjecturally be admitted to exist from the start, from the moment the newborn baby seeks the nipple and, on hearing mother's voice, seeks her gaze. Such perceptual awareness from the beginning is a valid lesson to be extracted from infant observations. But the point is that perceptual awareness does not by itself entail a tolerance for self–object emotional distinction and an acknowledgement of the other's otherness: this belongs to evolutions of unconscious levels of the mind, evolutions which come about much later, must be gained hardily, and are never fully accomplished.

To illustrate later vicissitudes of this long drawn-out process, we might take a Fourth Scene of a toddler nearly two years old, where the boy, playing quietly with some toy cars while in another room his mother was chatting with a friend, at some moment stepped on a toy car, fell on his face and got up angry and crying, ran straight to where mother was, and hit her furiously. Obviously enough, at the *perceptual level* separateness between them had been fully attained; at the *emotional unconscious level* that Freud would deem his psychic reality, despite being quietly playing by himself, the boy inhabited some sort of affective mother-space whereby mother, be she present or not, was felt to be in charge of his well-being, and was responded to on such a basis.

So, our response to the question, "Is there a primary separateness or not at the beginning of life?" is that in order to be fruitful, the issues of me/not-me separateness, as most issues in the realm of the mind, must be posed in terms of psychic levels. Our scenes illustrate the level of what Freud obscurely enough called "thing-presentations", of which the unconscious is built, and from which meaning is generated from the beginning.

The baby's relational "Truths" on which opening the road to maturity depends are primarily and fundamentally enacted affective-pragmatic Truths, which all through later life will pertain to the deeper levels of the unconscious, far removed from consciousness and difficult to access in psychoanalytic inquiry. Freud's use of the neutral gender for the unconscious, *das Unbewusste*, reflects the less or non-individualised character at these levels of psychic reality where the unconscious does not recognise individuals: this is most pertinent as to the initial fusional link to mother, which is never fully renounced. The Fourth Scene marks the striking distance between an already fully attained perceptual separateness and the yet-to-be-attained emotional self–object discrimination which will require, as Freud insists on, the renouncement to the omnipotent possession of the object.

Relinquishment of the fusional bodily-affective link to mother is no easy affair. Its most visible aspect, weaning, usually occurs in several stages: weaning from the breast, most often after a few weeks of life, weaning from the bottle perhaps a year or more thereafter, daytime weaning from the pacifier maybe after another year, and later on, final night-time renouncement, these later stages usually meeting diverse amounts of resistance. An akin adversarial conflict routinely occurs in our next of kin the chimpanzee: relinquishment of the breast at age four to five years, imposed by the mother, meets cheating and overt violence on the side of the infant (Goodall, 1986).

That, as Winnicott comments, infants do not remember when things went well, they remember when things went wrong and felt that suddenly the continuity of their life was snapped, and that it is difficult for them to keep alive the internal image of the mother during and after separations (Winnicott, 1986, p. 146), goes right across attaining tolerance to separation as well as against gaining a secure sense of self, which provides ample grounds for resentment and feelings of victimisation. Besides, ambivalence as to fusion arises soon enough and turns obvious as motility is being gained: the toddler enthusiastically shoves mother away, departing from her in a joyous euphoric run and then returns smiling to her embrace; but should she try to retain him, he will forcefully push her and again run enthusiastically away!

These conflicting issues (from which father has been excluded) that happen in early stages falling under infantile amnesia, are bound to remain unconscious and be re-enacted most diversely in daily life and in the transference link to the analyst. This grounds the expansion of the concept of truth necessary for psychoanalysis, where relinquishment of omnipotence and its denials open the way to truthfulness.

A relevant final question: is the daunting expansion of knowledge disclosed and required by psychoanalytic inquiry being done justice in the neurosciences and their in-house offshoot, neuropsychoanalysis?

References

Ahumada, J. L. (2011). *Insight: Essays on Psychoanalytic Knowing.* London: Routledge.

Ahumada, J. L. (2021). Unbridled: Thoughts on times of self-begetting and violence. *American Journal of Psychoanalysis, 81*: 301–325.

Ahumada, J. L. (2022). Omnipotence and the paradoxes of insight: A Darwinian look. In: J. Arundale (Ed.), *The Omnipotent State of Mind: Psychoanalytic Perspectives* (pp. 191–205). London: Routledge.

Aristotle (c. 350 BC). *Treatise on Rhetoric.* Amherst, NY: Prometheus, 1995.

Balint, M. (1968). *The Basic Fault: Therapeutic Aspects of Regression.* London: Tavistock.

Blackburn, S., & Simmons, K. (1999). Introduction. 1. Robust theories and deflationary theories. In: *Truth* (pp. 1–28). Oxford: Oxford University Press.

Busch de Ahumada, L. C., & Ahumada, J. L. (2017). *Contacting the Autistic Child: Five Successful Early Psychoanalytic Interventions.* London: Routledge.

Davidson, D. (1999). The folly of trying to define truth. In: S. Blackburn & K. Simmons (Eds.), *Truth* (pp. 308–322). Oxford: Oxford University Press.

Davidson, D. (2004). Truth. *International Journal of Psychoanalysis, 85*: 1225–1230.

Descartes, R. (1637). *Discourse on the Method.* G. Heffernan (Ed.). Notre Dame, IN: University of Notre Dame Press, 1994.

Einstein, A. (1945). A mathematician's mind. In: *Ideas and Opinions* (pp. 25–26). New York: Wings, 1954.

Einstein, A. (1949a). Autobiographical notes. In: P. A. Schilpp (Ed.), *Albert Einstein: Philosopher–Scientist* (pp. 3–94). New York: MJF.

Einstein, A. (1949b). Reply to criticisms. In: P. A. Schilpp (Ed.), *Albert Einstein: Philosopher–Scientist* (pp. 665–688). New York: MJF.

Ferenczi, S. (1913). Stages in the development of the sense of reality. In: *First Contributions to Psychoanalysis.* London: Hogarth, 1952.

Freud, S. (1915a). Observations on transference-love (further recommendations on the technique of psycho-analysis, III). *S. E., 12.* London: Hogarth.

Freud, S. (1923b). *The Ego and the Id. S. E., 19.* London: Hogarth.

Freud, S. (1926e). *The Question of Lay Analysis. S. E., 20.* London: Hogarth.

Goodall, J. (1986). *The Chimpanzees of Gombe: Patterns of Behavior.* Cambridge, MA: Belknap/Harvard University Press.

Grubrich-Simitis I. (1995). 'No greater, richer, more mysterious subject [...] than the life of the mind'. An early exchange of letters between Freud and Einstein. *International Journal of Psychoanalysis, 76*(1): 115–122.

Lindberg, D. C. (2007). *The Beginnings of Western Science* (2nd edn). Chicago, IL: University of Chicago Press.

Matte-Blanco, I. (1988). *Thinking, Feeling and Being.* London: Routledge.

Poincaré, H. (1902). *La science et l'hypothèse.* Paris: Flammarion, 1968.

Poincaré, H. (1908). *Science and Method.* New York: Cosimo, 2007.
Rorty, R. (1978). *Philosophy as a Kind of Writing: An Essay on Derrida.* Baltimore, MD: Johns Hopkins University Press.
Rorty, R. (1983). Pragmatism without method. In: *Objectivity, Relativism and Truth.* Cambridge: Cambridge University Press, 1991.
Russell, B. (1903). *The Principles of Mathematics* (2nd edn). New York: W. W. Norton, 1938.
Salomonsson, B. (2012). Has infantile sexuality anything to do with infants? *International Journal of Psychoanalysis, 93*(3): 631–647.
Spitz, R. (1945). Hospitalism: An inquiry into the genesis of psychiatric conditions in early childhood. *Psychoanalytic Study of the Child, 1*: 53–74.
Tustin, F. (1988). The "black hole": A significant element in autism. *Free Associations, 1*: 35–50.
Winnicott, D. W. (1967). *Thinking about Children.* R. Shepherd, J. Johns, & H. Taylor Robinson (Eds.). London: Karnac.
Winnicott, D. W. (1986). *Home Is Where We Start from.* C. Winnicott, R. Shepherd, & M. Davis (Eds.). New York: W. W. Norton.
Winnicott, D. W. (1987). *The Spontaneous Gesture: Selected Letters of D. W. Winnicott.* F. R. Rodman (Ed.). London: Karnac.

CHAPTER 5

Is truth an illusion? Psychoanalysis and postmodernism*

David Bell

The philosopher Susan Haack tells the following story:

> Not long ago I heard my dean, a physicist by training, express his unease at the suggestion that the mission statement for the College of Arts and Science included the phrase "concern for truth". The word makes people nervous he warned and they are bound to ask, "Whose 'truth'?" A sociologist colleague seconding the dean's reservations remarked that, while of course his research advances knowledge, he isn't concerned with "truth". A couple of us pointed out that unless your conclusions are true, they aren't really knowledge, only purported knowledge, and I did my best to explain that it doesn't follow from the fact that people disagree about what is true that "truth is relative to perspective" (Haack, 1999).

* This chapter was originally published as Bell, D. (2009). Is truth an illusion? Psychoanalysis and postmodernism. *International Journal of Psychoanalysis*, *90*(2), 331–345. https://doi.org/10.1111/j.1745-8315.2009.00136.x,

Such conversations represent an important sea change in attitude. The recognition of the fragility of truth claims, of how easily they are overloaded with individual, social, and political preconceptions, the resulting challenge to orthodoxy, are all essential to the pursuit of knowledge, which had undergone an important transformation and a peculiar new orthodoxy gained hegemony.

In a way that has truly advanced our knowledge, the link between what is held to be knowledge (that is, purported truth) on the one hand, and powerful interests on the other, has been increasingly subjected to deep and illuminating scrutiny. This exposed the importance of ideology and power in what is claimed as "knowledge". Social theorists have shown how often what is held to be true turns out to be a substitute for truth, that serves certain vested interests. Here the principal figure would be Marx. Similarly, Freud showed how, at an individual level human beings have a powerful tendency to substitute for truth wishful illusions, that serve certain deeper interests.

This explanatory structure is still underpinned by a conception of truth. Uncovering ideology and self-deception brings a world that is broader, truer than the one that preceded this understanding. And this is in line with the psychoanalytic explanation which endeavours, among other things, to show that individuals and groups have "vested interests" in perceiving, or more properly misperceiving, the world. From this perspective, a real freedom can arise from recognition of what the world is really like. But the relativisation of all truth is something entirely different. Postmodernism dispenses with any conception of truth, claiming that no distinction can be drawn between what is claimed as truth, and what is preference, fashion. Where there is no conception of truth, its various counterparts—deception, lies, misrepresentations—gain a foothold, and what a depth-psychology or depth-social explanation might look like without such concepts is very hard to understand.

The "relativisation of truth" brings not a recognition that there are no ultimate truths, but a world in which the very terms "truth" or "reality" are to be abandoned, on the grounds that they have no meaning and serve only to legitimise the power of those who claim to "know". There is, here, a slippage from the reasonable understanding that certain claims to truth might—and often do—turn out to be false, to the assertion that, therefore, there is no such thing as truth at all, only "purported truth", a plurality of perspectives, each said to have its own value. What had been accepted as "known fact" is then taken to imply that there are, in fact, no facts.

What is at issue here is a confusion between what is true and what is held to be true. Truths about the world, which may be very hard to come by, do not depend on perspective. But what we suppose to be true—what Susan Haack calls "purported truth"—may turn out to be false. What I hold to be true may be incompatible with what you hold to be true, but it does not follow from this that incompatible truths can both be true. When we speak of "your truth" and "my truth", we are speaking loosely, for truth is not something that can be possessed by any individual but something we apprehend with others.

The "relativisers of truth" seem, at one and the same time, to be saying that there can be no epistemic standards as to what is to count as knowledge—claiming, for example, that the shaman and the physician are both "true in their own ways", or that, understood within their own social contexts, we cannot judge between them—while also claiming that their "non-white, non-western, non-masculinist, non-scientific" standards are better (Haack, 1999).

In a similar way, the clearly correct assertion that any view is a view from somewhere—there being no perspective-free position, no "view from nowhere"—slips into the claim that all perspectives are equal and that objectivity does not exist, that one view cannot be more objective than another, and that no perspective should be privileged over any other. Instead, what is offered is a putative "democracy" of truth. Here, there can be no place for differentiating between the world "as it is" and the world "as we know it". All such discussions collapse into discourses about discourses, rather than discourses about the world. No perspective can clash with any other, for each is "right" from its own point of view; similarly, no perspective can clash with reality, for reality is said to be a fiction.

Thus, one of the fundamental bases of human conflict—between wish-fulfilling views of the world mistaken for reality and reality as it "really is"—is removed in one stroke. The apparent egalitarianism of this position, and its professed opposition to absolutes, is offset by the universalism and absolutism of its own stance: a tyrannical assertion that there are *no* truths and that *all* views are equal. It thereby takes itself to be in possession of a higher-order truth. There is, moreover, a certain higher moral tone—what Susan Haack has called a "higher dismissiveness". I shall have reason to return to this later in the chapter.

A further difficulty of such "perspectivism" can perhaps be seen from the following. I might have started this essay by saying that I am male, white, middle class, the implication here being that the claims I am about to make should be understood only within that sociocultural framework or context; that I am not necessarily making any claims that would be relevant, for example, to a black, working-class woman.

The difficulty here is, I think, immediately apparent. It lies in the issue of where to stop. I could perhaps sharpen my position further by adding that I am seventy-five, a doctor, a psychoanalyst, and live in North London. But maybe I should add that I live in Crouch End, in that Crouch Enders may have a different perspective on truth than those in Hampstead or Brixton … and so I could go on, as there is no obvious place to stop, until in the end I give such a complete picture of the perspective within which my assertions must be judged that the only person to whom they can be directed is myself. Extreme relativism thus reveals itself as a kind of solipsism.

The point here is that the place at which this stops—say, at being white and middle class—would rest on the unquestioned assumption that such a category is more important than, say, my being a psychoanalyst. Such an assumption could not be justified without appealing to a logic that has already been "outlawed" from this relativistic perspective.

It is also worth remarking here that the person who insists that he is only talking from his own point of view surrenders the possibility of being wrong. Making the stronger claim that one believes a statement to be true has an important modesty because implicit is the possibility that one may turn out to be wrong.

Psychoanalysis and postmodernism

The relativisation of all truth, an essential feature of postmodernism, marks a final break with the modernist project. Its influence has been wide, especially within the humanities, and it has been considered by some as a natural philosophical "home" for psychoanalysis. A number of authors have suggested that bringing psychoanalysis within the post-modern liberates it from what is characterised (or caricatured) as its naïve scientism, which makes omnipotent claims for objectivity and Truth. This view of psychoanalysis is, I think, a gross misrepresentation. Further, the celebration of multiplicity, pluralism, and the abandonment of a conception of truthfulness opposes some features of psychoanalysis that are central to its worldview.

"Modernism" is used, I think, in two distinct ways. First, and very germane to my theme, one might take modernism to refer, broadly, to the movement from the sixteenth century onwards that is characterised by the view that human knowledge derives from reason and that understanding of the world must be based on accurate observation of it—in other words, the project of the Enlightenment. Here, modernism is counterposed to religious and mystical notions which view knowledge and understanding as given by God (truth as struggled for, worked out, as opposed to Truth as revealed). An underlying credo of the modernist movement is that, through knowledge, human beings can emancipate themselves.

Another conception of modernism, sometimes called "High Modernism", refers to those momentous upheavals which, though beginning long before, have as their main scene of action the turn of the nineteenth century. This was the time of a major break with classical modes of thought—whether in music (with the break from classical form), in art (the break with realism and the birth of cubism), or in literature, with the psychological novel: the novel that locates its principal scene of action in the interiority of individuals. In this sense, psychoanalysis is a child of High Modernism.

Psychoanalysis occupies a paradoxical position in relation to the Enlightenment project. Its discovery of the existence, within all of us, of large areas of mental content and functioning that are beyond the reach of any ordinary awareness was the last of a series of crucial "de-centrings" of man. Freud's discovery of the importance and influence of the "irrational" in psychological life dealt, perhaps, the most devastating blow of all to man's narcissism: even in his own mind he is moved by forces beyond his control. Yet Freud, of course, did not hold up his hands and surrender to the dominion of the irrational but observed that, behind the apparently nonsensical, there lie deeper truths. In this sense, he reclaimed the "irrational" for the house of reason, giving an account of its history, its nature, and the laws that govern its functioning, while always maintaining that the knowledge arrived at—important though it is—is limited.

High Modernism, the soil from which psychoanalysis sprang, was not a break with certain core features of modernism—such as the belief that knowledge brings freedom—but brought about a revolution in our understanding of the limitations under which we labour to acquire such knowledge, and also put the seal on the impossibility of any such knowledge being absolute. The critical thinkers of this period, Freud and Marx, sought to expose the illusions we create and live by, which conceal from us necessary truths of our condition.

Postmodernism as an epistemology, then, is *not* a child of High Modernism that broke with old forms which constrained knowledge in order to discover deeper truths but instead stands in opposition to all claims of knowledge, truth, or reality. The postmodernist argument refers to all truth-claims, whether they be from the natural or the human sciences. Some may find this a difficult position to sustain in relation to the natural sciences but might find the argument more persuasive when it comes to human experience itself.

Given that psychoanalysis has, as its primary concern, inner experience, and that this is complex and often many-sided, it may appear to belong within such a postmodernist framework. This is, I think, profoundly mistaken. First, there is no necessary connection between complexity and the relativisation of truth. Second, psychoanalytic explanation asserts the enormity of the factor of subjectivity in determining any human being's understanding of his world, while at the same time maintaining a commitment to objectivity. In fact, this tension between the importance of subjectivity and the struggle for objectivity is an essential tension within our subject. One might add that it is also constitutive of what it is to be human.

I think it is important to disentangle a commitment to recognising the importance of the subjective, and a deep involvement with it, from the doctrine of subjectivism, which claims that subjectivity is all there is in the world (in other words, idealism). In fact, recognising the importance of subjectivity is part of an attempt to be more objective, while labouring under difficult conditions. There is no necessary connection between a deep involvement with human subjectivity and subjectivism as a philosophical position.

Some characteristics of psychoanalytic thought

There are a number of core features that are constitutive of psychoanalytic explanation, and which locate it firmly within modernism and as inimical to postmodernism. Psychoanalysis is a "critical activity", both at the level of theory and of practice. Appearance—that which is manifest—when probed, reveals deeper realities. And this is the way that knowledge advances, whether at the level of the individual patient or at the level of theory.

These deeper realities reveal causal structures which, if they are to be credited with real explanatory value, have to do work. They have to explain the phenomena addressed, and at the same time explain why these deeper causal structures are not self-evident. This is true in general of all scientific explanation. The laws of planetary motion show that the earth is not an unmoving body in the centre of a universe that rotates around it; they also show why it appears as if it does. Physics shows us that in solid matter there is more space than solid and can also account for the fact that this does not appear to be the case.

Similarly, Freud's understanding of symptoms suggests that the symptom is only the outward appearance of a deeper structure—a compromise between hidden forces within the mind. It both expresses and obscures this conflict. At one and the same time, the theory gives an account of the phenomenon and, through the concepts of repression and resistance, of why it is that we are pulled towards settling for appearance. Such forms of explanation are committed to the view that seeing behind appearances is potentially emancipatory.

A distinct but related feature of psychoanalytic explanation is its commitment to historical continuity. Where discontinuities appear, part of the task will be to show continuities functioning, but at a less apparent level. An important continuity will be that between "personality" and "illness". From a psychoanalytic perspective, illness will always be a personality development under the stress of particular internal and external conditions. A breakdown manifests itself as an apparently impressive discontinuity, but when examined more deeply and in more detail shows, in bizarre and distorted form, conflicts and preoccupations that were part of the personality prior to the breakdown. In fact, the capacity to help the patient integrate his pre- and post-breakdown states is an important part of the work, as is the less welcome discovery that recovery is *not* recovery from the difficulties that brought about the illness, which continue—though at a less manifest level—within the character structure of the individual patient.

This commitment to the restoration of continuity to that which appeared to be discontinuous reflects the developmental perspective central to psychoanalytic explanation. The finding of continuity in the apparently discontinuous extends beyond the individual patient to broader concerns, as Freud showed the continuing presence of the normal in the "abnormal": even the most bizarre symptoms had, as their content, concerns that are universal to humanity. Given that the continuities I refer to are not manifest, it becomes clear that the restoration of continuity is really another aspect of the appearance–reality distinction.

This type of understanding not only imparts meaning to symptoms but goes further. A man whose father has died recently develops his father's symptoms—and this may express his identification with his dead father, a way of keeping him alive, as well as his guilt (making himself suffer) arising from the realisation of his own death wishes towards the father. The understanding of the meaning of the symptom displays, at one and the same time, its causal structure and its causal history.

Wittgenstein (1953) viewed certain types of philosophical error as akin to a disease, and his philosophical approach as a kind of therapy. The cause of the disease was not the doctrine per se but the attitude to the world that it revealed. All of us suffer from various kinds of epistemological malaise when it comes to facing certain unwanted aspects of reality. What we have learnt, however, is that such problems cannot be dealt with without a deep appreciation of the powerful emotional factors that bind us to a worldview which, though not manifest, deeply influences our understanding of ourselves and of the world around us.

Case 1

> Mr A's thinking was dominated by a relativistic perspective, although he was not fully aware of this. For him, the reality of his objects could be altered purely by changing the way he thought about them. He was, in this sense, a subjectivist. He thought this view was quite consistent with the aims of psychoanalysis.

> He would avidly agree with any interpretation that he could take as implying that he was projecting aspects of himself into external objects. His understanding of analysis might be put in the following way: "Through analysis I can learn how I distort my objects by projecting into them aspects of myself, which analysis will make me own. Then I will become able to see my objects as good, instead of bad." There was a sort of energetic exposure of himself, this taking place in an atmosphere highly charged with "moralism".
>
> When this procedure was no longer available to him, he collapsed into the most terrible despair, trapped with objects whose badness was an unalterable fact.

My patient, who suffered from a kind of solipsism, also suffered from the related disorders of "perspectivism" and "multifaceted-ness". For him, there were no determining characteristics of an object—only "views" and "facets". He might decide that his objects had certain unpleasant characteristics, but then, in an apparently excessively fair-minded way, would treat this as "only an aspect". Having decided that his analyst was using him perversely, he also claimed that this was something that could be "put aside", as he might gain something from "the analysis". This view of "analysis" was completely abstracted from the human relationship within which it takes place.

Case 2

> Mr T led a very limited and utterly joyless life. He had relationships with women who had other partners, and his activities with these women consisted mainly of "going to the cinema". It did not seem to matter to him that these women had lovers, as he considered sexual intercourse as "another activity added on", no different from "going to the cinema". We might say that his vision was very limited. He knew of the primal scene, but that knowledge had no significance for him. His view was limited in this way for various profound and disturbing reasons. When he did apprehend the significance of the primal scene, it brought awareness of exclusion and the attendant unbearable pain but also ushered in a capacity to have a broader view of himself and thus of the world around him.

The point that I am making here is that, as a result of the psychic moves made possible through development, we all become able to have a more objective and more complex view of ourselves and of the world. The new perspective contains within it the old but is more inclusive; it transcends it. It does not exist alongside it as an alternative. We can conceive of someone having a truer relation to the world—at least one that is less untrue—without having to think that this new, expanded relation to the world provides truth in any ultimate sense.

I can examine the world from one particular point of view with which I am heavily invested, say an envious perspective, and then realise that my perspective has been very limited, as it did not take into consideration certain features of the world that, I now realise, I had not wanted to think about. Now that I think of them, I widen my frame of reference and so, relatively speaking, I am in a more objective position than I was before. This sort of move underlies the capacity to learn from experience.

This learning, however, depends upon the capacity to negotiate what Money-Kyrle (1971) described as certain facts of life. Central to his model is the recognition of certain truths of the world—such as the awareness of the object, which is both good and not under our control, and the awareness of our own mortality. Full recognition is an emotional experience and at one and the same time marks development and is a precondition for it. All of us have a tendency to put a kind of "spin" on these facts—to accept them and not accept them. The patients described above, in different ways, tried to accommodate certain difficult facts without being affected by them. Mr T knew of the primal scene as a fact but gave it no significance. Mr A could not bear the awareness of bad objects that could not be altered and tried to change their nature by thinking of them differently. Both patients made un-negotiable facts negotiable, and so inconsequential.

But the privileging of subjectivity, characteristic of postmodernism, raises a further thorny problem for any depth psychology. Can a person's consciousness of his position be false consciousness? Postmodernism provides no place for false consciousness, as such a category can only make sense in a world in which something may be true—or at least more true. The privileging of subjectivity, giving experience itself a special status that cannot be gainsaid, does not allow the possibility that experiences may derive from poor understanding. In a world that provides no place for a conception of truth, there is no place for illusion, self-deception, or lies: all of which derive their meaning from their contrast with truth or reality.

The attractions of relativism

When I tried to think about the excitement generated by postmodernism it struck me that what made it so attractive was the very fact that it claimed to transcend just those features of life which Freud viewed as central to the human condition. Perhaps the most important of these concerns the acceptance of the inevitability of limitation.

Postmodernism celebrates transitoriness, fluidity, and plurality. It sounds the death knell of "grand theory". As Terry Eagleton (1996) has put it, "Science and philosophy must jettison their truth claims and view themselves more modestly as just another set of narratives." Appearance is, so to speak, "all there is". In such a world, the idea of depth (in the sense outlined above in terms of explanatory structure) is a convenient myth for manipulating texts. The epistemological position of postmodernism is necessarily relativist, its ethic, pragmatism. Truth collapses into what works.

The epistemological problem addressed by postmodernism is not new; it is as old as philosophy itself (Aristotle, for example, tells us, "That which exists does not conform to various opinions, but rather the correct opinions conform to that which exists," and Plato's *Theaetetus* contains a prolonged discussion of whether "Man is the measure of all things"). What is new is its penetration into society and culture as a whole, defining, in Raymond Williams' memorable phrase, a new "structure of feeling" that informs the age (1977). Hassan, Eagleton, and others have pointed out that the world as depicted is profoundly schizoid (by which they mean fragmented and alienated). This form of existence does not bring the emptiness and despair one might imagine as its counterpart but instead becomes a basis for celebration. David Harvey writes: "Its total acceptance of ephemerality, fragmentation, discontinuity … it does not try to transcend it … or even define it … postmodernism swims, wallows in the fragmentary currents of change, as if that is all that there is" (Harvey, 1990, p. 44).

I will have something to say a little later concerning the basis of this.

Michael Rustin (1999) captures both the epistemological position and its personal implications when he says: "Reason floats free in this model without necessary limit or obstruction ... Only historical anachronism stands in the way of human autonomy and self-determination." Postmodernism minimises the obstacles to self-understanding and the inevitable constraints on self-realisation, positing "pure relationships of self-realisation established for their own sake, beyond the constraints of family and ascribed social roles" (Giddens, cited in Rustin).

The constraints that arise as a result of being human are, in the postmodern world, transcended. What is offered—an apparently limitless world without objective constraints—is clearly a very attractive proposition. This has important consequences for the understanding of identity. Identity as an enduring characteristic ceases to exist, as identities and beliefs can be chosen to suit one's needs.

But what manifests itself as freedom is, I think, really an enslavement to narcissism. Where choice does not impose limitations on further action—where ideologies, partners, commitments are all easily cancellable—then this is not really choice. It can only be choice where it is accompanied by the recognition of breaking with other possibilities, with the inevitable feelings of loss that this brings. Freud's tragic vision of man, engaged with the inevitable disappointments and pains of life, having to discard his illusions in order to become himself, is superseded in postmodernism by the illusion of infinite freedom: life as a shopping expedition. My reference to the shopping mall here is not accidental. Frederic Jameson (1991) has suggested that postmodernism is nothing more than the "cultural logic of late capitalism". As, in ever-accelerating ways, all human activities are brought under the dominion of the market, ideals, relationships, even philosophical positions can be chosen in the same way that one may choose any commodity. The market is a marvellous representative of the illusion of infinite freedom; it represents itself as gratifying desire in limitless ways.

Ideas and beliefs can be "bought into" to be used as we need them, and to be disposed of when they are past their "sell-by date". In this sense, postmodernism is the penetration of the commodity form into epistemology. The painful, difficult struggle for limited understanding is replaced by the shopping mall. This world of limitlessness bears all the hallmarks of omnipotence—a world where all "reality" is merely construction.

I think in this type of thinking there is a confusion between complexity and relativism. Truths about ourselves and the world are likely to be highly complex and difficult to grasp. This is a fact of life. When this fact is apprehended by a personality in which the forces promoting development are uppermost, the result is the painful struggle to comprehend this complexity—"the ragged, untidy process of groping for and sometimes grasping something of how the world is" (Haack, 1999). But when this is met by a personality dominated by more destructive forces, the apprehension of complexity becomes "the world can be what I want it to be", and so all painful struggle is disposed of at one blow. It seems to me that this is just the sort of error made by postmodernists.

The features that I described above as being central to the psychoanalytic form of explanation, such as the idea of depth and the appearance–reality distinction, only make sense if psychoanalysis is underwritten by a realist ontology.

There is an intrinsic relationship between a worldview that accepts inevitable limitation and an epistemology that is realist in the sense of being committed to the view that the world "as it is" is not reducible to the world "as I see it". From such a realist perspective, the observations we make of the world are causal effects of objects that have a reality independent of our experience of them. Thus, there is an inevitable limitation to what can be known, and what can be known is not coterminous with what we experience.

The mental structures investigated by psychoanalysis are, in this sense, real, and the assumption of such "unobservable" structures is necessary in order to make the project coherent. Further, in presupposing the existence of such structures, psychoanalysis captures, as Michael Rustin (1999) has pointed out, the "idea of unconscious constraints on individual psychic freedom".

Psychoanalysis, when underwritten by this realist position, emphasises the inevitable constraints on human freedom—not least those that derive from the materiality of our own bodies, our inevitable vulnerability, inescapable mental structures, and aspects of our own characters that we are not happy about but have to live with. There is a certain sort of deep freedom that arises when individuals who have spent their lives trying to escape all constraints come to accept some of the inevitable limitations of being human and to distinguish awareness of these ordinary limitations from imprisonment. Freedom is the recognition of necessity.

Theory and practice

These considerations are not abstract, for one's view of what psychoanalysis is, has profound implications for how we carry out our work. The close link between theory and practice is a further important defining characteristic of our subject. The postmodernist framework brings a view of analytic work well represented in the work of Renik (1998b). His paper given to the British Psychoanalytic Society and subsequently published in the *International Journal* was subject to a most penetrating critique by Marcia Cavell (1998). For our purposes here I will only pick out one or two points that are relevant to my main theme. Renik in a way that is quite uncontroversial emphasises the irreducible subjectivity of all interpretive work. But from this he derives the following:

He states, discussing his work with his patient, Ethan:

> We were trying to devise a new way for Ethan's life, present and past, that worked, that helped him feel better. We evaluated the validity of our understanding entirely on the basis of therapeutic efficacy. As I see it, in clinical psychoanalysis, as in the rest of science, truth *is* what works [italics in original], or objectivity is a pragmatic concept; it refers to objectives … (Renik, 1998a, p. 492)

For Renik, there are no truths that are there to be discovered, but only "what works". The problem this creates is, I think, immediately obvious: how are we to distinguish truth as "what works" from illusion and wish-fulfilment? Those who view psychoanalysis as involving only narrative truth face exactly this problem, for a coherent, consistent narrative of one's life that serves one well and promotes happiness may arise from self-deception—and thus cannot promote development (see the argument about false consciousness above).

Cavell (1998) says: "the view of truth as what works (cannot do the) work that the concept of truth does, in both ordinary and scientific talk. (It) would need to distinguish good reasons for holding a belief from bad reasons". I would add would have to recognise the difference between thinking wishfully and thinking realistically.

There is a further problem in Renik's position. Relativism cannot distinguish different levels in a theory. All scientific explanatory systems are layered: at certain levels what appears to be true or real may be highly conjectural and capable of being replaced without causing any serious problems to the general theory, while postulates at other levels within the system may be much more robust. This is true for our subject: the understanding of a session might be easily changeable as things develop, but we may have considerably more confidence about the anxieties and conflicts that dominate an individual's character. At another level still, there are clinical facts such as transference and projection. Lastly, there is the theory of mind that psychoanalysis offers.

For Renik, nothing in the theory or the practice appears to have more grounds for belief than anything else, as "what works" is all that matters. The insistence on the importance of truth is misunderstood by relativists such as Renik as claims to possess it—omnipotent assertions of truth with a capital "T", in other words, a crude scientism.

This misunderstanding at the level of theory has its counterpart at the level of practice, where the recognition of the need to maintain ordinary boundaries as part of the psychoanalytic setting is misunderstood as a rigid assertion of authority and disregard for the patient. Goldberg (2000), in his paper "Postmodern psychoanalysis" to the IPA Congress in Nice, suggested that the analytic setting is too rule-bound and that we need to be more flexible and adapt our procedures to suit the patient's needs. Irma Brenman Pick pointed out that the speaker misrepresented rules of analytic procedure as deriving from a position of omnipotent authority. Having (mis)represented the matter in this way, she argued, leaves only two possibilities available: either mindless submission to the "law" (father) or complete opposition to all law (psychically equivalent to the murder of the father). My argument is that the former is crude scientism, the latter, relativism.

The last point I wish to make, I have made before and will touch only briefly on it here. A view of psychoanalysis that collapses its truth-claims to merely pragmatic concerns creates serious difficulties for understanding the validity of the theory of mind that it represents. How could one decide, on purely pragmatic grounds, whether or not unconscious fantasy is an important part of mental life? For if the only criterion is pragmatic, then how could such knowledge have any existence independent of its practical use?

In discussion of his paper, Renik made it clear that, given he equated psychoanalysis with therapeutic activity, judgement of its value lay only in its success in helping patients, and, following his own logic, he had to assert that psychoanalysis can have no distinct status as a body of knowledge separable from its use in treating patients (Renik, 1998b). The "pragmatic" version of truth of psychoanalytic interpretations is wedded to an epistemological position which is, I believe, quite implausible, within which the objects to which psychoanalytic theories refer exist only within the psychoanalytic setting. It thus situates psychoanalysis within an epistemological framework that cannot encompass the idea of psychoanalysis as a body of knowledge logically quite separate from the effectiveness of that knowledge in treating patients. No place is available, within this framework, for what is usually termed "applied psychoanalysis".

Conclusion

By way of conclusion, I will first summarise the main argument. I have suggested that the postmodernist relativisation of truth cannot provide a framework for psychoanalysis, which I believe is committed to a realist ontology. I have attempted to outline certain core features of psychoanalysis that locate it within modernism—here I have emphasised the idea of depth explanation, the crucial distinction between appearance and reality, and the commitment of psychoanalytic explanation to continuity beneath discontinuity. I have further suggested that the meaning of the symptom displays both its causal structure and its causal history. This again commits it to a realist ontology.

I have attempted to discuss postmodernism and its relativising discourse from a psychoanalytic perspective, suggesting that its celebration of plurality, fluidity, and limitlessness reveals an omnipotent system of "knowledge" freed from the constraints of reality—a world where claims can never, by definition, be right, and so can never be wrong. Following Jameson, I have suggested some links between postmodernism and the market form. These forces support the powerful human tendencies to discard the limitations of reality and seek solace in a world of infinite possibility.

The collapse into pragmatics and subjectivism (where psychoanalytic knowledge can be judged only by its effectiveness in helping patients) leaves no place for psychoanalysis as a body of knowledge of mind separable from the effectiveness of that knowledge in helping patients and so creates great difficulty in accounting for its broader relevance.

The celebration of subjectivity and plurality—the hallmark of postmodernism—appears to be a long way from the absolutist assertion of objective reality. Yet it seems to me that they are really opposite sides of the same coin. Relativism opposes itself to a crude scientism seen as authoritarian and absolutist, yet relativism can be asserted with an absolutism that betrays its origins. Often the personality which at one moment appears to accept only subjectivism, in the next reveals itself to be threatened by an absolutism which can easily become the basis for identification.

Wittgenstein points out, in connection with the problem of other minds, that we do not *decide* whether or not a person is a person like us: "My attitude towards him is an attitude towards a soul. I am not of the opinion that he has a soul" (1953, p. 178). Hilary Putnam (1995) echoes this sentiment when he says, "Whether there is a reality or not is not something on which we can form an opinion, it is just a given of our lived life." He goes on to say that such a (radical) scepticism as Rorty's is "the flip side of a craving for an unintelligible kind of certainty".

It is at least plausible that relativism is a radical turning away, in disappointment, from the unfulfillable demand for certainty—but the disappointment and living with uncertainty that might be the result is instead replaced by an attack on all truth claims, equalising them all. If then, the original demand was a fundamentalist one, the turning away in radical scepticism retains the fundamentalism of its origins.

I do not think that whether there is truth or not is a purely scholastic question. "The ragged, untidy process of groping for and sometimes grasping something of how the world is", as Susan Haack (1999) says, "not a male thing or a white thing but a Human thing." The distinctions between objective and subjective, inner and outer, appearance and reality, the world as it is and the world as we perceive it, are all inescapable—and our struggle with them is constitutive of our humanity. Like Putnam, I do not think these are matters on which we can have an opinion. I am reminded of Isaac Bashevis Singer who, when asked the question: "Given that you clearly value human freedom so highly, it seems strange that the fate motif figures so strongly in your stories. Do you believe in Free Will?" Singer replied, "You gotta, you got no choice" (quoted in Kanfer, 1997).

Postscript

I first started thinking about this a long time ago, when looking at the implications for psychoanalysis of the new relativism. But a more direct engagement in this process came from the part I was to play in the so-called "gender wars". As a governor at the Tavistock Clinic, I became increasingly aware of the damage being done to children and adolescents as a result of the capture of the gender service (GIDS) by a peculiar ideological position which characterised itself as liberal and emancipatory but soon revealed itself as a new form of tyranny that would not permit any doubt or opposition. I subsequently wrote a report highly critical of the service, and this gained wide public attention and, alongside other critical voices, became part of a chain of circumstances leading to widespread public concern and eventually to the decision by NHS England to close the service (see Bell, 2020).

Relevant to the dominant thesis of this chapter, I will elaborate on some aspects of the peculiar form of thinking—or rather non-thinking—that has come to dominate the discourse in this area. In this climate, thoughtful engagement is treated as a kind of enemy, and this is certainly the experience of many clinicians working in gender services. The wish to think over time and understand why a particular child has developed gender distress comes to be seen as an expression of "transphobia", creating a world where "you are either with me or against me"—that is, a paranoid universe in which there is no room for a mind that simply wants to think about things. The intolerance of doubt and thought that characterises certain kinds of mental states leaks out and becomes a force in the institution itself.

The term "transphobia" has, for our community, a particularly unfortunate resonance—namely, the homophobia that is part of our own history. I have in mind that dark history of conversion therapies for homosexuals (particularly, though not only, in the USA). I believe the fear of repeating this has interfered with our capacity to think through these issues and has led us to turn a blind eye to the damage being caused to young people. But it is vital to distinguish between conversion therapy and a wish to think. As I see it, the rapid decisions regarding the provision of medical and surgical intervention are themselves a form of conversion therapy: like the past "treatments" for homosexuality, they seek to refashion the body as the only permissible solution to painful conflicts about gender and sexuality. That is, they bring about transformations in the body, converting it in order to satisfy insufficiently examined individual, family, and social agendas.

Lastly, the possession of a particular identity is taken as supplying one with a peculiar kind of higher authority. Let me explain: if, for example, a person says, "as a gay man", or "as a Jewish man", or "as a disabled man", or "as a black woman" … it would be reasonable to accept that such a person, because of their specific experiences, will enrich any discussion of the world with which they identify. But this does not bring entitlement to an unquestioned higher authority. That is, by belonging to group X or Y, my views as to what is true of the world—particularly about the group to which I belong—remain as open to question as the views of any other person. However, in these discussions, membership of the relevant group is assumed to grant a "higher authority", exhibiting a kind of entitlement (that can in part derive from the link between a particular identity and the experience of victimhood), an entitlement that must not be questioned. This is, in other words, a demand to be exempt from the ordinary canons of what counts as good judgement. There can be no personal or group sovereignty over what counts as true. There is here, I believe, a link to the attack on truth-value that is also a characteristic of our "postmodern" age.

If we take it as a fact that gender identity is largely socially constructed, then there is a paradox at the heart of the "trans" phenomenon. The apparent freedom or liberation it expresses is totally undermined by locating all possibility of change only concretely, in material alteration of the body, rather than in the mind.

There has been a peculiar regression in thinking. In our contemporary world we are generally tolerant of, even celebrate, a certain fluidity in the expression of gender and sexuality. We are less interested in who a person goes to bed with, less bothered by a man being somewhat feminine or a woman being somewhat unfeminine. This exists alongside a toleration of certain limitations arising from the body. In the ideology of the militant trans lobbies, however, there is a marked rigidity of gender identity coupled with a belief in the total fluidity of the body—a most peculiar reversal. This is coupled with a peculiar essentialist mode of thought: that is, gender identity is confused with anatomical sex.

References

Bell, D. (2020). The Fitzjohn's Unit. In: M. Waddell & S. Kraemer (Eds.), *The Tavistock Century: 2020 Vision* (pp. 229–230). Bicester, UK: Phoenix.

Cavell, M. (1998). In response to Owen Renik's "The Analyst's Subjectivity and the Analyst's Objectivity". *International Journal of Psychoanalysis, 79*: 1195–1202.

Eagleton, T. (1996). *The Illusions of Postmodernism*. Oxford: Blackwell.

Goldberg, A. (2000). Postmodern psychoanalysis. *International Journal of Psychoanalysis, 82*: 123–128.

Haack, S. (1999, July 9). Staying for an Answer: The Untidy Process of Groping for Truth. *Times Literary Supplement*.

Harvey, D. (1990). *The Condition of Postmodernity*. Oxford: Blackwell.

Jameson, F. (1991). *Postmodernism, or The Cultural Logic of Late Capitalism*. Durham, NC: Duke University Press.

Kanfer, S. (1997). Isaac Singer's promised city. *City Journal*, Summer. https://city-journal.org/article/isaac-singers-promised-city (last accessed 18 February 2026).

Money-Kyrle, R. E. (1971). The aim of psychoanalysis. In: D. Meltzer (Ed.), *The Collected Papers of Roger Money-Kyrle* (pp. 442–449). Strathtay, UK: Clunie, 1978.

Putnam, H. (1995). The question of realism. In: *Words and Life* (pp. 295–312). Cambridge, MA: Harvard University Press.

Renik, O. (1998a). Practical psychoanalysis: The relevance of clinical efficacy. *Psychoanalytic Quarterly, 67*(3): 492.

Renik, O. (1998b). The analyst's subjectivity and the analyst's objectivity. *International Journal of* Psychoanalysis, *79*: 487–497.

Rustin, M. (1999). Psychoanalysis: The last modernism. In: D. Bell (Ed.), *Psychoanalysis and Culture: A Kleinian Perspective* (pp. 105–121). London: Duckworth.

Williams, R. (1977). *Marxism and Literature*. Oxford: Oxford University Press.

Wittgenstein, L. (1953). *Philosophical Investigations*. G. E. M. Anscombe (Trans.). London: Penguin, 1968.

CHAPTER 6

What does research have to do with psychoanalysis?

Gregorio Kohon

Humility in the presence of the unconscious ... Let's not be in a hurry to translate ... Let's agree to be exposed to this passion, to this rage, to this wailing, to these silences, to all forms of this excess, in full ignorance of what incited it. Allow ourselves to be touched, wounded and demolished in our own being. Keep company with the shadows so that we may dream, if possible, in this darkness interrupted by flashes of light, in order to approach what is radically other, what the other feels as being foreign but from which they cannot escape.

— J.-B. Pontalis (2000, p. 11)

In the United Kingdom, Thatcherite policies of the late 1970s and 80s forced society to face the crude realities of an ideology of self-interest, ruthlessness, lack of compassion, materialism, and corruption. Political optimism and enthusiasm of earlier times were badly affected. Intense political pressure to produce only good news was developed by successive British governments as an attempt to deny a harsh and inhospitable reality (Cooper & Lousada, 2005, p. 61). Pressed to prove their worth, professionals in many areas became alienated by the demands created by an audit culture, in the midst of an atmosphere of discouraging political control.

The area of mental health became a particularly critical target: the emphasis placed on quick results and "efficacy" came into conflict with the needs for proper and prolonged assessments of patients and the appropriate treatment required for each of them (Beck, 1986; Slade & Priebe, 2006). Clinicians were urged by a new class of factitious institutional managers to conform to protocols and treatment plans in order to keep targets on track. Financial pressures produced an urgent, generalised demand for "evidence of effectiveness". Psychoanalytic practitioners, while not stopping to contribute to the development of new psychoanalytic ideas, did not escape the demand to produce empirically demonstrable results—the need for so-called "scientific" research became a priority.

Psychoanalysis is neither a science nor an art—it inhabits a place of its own, with its own rather peculiar characteristics and particular approaches. This should never be an excuse to claim a misguided kind of exceptionalism. There are no excuses: psychoanalysts are, must be, and should always be accountable for what we do—no mitigating circumstances here. Nevertheless, the knowledge of what we do and practise in the clinic is not easily describable or accessible, nor can it be clearly or exactly understood.

As a rather extreme example of a response to negative criticisms, computational psychiatry came to occupy an intersectional point between computational neuroscience and psychiatry, emerging as a beacon of promise in the 2010s. While incorporating methods and insights from a mixture of neuroscience, behavioural economics, and machine learning, computational psychiatry aimed at the development of computer systems with the ability to learn, thus progressively improving performance in order to provide a deeper understanding of mental health conditions and supposedly helping to develop more effective diagnoses and treatments.

Psychoanalysts too faced demands to produce empirically demonstrable results. This was not new—but the need for evidence-based scientific research became a pressing priority. For the last couple of decades, the notion of research in psychoanalysis has been mostly reduced to measuring the outcomes of therapeutic interventions. Peter Fonagy, after reviewing the results of outcome studies and meta-analyses of the effectiveness of psychodynamic therapy, suggested that there was little evidence to indicate that psychodynamic therapy was superior to other therapeutic approaches; any "apparent superiority … is attributable to the prolonged contact between patient and therapist". He suggested that there was "considerably more to achieve by 'playful' experimentation, probably driven by advances in bioscience and computational psychiatry" (2015, p. 145).

It might be a possibility. But what does research have to do with psychoanalysis? What kind of research are we talking about?

This chapter is principally concerned with the nature of clinical psychoanalysis in a very specific sense: the individual treatment of single cases as the most appropriate source of psychoanalytic research. This does not imply a refusal or a denial of the need for measuring outcomes. I would like to start from offering you a brief characterisation of what I believe psychoanalysis to be:

1. Psychoanalysis constitutes a body of knowledge, the object of which is the psychic reality of the human subject.
2. Psychic reality, as understood in psychoanalysis, includes and contains the unconscious as a constituent part. Given this inclusion, psychic reality cannot be reduced to either the mental or the physical: the psychoanalytic object is neither exclusively psyche nor soma; it has its own characteristics, categories, and laws.
3. Psychoanalytic models and theories are based on fundamental hypotheses and basic assumptions that have been arrived at through a mixture of clinical experience and self-reflection, speculative intellectual activity and intuition, free-floating attention and deduction, and the attribution of retrospective meaning and abstract representations.
4. Psychoanalysis is also a psychotherapeutic treatment, acquired and developed by clinicians through study, personal analysis, and clinical supervision. As a form of therapy, it is applicable to a selected number of clinical cases. Historically, it has become the source of considerable influence on other psychotherapeutic approaches and in a multiplicity of other fields: social work, education, general medical practice, paediatrics, and institutional conflicts.
5. In the words of Cornelius Castoriadis, human beings are not characterised by logic and rationality but by a radical "unbridled imagination", which exercises a central role in our psyche, distinguishing us from the rest of the animal world (1988). Primates may be able to

suck their thumbs but have not yet been capable of creating an extensive language for sophisticated communication, or music, or science, literature, and art.

6. In attempting to give account of this unbridled imagination, psychoanalytic theory oversteps the limits of moderation. It describes the existence and persistence of incestuous wishes in human beings. It speaks in terms of life and death; it deals with uncontrollable passions and the potential presence of murderous feelings towards our loved ones. It attempts to give account of unconscious phantasies while demonstrating that what sometimes appear as "good intentions" can be the disguised expression of destructive envy. It has amply shown the inevitable splitting of the ego, and the negation of that which we consciously might already know. It proposes the existence of infantile sexual theories which persists beyond infancy, continuing to influence our adult psychic life.
7. It is fair to describe psychoanalysis as a literature of excess. As a theory, psychoanalysis can be characterised as a deconstructing method which never reaches an absolute conclusion. It can be understood as an attempt to develop an objective knowledge of subjectivity, but this knowledge is always under the inevitable influence of the subject's unconscious (Kohon, 1999, p. 150).

When we move from psychoanalytic theory to clinical practice, psychoanalysis finds its purpose in a therapeutic process which takes place in the exclusivity of a consulting room, where patient and analyst gain access to the patient's unconscious in an encounter through language, always marked by the dynamics of transference and countertransference—two expressions of the said unbridled imagination. Clinical psychoanalysis owes its existence to it.

I would like at this point to highlight four important concepts, all of them with special resonance in different fields, scientific and otherwise. I hope they might help us to establish certain parameters, let us say, a framework, which we could use to draw an accurate account of the complexity of the quest for knowledge—*any* knowledge.

The first concept is *indeterminacy*, one of the fundamental discoveries of quantum theory. In describing the physical properties of nature, Rovelli, a physicist, stated that "it is not possible to predict exactly … where an electron will appear tomorrow. Between one appearance and another, the electron has no precise position, as if dispersed in a cloud of probability" (Rovelli, 2017, pp. 75–79). This refers to the ability of a quantum system to be in multiple states and in different locations in one given time. It is only when a measurement occurs that the superposition collapses onto a single state. This allows for a clear and systematic approach to understanding complex systems: the state of one particle is directly related to the state of another, no matter how far apart they are.

For many of us, not being physicists or scientists, this is difficult to understand fully. Nevertheless, from knowing about this lack of predictability, we are then confronted with yet another, complementary principle—that of *uncertainty*. Fundamentally, indeterminacy and uncertainty challenged all possible areas of human knowledge: our traditional, long-established intuitions and beliefs of how the world works, how we observe and perceive it, how we interpret the nature of reality, and how we understand the role of the observer, all come into question. In fact, each single interpretation of reality follows different perceptions and insights, which reflect the deep complexity and counter-intuitive nature of the perceived phenomena. This has profound implications for our understanding of what we observe and study, not just in physics but in every other field.

Important questions followed: does reality exists independently of our perception or is it intrinsically linked to the observer's experience? Do perception and interpretation vary from person to person? Can we clearly draw a perfect and clear line between reality and possibility, or do events have multiple, coexisting outcomes? What is the nature of causality? Is everything caused by something else, or could events happen spontaneously? How do we conceive the concept of free will, destiny, the nature of choice? How do we come to know our objects of study? What is the relationship between consciousness and the physical body? Is the mind a separate entity from the body? What is the nature of space and time? Are they constructs of human understanding, or do they exist independently of our perception?

The combination of these two principles of indeterminacy and uncertainty critically questioned our notions of identity, and the existence and the nature of the self—none of which are just the result of philosophical speculation: they challenge the rather naive notion that knowledge can be objective and exhaustive. Different perspectives can yield different insights into the same reality; conflicting or contrasting interpretations may all hold certain validity, confirming the limits of human understanding. Thus, certainty is not achievable—it may be an illusion.

So, how does all this affect the theory and practice of a psychoanalyst? What happens when a psychoanalyst makes an interpretation?

We may want to compare the task of a clinician to the work of a musician. Composers provide written scores which usually include extra comments and instructions, providing dynamics (loudness and softness), tempo (speed), and articulation marks. We are aware though that there is never an exact faithful execution of these instructions. It is left to the musicians to emphasise certain things and not others; the musical notes are clearly there but the musicians' interpretation of the score will be based on their own perception and understanding of the piece—including their always individual emotional connection and artistic vision to the music, the object of their art.

Like a musician, every psychoanalyst has a unique, individual style and a particular technique. In the act of making an interpretation, there will be variations of psychoanalytic significance in the content, phrasing, timing, and dynamics of an interpretation. Interpretations will inevitably include a particular personal sound through their unique voice. On the other hand, each patient would equally represent and evoke an individual and particular culture, which would also influence how the analyst performs his or her interpretations. Like a musician, it will never be the same interpretations: even the interpretation of one historical event in the life of a patient might change over time; new information that appears during a treatment might lead to different, and yet complementary interpretations in the future. And to make things more complicated: not one analyst would treat all of his or her patients the same.

John Cage was an American composer who created the indeterminacy movement in New York in the 1950s. He originally defined indeterminacy as "the ability of a piece to be performed in substantially different ways" (Pritchett, 1993, p. 108). In a similar fashion, interpretations given by a psychoanalyst are not clearly or precisely specified beforehand; in the best clinical moments of a session in the consulting room there is an "indeterminacy of performance" (Simms, 1986, p. 357). According to Cage, the only true form of indeterminate music is when chance elements intervene in the very moment of performance. A psychoanalytic interpretation is not chosen solely by chance, but the analyst does not have a written, analytical "score". There is no sheet music, no prior representation of the interpretation, no pre-published, noted text. Analysts have to follow, if not chance, certainly their own gut feelings; interpretations will come from a mixture of instinctive emotional responses, creative imagination, the capacity to identify with the other, and from the analyst's own intellectual courage.

This list should also include intuition, defined as the ability to understand or know something without the need for conscious reasoning. It often manifests as an instinctive response to a situation, which draws on personal experiences, insights, and unconscious knowledge, allowing individuals to navigate complex situations where rationality might be insufficient.

I would argue that indeterminacy, a concept which describes something that cannot be clearly defined or completely known, applies, first, to the *object* of psychoanalytic study; second, to the *knowledge* of that object, and, third, to the *therapeutic implications* derived from it. What would it mean to research them?

The second concept that I would like to refer to is *undecidability*, which should also help us to consider the nature of the psychoanalytic discipline. It originates in the field of mathematical logic and computational complexity theory: an undecidable problem is a decision problem to which it is impossible to construct a single algorithm leading to a correct answer, whether negative or positive; in simpler words, there are specific questions for which there is not one single answer.

In science, this is closely linked to the questions originally posed by Gödel's theorems in 1931 (1931, pp. 44–195): within a specified deductive system, a statement is neither provable nor refutable. The undecidability of a statement in a particular deductive system does not, in and of itself, address the question of whether the truth value of the statement is well defined, or whether it can be determined by other means. Undecidability only indicates that the particular deductive system being considered cannot prove the truth or falsity of a statement. Gödel showed that it is impossible to be completely truthful and completely universal; one can never say a true statement without saying some false ones. Alternatively, one can never say only true things without being forced to withhold some other equally true statements (Berto, 2009).

Undecidability has important implications in various fields. It raises the same question as the principle of indeterminacy: can anything be proven with certainty?

In psychoanalysis, we can only claim that psychoanalytic interpretations are interpretative constructions: the value of any interpretation cannot be fully known—they are interpretations, not "discoveries" or "truths" in any conventional sense. They become validated when the individual subject in analysis makes his or her own the interpretations offered by the analyst. Every interpretation is tried and tested, as it were, in every new situation in which it appears; if accepted by the patient, it is then that theoretical ideas become personal knowledge. Interpretations help patient and analyst to make visible what otherwise is not comprehensible or understandable; they develop the conditions through which psychoanalytic theory organises itself so that the unconscious of the other, as expressed in the clinic, can be revealed. Of course, interpretations offered by an analyst can also be rejected by the patient.

We need to imagine our psychic world in order to be able to think anything about it. To imagine, to fantasise, to create new ways of thinking. This form of proceeding is not alien to science—just the opposite. To quote Rovelli again, "The ability to understand something *before* it's observed is at the heart of scientific thinking" (2017, p. 10). Theoretical frameworks and imaginary *constructums* guide the scientist's observations and experimentations. This makes sense: to understand phenomena before they are directly observed often involves formulating *a priori* hypotheses and models, with no previous evidence provided.

In the case of Little Hans, Freud told us that for many years he had asked his colleagues and students to collect observations of the sexual life of children for a "more direct and less roundabout proof of these fundamental theorems". Surely, he argued, "there must be a possibility of observing in children at first hand and in all the freshness of life the sexual impulses and wishes which we dig out so laboriously in adults from among their own debris …" (Freud, 1909d, p. 6). Freud wanted to compare the observations contributed by his colleagues with the hypotheses previously put forward by him in the *Three Essays on the*

Theory of Sexuality (1905d). In his conclusion of the Little Hans paper, Freud stated that, "Strictly speaking, I learnt nothing new from this analysis, nothing that I had not already been able to discover ..." (1909b, p. 147)—that meant: already learnt from the hypothesis that he had developed from the analyses of adult patients. Rosine Perelberg describes how in Freud's clinical presentations there is a simultaneous study of structure and history. In each of his clinical cases, says Perelberg, "Freud constructed hypotheses about the successive stages that gave rise to the structure" (2005, p. 14).

The third concept I would like to mention is *overdetermination*, which should help us to describe the many and diverse formations of the unconscious. Psychoanalytic formations are dreams, slips of the tongue, symptoms, etc., always "related to a multiplicity of unconscious elements which may be organised in different meaningful sequences, each having its own specific coherence at a particular level of interpretation" (Laplanche & Pontalis, 1967, p. 292). Introduced by Freud in *Studies on Hysteria* (1895d), overdetermination operates at all levels of human life. In psychoanalysis, it refers to the idea that a single psychological symptom or behaviour would be always traced back to that multiplicity of unconscious causes, motives, or conflicts just mentioned. There is no room for a simple understanding in terms of cause and effect. The meaning of a symptom, a dream or a slip of the tongue is never straightforward, it is always a complex and multilayered affair; it stems from various sources from the past as well as from the present. In the therapeutic context, patient and analyst explore them and work hard at understanding these multiple layers.

Overdetermination operates in other fields of knowledge. In genetics, for example, scientists have long known that there is always a variety of genes interacting with internal and external environmental factors, which determines biologically important consequences: "Genes do not operate in a vacuum, but, rather, each has its role to play in the complex machinery of development" (Neel & Schull, 1954, p. 27). Examples of traits influenced by overdetermination include height, skin colour, and the susceptibility to certain diseases. Different combinations of multiple genes can lead to similar phenotypic outcomes, making it difficult to predict the inheritance patterns and the exact contributions of individual genes to the overall trait—they are overdetermined.

Finally, I would like to mention the concept of *hypercomplexity*, which has been developed in the contemporary sciences, confirming the idea of a totalising or unitary knowledge as an illusion. At present, we are witnessing the displacement of epistemological questions by ontological realities in sciences like biology, where scientists find it difficult to describe different levels of complexity in cells and in systems. Such systems represent complex configurations of parts, factors, and forces that interact with each other. In trying to study this kind of hypercomplexity, biologists find it difficult to think of models adequate enough to describe the hypercomplexed systems; they have to predict responses without being able to explain the properties of the systems causing the response. For them, reality seems to defeat their imagination.

In *algebra*, contemporary mathematicians speak of hypercomplex numbers, extensions of the complex numbers previously constructed by means of abstract algebra (Kantor, Solodovnikov, & Shenitzer, 1989). And there seems to be more complicated matters coming up their road: mathematicians have of late described more than one type of hypercomplex numbers. In the *social sciences*, authors (Qvortrup, 1998) describe a complexity inscribed in complexity, which has emerged as a new social paradigm. By this, it is agreed that there is no one single and universal position from which to observe social phenomena; instead, there are many observation points, each of them using an individual observational code specific to its own social complexity. Similarly, in *astronomy* the parallax or peripatetic view refers to the apparent position of a star among more distant stars, a position that changes when viewed from opposite sides of the earth's orbit. In *general physics*, it refers to an apparent change in the position of an object resulting from a change in the observer's position (see Kohon, 2016, pp. 87–88). Furthermore, in many of these disciplines, observations are observations of observations, making them not only polycentric but also polycontextual.

So, here we have: *indeterminacy*, *undecidability*, *overdetermination*, and *hypercomplexity*, concepts that might help us to consider and understand the complexity of the quest for psychoanalytic knowledge as much as the complexity of the psychoanalytic object of study. This formidable challenge has been approached in psychoanalysis through the detailed study of single clinical cases.

Psychoanalytic case studies originated in clinical medicine, traditionally representing an in-depth investigation over an extended period of time; it comprised the history of the patient, a clinical description of the medical complaint, and its treatment. It is characterised as the idiographic approach, emphasising the unique personal experience of the subject. However, in psychoanalysis, in contrast to medicine, data are not gathered using several different methods from a variety of sources—the only source of information originates from the dialogue between patient and psychoanalyst.

Thomas Ogden argues that "psychoanalysis [is] a process of inventing itself as it goes" from one session onto another (2005), taking into consideration not only the patient's subjectivity but also that of the psychoanalyst. The effectiveness of psychoanalytic interventions is assessed by the movement of the analytic process itself, by the changes from session to session as well as within one single session. The analyst registers these movements by paying special attention to the dynamics of transference and countertransference—and to the responses of the analysand to interpretations: have they produced new, meaningful information? Have new memories been uncovered? Is the process of free association being helped by the analyst's intervention? Is the patient's narrative creating new meanings? Do they indicate psychic change?

The idiographic approach is radically opposed to the nomothetic view, which uses experimentation and testing to observe patterns in order to be able to predict behaviour. Outcome studies and empirical forms of research, as valuable as those studies may be for the evaluation of a treatment, are radically different from the studies of single cases of psychoanalysis. In the latter, analysts attempt to share their clinical experience with colleagues, communicating their own personal and professional findings. If there were new psychoanalytic breakthroughs proposed by a psychoanalyst, whether theoretical or therapeutic, they would emerge from the work carried out by that particular psychoanalyst in the consulting room with a given patient.

Since there is no single model to describe or convey the specificity of psychoanalysis, two psychoanalytic observers witnessing the same phenomenon may be steeped in two different theories; thus, they may see two different things. Such methodological incommensurability excludes any universal mode of making inferences from the observed.

Furthermore, the observed themselves are changed by the observer; there is no possibility of making references to a fixed, permanent goal (Kuhn, 1962, p. 173).

There seems to be good and searching reasons to believe that so-called "scientific" research in psychoanalysis is inherently limited. However, not all psychoanalysts agree. A number of professionals working within the world of psychoanalysis have suggested that if psychoanalysis is going to become closer to being a science so as to become more accepted by society, we then need more research, more empirical studies, more formal methods, more transparency, more sensitive measurement systems as well as new approaches to measurement—and above all more "solid" proofs of effectiveness. They find it difficult to move away from a conventionality in the world of research, thus attempting to ignore the ontological problems presented to them by the psychoanalytic object of study. They hope to arrive to "scientifically" acceptable explanations and generalisations which would, in turn, create the possibility for predictions, further experiments, and controlled studies. Their approaches move away from singularity and difference, producing an illusion of knowing—a form of scientism.

For example, Otto Kernberg argued that:

> Our research efforts obviously need to move both into the comparative study of groups subjected to naturalistic and empirical conditions, as well as to the intense study of individual patients (N = 1), based on the direct observation of the psychoanalytic process, as well as studies where significant aspects of the psychoanalytical process can be evaluated experimentally under different conditions and in alternative clinical designs. (Kernberg, 2006, p. 933)

Transparency and measurement are taken to be universal characteristics of a method of research which would allow a given study to be qualified as scientific, appearing to validate its conclusions through "naturalistic and empirical conditions", promoting "direct observation of the psychoanalytic process", and evaluation through experimental conditions. Most of these recommendations would be considered completely anti-psychoanalytic. There also is a frequently repeated recommendation for more "*sensitive measurements systems* that identify changes in psychological functioning ..." (Fonagy, 2004, p. xxii, original italics); or, "a new approach to measurements of individual difference" (ibid., p. xxxiii); or that our aim should be "to assist the movement of psychoanalysis toward science ..." (Fonagy, 2003, p. 78), and that "some changes [are] necessary in order to ensure a future for psychoanalysis and psychoanalytic therapies within psychiatry" (ibid., p. 73).

Wilfred R. Bion described the capacity to think in human beings as "rudimentary", arguing that given this human inadequacy, any field of investigation is essentially limited only "to those phenomena that have the characteristics of the inanimate". He declared that,

> We assume that the psychotic limitation is due to an illness: that of the scientist is not. Investigation of the assumption illuminates disease on the one hand and scientific method on the other. It appears that our rudimentary equipment for "thinking" thoughts is adequate when the problems are associated with the inanimate, but not when the object for investigation is the phenomenon of life itself. Confronted with the complexities of the human mind the analyst must be circumspect in following even accepted scientific method; its weakness may be closer to the weakness of psychotic thinking than superficial scrutiny would admit. (1962, p. 14)

Antonio Damasio, a professor of neurology, argued that conscious and rational decisions are not easily available to people. Human beings are not capable of coping well with the "uncertainty and complexity of personal and social problems" (1994, p. 191). He asserted that the concept of rationality should include the personal desires, unconscious drives, and biological instincts of the subject, which always make rational decisions complicated (1994, pp. 165–201)—including the rational decisions involved in scientific research.

Well-known psychoanalytic cases, like all great works of literature, possess the "uncanny ability to evolve endlessly diverse readings" (Bloom, 1986, p. 26). They may never yield what is known as "scientific generalisations", but this is not, to my mind, a necessarily negative aspect of psychoanalytic literature. The unconscious is an intricate object of study, and although it belongs to one particular individual, its influence affects an area between the individual and the social, between self and others, between the inside and the outside, at the very limit of the distinction between the body and the mind. In spite of difficulties and limitations, including the diverse readings that they can offer, case studies, which include considerations concerning the unconscious, have been the very type of study and method of research which has pushed psychoanalytic theory forward.

A distinction can be made between, on the one hand, *clinical research* based on the consideration of single case studies, hopefully leading to revisit relevant issues of technique and approaches concerning the treatment of patients, and, on the other hand, intense, profound, and extensive *conceptual research* through the comparative study of theoretical concepts originally created from, and developed through, the treatment of single cases. In either type of research, clinical or conceptual, we are still inhabiting the realm of single case studies.

In trying to evaluate the achievements reached by psychoanalysis in the consulting room, we come to results that appear on the surface rather modest. For example, psychoanalysts would consider it to be progress whenever the patient on the couch responds to the analyst's interpretation by saying, "that makes me think of …", followed by a genuine, free association (André Green, quoted in Caldwell, 1995; see also Browne & Streeruwitz, 2017). This is not what is commonly thought to constitute "scientific" evidence—but it *is* psychoanalysis.

How do we account in psychoanalysis for the fact that whatever insights and findings we might come across in the psychoanalysis of a subject, they do not constitute "discoveries"—they are either *reconstructions*, or psychoanalytic *constructions*?

And even when we would want to measure the efficacy of the treatment, would we base the measurement on what the patient says when, in fact, his speech is the very thing that a psychoanalyst is supposed to question? Parameters used in psychology or in psychiatry are not necessarily relevant in psychoanalysis. Would we be interested in quantifying the "amount of contentment", even were it possible, that a person has achieved through his analysis? Or should we rely on the disappearance of his symptoms? Or perhaps on his life achievements—becoming a banker or a dentist or, for that matter, a psychoanalyst?

All such criteria are external to the process of psychoanalysis. How, for example, does the psychoanalyst describe or narrate the unique and intimate relationship whereby a patient tells a psychoanalyst phantasies, thoughts, and events of his or her life that they would never dare tell anyone else? How, indeed, can I account for my own responses as an analyst, responses that will have been inspired not only by what I already know but by what I did not know until I said it, until I happened to utter the words that became my interpretation? How do we pay special respect to the complications, subtleties, and variations of a psychoanalytic relationship, evident both on the patient's side as much as on the analyst's side?

The practice of psychoanalytic listening resists codification; its technique cannot be prescribed, nor can it be restricted to the contents offered by manuals of therapeutic intervention. Psychoanalysis works through abductive inference. This is a type of non-deductive inference, which in contrast to an inductive inference, consists in a process of forming explanatory hypotheses that are held awaiting further confirmation; they are only put forward as questions and only a few would be viewed as satisfactory. That an explanation might make meaningful sense does not suggest that there is only the one explanation or even that it would be the best one. There might be many possible explanations for any process that we observe, but we tend to abduce, to take away one single explanation, developing a form of reasoning through successive approximation. Under this principle, an explanation is valid if it is the best possible explanation for a set of known data (Peirce, 1903; see also Eisele, 1985; Fabbrichesi & Marietti, 2006).

Psychoanalysis is not alone: anthropology, history, and other social sciences share a similar stance: they study a singular being (in the consulting room), a particular culture (in the jungle, mountain, island, etc.), or unique significant event from the past. They arrive at findings and insights only through being open to the strangeness of each individual object of study. Elizabeth Spillius (2003) argued that, in psychoanalysis, it would be futile to promote a type of research based on methods borrowed from other areas of knowledge: psychiatry, developmental psychology, infant research, attachment theory, etc.

Included as a praise in the book that David Tuckett and others edited in 2024, entitled *Knowing What Psychoanalysts Do and Doing What Psychoanalysts Know*, the late Dana Birksted-Breen wrote that the authors included in the book had set out, "to research the different basic modes of doing psychoanalysis, which would lead us to the identification of those significant moments when the unconscious maximally reveals itself in the disturbing phenomena which occur unexpectedly" (Birksted-Breen, 2024, p. ii).

She spoke of "different basic *modes* of *doing* psychoanalysis …" This acknowledged that each clinician may practise psychoanalysis in different ways to other psychoanalysts; there is not just one rigid method to be followed, in fact psychoanalysts may not even treat all of their patients in the same way. The concept of "modes" implies that there are alternative ways in which something exists, a task is done, an event is experienced. It is not a "method", which refers to a much more systematic or organised approach in achieving a goal. In scientific disciplines, methods are systematic steps for conducting experiments, gathering observations, and making conclusions, hoping for a "sure road [a *method*, a path] to knowledge" (Agamben, 1978, p. 33). While a "method" is planned and follows a structured approach used to achieve a specific objective, in psychoanalysis, a "mode" refers to a way of doing or experiencing something without such a given method: nevertheless, the psychoanalyst's mode is not arbitrary, it will follow clinical reasons, which would always be a combination of the familiar and the extraordinary. Dana emphasised that there will be a clinical focus on recognising crucial points during the therapeutic process that become significant, highlighting the idea that there could be disturbing unconscious elements which might become clearer at unexpected times.

Thomas Kuhn's book on *The Structure of Scientific Revolutions* (1962) represented a historical landmark in the philosophy of science. Twenty years later, he presented a paper entitled, "What are scientific revolutions?", where he argued that,

> Revolutionary change [in science] is defined in part by its difference from normal change … [They] involve discoveries that cannot be accommodated within the concepts in use before they were made. In order to make or to assimilate such a discovery one must alter the way one thinks …. (Kuhn, (1987), quoted in Patton, 2014, p. 72)

This enabled us to understand that the evolution of scientific theory did not emerge from a straightforward accumulation of facts, which was an early positivist view of science. Instead, there were genuine epistemological jumps which represented a revolution, a change of intellectual circumstances and possibilities bringing new paradigms into play.

Kuhn suggested a different view in his philosophy of science: a necessary conceptual change from speaking *only* in terms of *paradigms* (which represented examples of successful practices that served to keep the coherence of a given research community), to thinking *also* in terms of *exemplars*, which set up a standard for others to follow (1969, p. 187). In psychoanalysis, an exemplar would serve to represent a certain quality or trait which would identify clinical problems and challenges posed by patients, thus hopefully helping to guide psychoanalysts in their own efforts in treating their patients. This does not imply that the cases have to be always successful; on the contrary, psychoanalysts learn from their colleagues' mistakes, not necessarily from their successes—the representation of the singular becomes an authentic possibility for other cases.

Following his rendering of Kuhn's ideas, the late John Forrester described the concept of "reasoning in cases" as a method of learning in psychoanalysis (2017, pp. 1–24). The analyst never tells the "full story" of a psychoanalytic treatment by writing a case study; a completely accurate picture of a patient's predicament and/or pathology would never be created. Nevertheless, the idea of *reasoning in cases seems right to me.* It consists in a first-hand method of learning, which shows how Freud and his followers thought and continue speaking and thinking with their patients, in the context of a mutual, although asymmetrical psychoanalytic relationship. Psychoanalytic single cases have one great distinctive advantage over other medical and/or psychiatric case histories: from as early as *Studies on Hysteria* (1895d), Freud believed that they are always characterised by the close connection between the stories of the patients' sufferings and their symptoms.

Carlo Ginzburg (1989) argued that psychoanalysis is a form of conjectural knowledge, an indirect, intuitive knowledge based on the study of individual cases. In this sense, one could bring psychoanalysis together with history, ethnography, and anthropology; in all instances, the concept of science or art as references to be used and/or applied, would be wrong and misleading. Nevertheless, each of them represents different forms of knowledge: psychoanalytic knowledge is a form of knowledge peculiar, specific, and exclusive to psychoanalysis—and the same applies to the others.

As psychoanalysts, we cannot simplify what is extraordinarily multilayered and exceptionally complex. A psychoanalytic case study can never be a simple narration; there would always be a multiplicity of stories within the clinical history.

Given what psychoanalysis *is*, it could never aim at reaching a position where its theory and practice will be able to give a full and final account of its subject. Scientific evidence will never be given. Proofs cannot be provided.

Not now. Not in the future.

References

Agamben, G. (1978). *Infancy and History: The Destruction of Experience.* London: Verso, 1993.

Beck, U. (1986). *The Risk Society*. London: Sage.

Berto, F. (2009). *There's Something About Gödel: The Complete Guide to the Incompleteness Theorem*. Chichester, UK: Wiley-Blackwell.

Bion, W. R. (1962). *Learning from Experience*. London: Heinemann.

Birksted-Breen, D. (2024). Praise. In: D. Tuckett, E. Allison, O. Bonard, G. J. Bruns, A. L. Christopoulos, & M. Diercks (Eds.), *Knowing What Psychoanalysts Do and Doing What Psychoanalysts Know*. Lanham, MD: Rowman & Littlefield.

Bloom, H. (1986, March 23). Freud, the greatest modern writer [Review of the book *Freud*]. *New York Times*, p. 26.

Browne, H., & Streeruwitz, A. (2017). Foreword: Reflections on The Greening of Psychoanalysis Conference. In: R. Perelberg & G. Kohon (Eds.), *The Greening of Psychoanalysis: André Green's New Paradigm in Contemporary Theory and Practice*. London: Karnac.

Caldwell, L. (1995). An interview with André Green. *New Formations, 26*: 15–35.

Castoriadis, C. (1988). Logique, imagination, reflexion. Lecture presented to the colloquium on The Unconscious and Science, University of Paris-X (Nanterre), March 5–6. In: R. Dorey (Ed.), *L'inconscient et la science*. Paris: Dunod, 1991. Reprinted 1992 as Logic, imagination, reflection. D. A. Curtis (Trans.). *American Imago, 49*: 3–33.

Cooper, A., & Lousada, J. (2005). *Borderline Welfare: Feeling and Fear of Feeling in Modern Welfare*. London: Karnac.

Damasio, A. R. (1994). *Descartes' Error: Emotion, Reason and the Human Brain*. London: Papermac, 1996.

Eisele, C. (Ed.) (1985). Peirce, the scientist. In: *Historical Perspectives on Peirce's Logic of Science: A History of Science*. Amsterdam, the Netherlands: Mouton.

Fabbrichesi, R., & Marietti, S. (2006). *Semiotics and Philosophy in Charles Sanders Peirce*. Newcastle-upon-Tyne, UK: Cambridge Scholars, 2008.

Fonagy, P. (2003). Psychoanalysis today. *World Psychiatry*, *2*(2): 73–80.
Fonagy, P. (2004). Foreword. In: P. Richardson, H. Kächele, & C. Renlund (Eds.), *Research on Psychoanalytic Psychotherapy with Adults*. London: Karnac.
Fonagy, P. (2015). The effectiveness of psychodynamic psychotherapies: An update. *World Psychiatry*, *14*(2): 137–150.
Forrester, J. (2017). On Kuhn's case: Psychoanalysis and the paradigm. In: *Thinking in Cases*. Cambridge: Polity.
Freud, S., with Breuer, J. (1895d). *Studies on Hysteria*. *S. E.*, *2*. London: Hogarth.
Freud, S. (1905a). On psychotherapy. *S. E.*, *7*. London: Hogarth.
Freud, S. (1905d). *Three Essays on the Theory of Sexuality*. *S. E.*, *7*. London: Hogarth.
Freud, S. (1909b). Analysis of a phobia in a five-year-old boy. *S. E.*, *10*. London: Hogarth.
Freud, S. (1909d). Notes upon a case of obsessional neurosis. *S. E.*, *10*. London: Hogarth.
Ginzburg, C. (1989). *Clues, Myths, and the Historical Method*. J. & A. C. Tedeschi (Trans.). Baltimore, MD: Johns Hopkins University Press, 2013.
Gödel, K. (1931). Über formal unentscheidbare Sätze der Principia Mathematica und verwandter Systeme, I. In: S. Feferman (Ed.), *Kurt Gödel: Collected Works*, Vol. I. Oxford: Oxford University Press, 1986.
Kantor, I. L., Solodovnikov, A. S., & Shenitzer, A. (1989). *Hypercomplex Numbers: An Elementary Introduction to Algebras*. New York: Springer.
Kernberg, O. F. (2006). Research anxiety: A response to Roger Perron's comments. *International Journal of Psychoanalysis*, *87*(4): 933–937.
Kohon, G. (1999). *No Lost Certainties to Be Recovered*. London: Karnac.
Kohon, G. (2016). *Reflections on the Aesthetic Experience: Psychoanalysis and the Uncanny*. London: Routledge/The Institute of Psychoanalysis.
Kuhn, T. (1962). *The Structure of Scientific Revolutions*. Chicago, IL: University of Chicago Press.
Kuhn, T. (1969). *Postscript*, in the 2nd edition, *The Structure of Scientific Revolutions*. Chicago, IL: University of Chicago Press, 1970.
Kuhn, T. (1987). What are scientific revolutions? In: J. Conant & J. Haugeland (Eds.), *The Road Since Structure: Philosophical Essays, 1970–1993, with an Autobiographical Interview*. Chicago, IL: University of Chicago Press.
Laplanche, J., & Pontalis, J.-B. (1967). *The Language of Psychoanalysis*. London: Hogarth, 1973.
Neel, J. V., & Schull, W. J. (1954). *Human Heredity*. Chicago, IL: University of Chicago Press.
Ogden, T. (2005). *This Art of Psychoanalysis: Dreaming Undreamt Dreams and Interrupted Cries*. London: Routledge/The Institute of Psychoanalysis.
Patton, L. (2014). *Philosophy, Science and History—A Guide and Reader*. New York: Routledge.

Peirce, C. S. (1903). *Collected Papers of Charles Sanders Peirce (Vol. 5).* C. Hartshorne & P. Weiss (Eds.). Cambridge, MA: Harvard University Press, 1958.

Perelberg, R. J. (2005). Introduction. In: R. J. Perelberg (Ed.), *Freud: A Modern Reader.* London: Whurr.

Pontalis, J.-B. (2000). *Windows.* Lincoln, NE: University of Nebraska Press, 2003.

Pritchett, J. (1993). *The Music of John Cage.* Cambridge: Cambridge University Press.

Qvortrup, L. (1998). *The Hypercomplex Society.* New York: Peter Lang, 2003.

Rovelli, C. (2017). *The Order of Time.* S. Carnell & E. Segre (Trans.). London: Allen Lane, 2018.

Simms, B. R. (1986). *Music of the Twentieth Century: Style and Structure.* New York: Schirmer.

Slade, M., & Priebe, S. (Eds.) (2006). *Choosing Methods in Mental Health Research: Mental Health from Theory to Practice.* London: Routledge.

Spillius, E. B. (2003). Anthropology and psychoanalysis: A personal concordance. *Bulletin of the British Psychoanalytical Society*, 39: 7–24.

CHAPTER 7

In the space of conjunction: Discussion of Gregorio Kohon's "What does research have to do with psychoanalysis?"

Alessandra Lemma

Psychoanalysis and empirical research have always been uncomfortable bedfellows. In this thought-provoking paper, Gregorio stresses that as psychoanalysts we must be accountable for what we do but also invites us to challenge the applicability of the dominant scientific paradigm to the unique nature of psychoanalytic work. I am grateful for the opportunity to engage further with Gregorio's thinking on this important question.

Gregorio sets out very clearly four principles that challenge all established areas of human knowledge, and which confirm, in his words, that "totalizing or unitary knowledge is an illusion", namely the principles of indeterminacy, undecidability, overdetermination, and hypercomplexity. I will not elaborate on these further as I am approaching my discussion from a starting point of agreement over these core principles. However, from this shared set of presumptions, there are several possible directions of travel.

Reading Gregorio's chapter, I was taken back to my days in the NHS in 2007 when Lord Layard (an economist) put forward his proposal to increase access to psychological therapies and hence reduce the cost to the economy due to mental ill health. His goals and those of the IAPT programme (Improving Access to Psychological Therapies, as it was then called) were economically inciting to politicians. The proposal had the appeal of simplicity: look at the extant evidence base, select the approach that ticks the evidence-based boxes—CBT in this instance—and offer it to as many people as possible. Layard's proposal all too neatly embedded itself in a pre-existing evidence-based psychotherapy movement that elevated the RCT (randomised controlled trial) as the "gold standard" in psychotherapy research.

The hype around RCTs revealed the significant investments made in the promise of research to deliver an unbiased, definitive guide to "what works" and what should therefore be funded. Between 2008 and 2011, as I sat in many meetings at the Department of Health discussing how to protect psychoanalytic interventions in the NHS, it was all too clear how research can become an idealised object that defends against the messy, complex, and painful reality of psychic pain, and against the very real challenge of how we can alleviate it and how we can meaningfully evaluate our attempts to do so.

The dominant culture of evidence-based practice has subjected the providers of psychoanalytic interventions to the requirement to justify the effectiveness of this mode of therapy in the public health sector. Gregorio invites us to not be intimated by this requirement. In an established tradition of psychoanalytic critiques focusing on the inappropriateness of many research methods to the very particular nature of the psychoanalytic encounter, Gregorio argues that we must respond to the evidence-based external culture from a vantage point that is distinctively psychoanalytic and practice-based. From this perspective, Gregorio believes that "experimental conditions" that move away from "singularity and difference" are simply not psychoanalytic. This raises an interesting question regarding whether psychoanalysis can only ever be investigated by methods that are deemed to be "psychoanalytic"—a definition which in itself might not be so easy to agree upon.

Notwithstanding a shared concern around what Gregorio rightly refers to as "the illusion of knowing" that we can easily succumb to if we are in the thrall of "scientism", I fall in the group of colleagues that Gregorio addresses when he writes:

> a number of professionals working within the world of psychoanalysis believe that if psychoanalysis is going to become accepted

> by society, what is needed is more research … more transparency, more sensitive measurement systems … (p. 98)

Although I am certainly not of the view that what we need are only more RCTs or brain scans, I believe that research conceptualised broadly (i.e. as a systematic, transparent approach focused on investigating a given question) and more narrowly (i.e. as referring to specific research methodologies) is essential to further our understanding of the human mind. Whichever means we use to arrive at this understanding, the conclusions we reach are always best conceived of as provisional, under constant evolution. We should be suspicious of the use of scientific claims presented as absolute. But we must be careful to distinguish the use we make of empirical research findings from the nature of scientific investigation at its best, which does not necessarily default to making inviolable, final knowledge claims. To claim that research can provide "absolute proof" is one way of using a scientific paradigm that leads to the "scientism" Gregorio rightly invites us to be sceptical of, but it is not the only way.

I could not agree more with Gregorio when he writes that: "We cannot simplify what is extraordinarily multilayered and exceptionally complex" (p. 104).

Indeed, public mental health programmes, with their focus on population health and statistical analysis, are certainly problematic and can run counter to a recognition of the complexity of psychic pain and psychopathology. The development of evidence-based interventions may result, for seemingly sound "scientific" reasons, in screening out complexity in research studies or patient groups. This can lead to a focus on simple interventions for so-called "simple" (or non-complex) conditions. And yet, within clinical practice, one rarely sees such non-complex conditions. The idea that they exist, and are amenable to simple and cheap interventions, is immediately politically attractive.

Recurrent criticisms of psychoanalytic approaches are that they prioritise the individual above the population need and that as treatments they are long, intense, and expensive. In a public health context where resources are limited, these are reasonable challenges to which we must respond, assuming we want to ensure that more people have access to this kind of intervention. It will not suffice to respond to this requirement by only criticising the dominant methods for evaluating what we do even though it is essential that the perspective that Gregorio has carefully outlined is central to these discussions, in order to underscore the complexity of what we are grappling to understand. It is worth noting that today we are in a stronger position to argue the case for psychoanalytic interventions thanks to the research efforts of colleagues in the UK and internationally, many of whom share similar concerns to Gregorio's but have nevertheless engaged in empirical research, mindful of its limitations.

If psychoanalysis claims to be a treatment for psychological problems, *and* it seeks public funding for its provision, then we have a responsibility in that context to evaluate its effectiveness and to understand the specificity of its impact. How we address these questions in a manner that respects the individual subjectivity of the patient, and of how the analyst does indeed need to approach each patient differently, as Gregorio helpfully reminds us, remains an ongoing but perhaps not altogether impossible challenge. Gregorio's important emphasis on psychoanalysis as a "mode" rather than a "method"—a "mode" that must be carefully titrated to the individual patient—can be captured, admittedly in a rather unpoetic manner, by the kind of approach that he is critical of when applied to our work specifically. A group I was involved with at UCL attempted to do this when we worked on developing the competence framework for psychoanalytic psychotherapy (Lemma, Roth, & Pilling, 2008). Through a systematic, evidence-based process we identified as a core "meta-competence" the clinician's capacity to adapt to the patient's individual needs and to be able to deviate from a prescribed "method" to attend to specific relational dynamics in the moment. This competence is now embedded in standards for training. I imagine the language of competences is not to everyone's taste, but I mention it here as an example of how an empirical approach need not deny complexity or the unique interaction of each analyst–patient dyad. Instead, it can be used to describe what we do in a language that creates bridges and facilitates the development of psychoanalysis in contexts other than private practice.

Gregorio selects the single case study as the most appropriate way to capture our work. I share his belief in the merits of this approach and how it allows us to distil "exemplars", which he evocatively captures as "a knowledge in permanent development". I am interested to hear more from Gregorio about how he suggests we approach the process of writing up our cases if we are to use them in this manner. Gregorio does not use the term "single case methodology", which refers to a very particular systematic way of approaching single case studies (Hinshelwood, 2013). The cases we typically write up and publish or present to each other very rarely meet the more stringent criteria of a single case methodology. Preserving the "singularity and difference" of each case as Gregorio puts it, is essential, and the single case study is indeed ideally suited to this, but unless we follow a disciplined, robust process for describing our work and challenging the conclusions we draw, we are at risk of perpetuating building psychoanalytic understanding on the well-known logical fallacy of assuming that if something has happened once before, and if this same pattern is observed again, this supports the proposed theory. As clinicians we find it hardest to identify negative instances when the patient's reaction is *not* as we would have hypothesised it to be.

So, even if we want to rely on the single case study to generate "exemplars", this will require consideration of how we approach this task. The outstanding work by David Tuckett and colleagues (2024), that Gregorio refers to, followed a clear research methodology. In so far as single cases are deemed the most appropriate to our field, we must ensure that we apply rigour to our abductive reasoning and that we follow a method that can be described and replicated, which is really another way of describing a good scientific method.

I welcome Gregorio's challenge to simplistic notions about the status of scientific findings. Science is all too often idealised as the only respectable path to knowledge. Equally, we cannot escape the fact that *all* knowledge—irrespective of how we arrive at it—is subject to both rational and irrational forces. No research is exempt from the self-serving bias of the researcher's own interests and allegiances. Luborsky et al.'s (1999) much-cited paper showed that we can reliably predict the conclusions of a paper on psychotherapy outcome just knowing the theoretical allegiance of its first author.

The endeavour to understand something or someone is anything but neutral or dispassionate. Behind all knowledge claims lie human beings fuelled by passions and their own unconscious. Our clinical "knowledge" is similarly compromised so that from whatever perspective we approach the task of understanding a person or a phenomenon we invariably need another perspective to act as a corrective and to provide some triangulation. Larger-scale research can provide one such "other" perspective for the clinician, just as the psychoanalyst's emphasis on individual subjectivity can alert the researcher to potential blind spots in their scientific field of vision and remind them of the perils of generalisation. I don't see these approaches as incommensurable with one another, which leads me finally to Freud's metaphor of the whale and the polar bear that Gregorio draws on.

Freud famously compared the dialogue between psychoanalysis and other disciplines to a metaphorical encounter between a whale and a polar bear: these two creatures are different, and they inhabit two separate environments. Both Freud and Gregorio appear to share the view that while the polar bear and the whale should respect one another, we must accept that their different points of view remain at odds. This tension is apparent, for example, in the discomfort some analysts feel with the rapprochement between psychoanalysis and the neurosciences. Quite understandably, the concerns centre on the neglect of subjectivity and first-person accounts in neuroscientific theories and research. However, a focus on the neurobiology of the mind does not mean that we reduce it to something that can ever be fully known objectively, thereby making psychoanalysis redundant. Solms (2020), for example, emphasises that the brain in the scanner and the experience of awareness are two different perspectives about the same one "thing". I agree that we need both perspectives because they *amplify* our understanding of the complexity of the human mind, not reduce it.

Freud's metaphor speaks to the challenges of interdisciplinary dialogue such as that required by research in psychoanalysis. It is true that different academic fields develop specialised languages, methods, and perspectives. Bringing them together requires creating a common space where both can communicate and collaborate, despite their contrasting natures. This is hard work. Basil Bernstein's (2000) concept of "hierarchical" and "horizontal" knowledge structures sheds light on why this is so.

A *hierarchical knowledge structure* is typical in the physical sciences. Bernstein suggests that this comprises very general propositions and theories, which integrate knowledge at lower levels, and track underlying uniformities across an expanding range of apparently different phenomena building towards greater and greater integrating propositions, at ever more abstract levels. By contrast, the typical *horizontal knowledge structure* found in the social sciences, arts, and humanities consists of a series of specialised languages and modes of interrogation which emerge and develop segmentally. So, *integration* is the key developmental concern within the physical sciences, resulting in hierarchical structures, whereas development in the social sciences results in *accumulation*—a series of segmented languages. This differentiation of internal knowledge structures—hierarchical or horizontal—has clear implications for interdisciplinarity. Significantly, Bernstein draws our attention to the socialising process of "becoming" in disciplines built on hierarchical structures where "mastering" the procedures of investigation and instruments of observation matters most. By contrast, initiation into a discipline with a horizontal knowledge structure—like psychoanalysis—is more likely to involve the acquisition of what he refers to as a "gaze": "what counts in the end is the specialised language, its position, its perspective, the acquirer's 'gaze', rather than any one exemplary theory … 'truth' is a matter of acquired 'gaze'" (1999, p. 165).

Appreciation of the original episteme of a discipline is critical then to understanding the methods, techniques, and procedures that a discipline adopts in knowledge production, of what counts as an object of study, and how the discipline treats its own nature as the subject of reflexive analysis. This is what Gregorio has articulated so clearly and evocatively in his paper in relation to the psychoanalytic "gaze".

Interdisciplinary dialogue is demanding precisely because everything we say operates at the intersection of two opposing forces: on the one hand, a relatively stable platform of communication that supports mutual understanding; but, on the other, the power of different discipline-specific socialising processes and beliefs to refract understanding. This is why I stated earlier that interdisciplinarity is "hard work", but I also believe that psychoanalysis and empirical research can collaborate creatively and be mutually strengthened if they are open to learning new languages and methods of investigation from each other.

To conclude, I want to return to Gregorio's important and unequivocal acknowledgement of the need for accountability. Accountability essentially refers to the quality or state of being responsible or answerable for one's actions. Gregorio has made a compelling case for the single case study as a way of addressing this requirement. This approach supports us in the endeavour to be accountable to the singularity of each patient. However, if we want psychoanalytic interventions to continue to be accessible to diverse patient groups who cannot afford this privately, we must secure a seat at the tables where decisions are being made about what type of therapy will be provided in the public sector. In this context, it is not unreasonable to be asked to demonstrate, somehow, our value. The indisputable complexity of this task that Gregorio underlines is not, in my view, an argument against applying an experimental method; rather, it is an invaluable reminder of the need to question *how* we use it and to be mindful of its limitations.

The fabric of the dialogue that will allow psychoanalysis to secure its place in public health settings and to remain more broadly "relevant" is one of conjunction: yes, to the single case study … AND … yes, to other types of research too. We have two equal duties: a duty of responsibility to the singularity of "any one Other", AND a duty of responsibility to "every Other". Deconstructing the illusion of scientism, as Gregorio so elegantly achieves in his chapter, need not result in stepping away from empirical research. Rather, the two equal and imperative duties to which we are required to respond, produce a tension: a paradox not resolved by a simple decision or choice between the two, but rather a commitment to an ongoing dialogue about the limitations of all research methodologies. Fundamentally, it is about our willingness to question our relationship to all types of "knowledge".

References

Bernstein, B. (1999). Vertical and horizontal discourse: An essay. *British Journal of Sociology of Education, 20*(2): 157–173.

Hinshelwood, R. D. (2013). *Research on the Couch: Single Case Studies, Subjectivity and Psychoanalytic Knowledge*. London: Routledge.

Lemma, A., Roth, A., & Pilling, S. (2008). *The Competences Required to Deliver Effective Psychoanalytic/ Psychodynamic Therapy: Clinician Version*. Department of Health. www.ucl.ac.uk/CORE (last accessed 6 February 2026).

Luborsky, L., Diguer, L., Seligman, D. A., Rosenthal, R., Krause, E. D., Johnson, S., Halperin, G., Bishop, M., Berman, J. S., & Schweitzer, E. (1999).

The researcher's own therapy allegiances: A "wild card" in comparisons of treatment efficacy. *Clinical Psychology: Science and Practice*, 6: 95–106.

Solms, M. (2020). Response to the commentaries on the "New Project". *Neuropsychoanalysis*, *22*: 1–2, 97, 107.

Tuckett, D., Allison, E., Bonard, O., Bruns, G. J., Christopoulos, A. L., & Diercks, M. (2024). *Knowing What Psychoanalysts Do and Doing What Psychoanalysts Know*. Lanham, MD: Rowman & Littlefield.

Part II

The whole truth and nothing but the truth?

CHAPTER 8

Psychoanalysis and freedom of thought*

Hanna Segal

Psychoanalysis belongs to the great scientific tradition of freeing thought from dogma, whether religious or arising out of an established scientific tradition itself. Claude Bernard said: "An idea must always remain independent. It must not be chained by scientific beliefs any more than by those that are philosophical or religious" (quoted in Segal, 1987, pp. 217–218). Such freedom, however, is hard to attain. In any culture certain thoughts or ideas are inadmissible.

Copernicus' and Galileo's work met with emotional resistance. It was unthinkable that the earth should be anything but the centre of the universe, with stars revolving round it. Darwin's work was equally inadmissible. Of course, I know that I am oversimplifying here. Copernicus, Galileo, and Darwin, like Freud, had predecessors. And in the case of astronomy there was the added problem that scientific conclusions ran against the evidence of the senses. The earth is flat. But be that as it may, however well documented was the evidence, their discoveries were

---

* This chapter was originally published as Segal, H. (1989). Psychoanalysis and freedom of thought. In: J. Sandler (Ed.), *Dimensions of Psychoanalysis* (pp. 51–64). London: Karnac. It is reproduced from *Dimensions of Psychoanalysis*, 1st Edition by Joseph, Sandler, published by Routledge.

resisted because they conflicted basically with the accepted view of the place of God and man in the universe.

Before Freud, it was unthinkable that incestuous wishes were part of human nature and not the privilege of a few perverts. It was unthinkable that children, and even infants, had sexual wishes, phantasies, and even activities, even though, unlike in the case of astronomy or biology, much of the evidence was around, both from observation and self-observation. The notion of infantile sexuality was so unthinkable that Freud himself, when first coming upon the evidence, assumed that all his patients had been seduced in childhood by an adult. Judging from a letter to Fliess, he was helped in allowing himself to contemplate the new idea because it released him from the burden of another inadmissible idea. In this letter he says that when his views about childhood seduction were disproved by his own evidence, instead of feeling depressed about it, he felt surprisingly excited and relieved. The excitement was due to the feeling of being on the brink of a great discovery. But the relief came from being able to discard another horrifying thought, namely, that so many respectable fathers, among them his own father, had been perverts. So, his acceptance of one painful idea was somewhat facilitated by his relief at its freeing him from another. But it is important to note that while both thoughts were painful, to Freud they were not unthinkable. He could think about them and test them against the evidence. The acceptance of the hitherto unthinkable thoughts about the child's sexual nature was a major breakthrough in his thinking.

Before Freud, it was unthinkable that human beings regularly held, not only incestuous, but cruel wishes and death wishes against their nearest and dearest and that they invariably harboured death wishes against their parents. To make such unthinkable thoughts thinkable, it takes a genius and a hero of the stamp of Copernicus, of Darwin, of Freud, someone of his time and yet stepping sufficiently outside what is thinkable in his time, to formulate hypotheses hitherto unthinkable.

Once such hypotheses are formulated, there is a long battle with emotional resistances and a long process of working through, of overcoming, first one's own inner resistances, then those of the scientific establishment, then the world at large, until, finally, they may become part of accepted scientific thought and eventually of the general culture.

With psychoanalysis, however, the problem is not only a social one. Even though psychoanalytic ideas gained some general acceptance, the battle for the freedom of thought has to be fought individually with every analysand on the couch, as well as within oneself. And that is where it started. Freud did not set out to revolutionise culture; he set out to treat patients. Recognising that the hysterical pathology hinged on the conversion into symptoms of thoughts that were not allowed into consciousness, he set about to free his individual patients' thoughts from inner resistances and prohibitions. His work, even the early work before his elaboration of the psychoanalytical method, abounds in examples.

What is the origin of such inhibitions of thought? Most immediately evident is the fear of the superego. In the same way in which the fear of an external authority can make us afraid to speak, the fear of an internal authority can make us afraid to think. The superego, according to Freud, is the internalised parental figure carrying the parental prohibitions, which becomes a structure in our unconscious mind, but while the external authority can forbid only actions, including speech, this internal authority can forbid thought. The prohibition may be directed not only to certain thoughts, say, hostile thoughts, directed against the parents and siblings, it may also be against searching for knowledge, and thought itself. Some myths lead themselves to this interpretation, for instance, the myth of the Garden of Eden. Eating from the tree of knowledge is the first sin and leads to a fall from grace. The myth of the Tower of Babel, the pursuit of knowledge of god is punished by an attack on language, that is, verbal thought, an attack that leads to confusion of thought. The myth of Prometheus, punished for stealing fire from the gods and giving it to mankind. One root of the inhibition of thought and searching for knowledge is the demand felt to emanate from the superego that it be deified. The superego becomes a god who cannot tolerate enlightenment. When Oedipus finds the answer to the riddle of the Sphinx, the Sphinx has to kill herself. A god cannot survive being known too well. Such a god is also a terrible god. The Sphinx ate her victims. That aspect of the superego felt to be directed against knowledge and thought was particularly investigated and described by Wilfred Bion.

The superego is, however, a complex structure. It is more than the sum total of parental prohibitions, and its savagery goes far beyond that of most parents. In his later works Freud expressed the view, partly in agreement with Melanie Klein and others, which emphasised the point that the superego is not only an internalisation of parental prohibitions, but that it is also and mainly a result of the projection into those parental figures of some of one's own impulses and phantasies. Both the ideal and the persecutory aspects of that superego have their roots in the infant's own impulses. For example, in the case of the Wolf Man, if his superego was a wolf with staring eyes, we would now say that this was largely because he attributed to his internal parents his own biting and voyeuristic impulses. Similarly, the demand of the superego to be treated as a god, never exposed to critical thought, is rooted in the infant's own needs for such a perfect parent.

The prohibition against thoughts that seem to emanate from the superego is also in part a projection of the infantile self's own antagonism to thought. If we eat from the tree of knowledge of good and evil, we exile ourselves from paradise. Copernicus and Darwin dealt great blows to human vanity. It was not only the superego vested in religion and authority that protested against their discoveries, but also human vanity and egocentricity. Man does not like losing his special and august place in the universe as god's elect. Freud refers in several papers to the blow Darwin and Copernicus dealt to man's self-love, and he adds: "But human megalomania will have suffered its third and most wounding blow from the psychological research of the present time, which seeks to prove to the ego that it is not even master in its own house" (1916–17, p. 285). And the third blow is of a more personal nature. It is easier to accept Freud's theories in general than to accept the knowledge of oneself individually and specifically: "Thinking puts a limit on the omnipotence of phantasy and is attacked because of our longing for that omnipotence" (Freud, 1911b, p. 219).

A patient dreamt that he was breaking the links in a chain with great fury. He associated to it that in the previous session the analyst had referred to a train of thought and had also used the expression, links, in pointing something out to him; when she had said, a train of thought, he had had the angry thought that he had not verbalised: it's not a train, it's a chain. He had been in a temper after the session. He did not want, he said, to be chained by his thoughts. He wanted to tear the chain apart and to be free of it. He felt his own train of linked thoughts as a prison and a persecution because it interfered with the belief in his omnipotence. It led him to realise things he did not want to know. Paradoxically, the freedom of thought that gradually emerged in his analysis was felt by him as a chain on his freedom to think what he liked. Free thought becomes, for instance, subject to perceptual evidence, laws of consistency, logic, and so forth.

I think that at this point I have to say something about what I mean by those terms "omnipotence", "omnipotence phantasy", and "thought", and how they are related. In Freud's view, expressed most tellingly and succinctly in his paper "Formulations on the two principles of mental functioning" (1911b, pp. 213–226), it is related to the emergence of thought, to the loss of omnipotence, and the experience of frustration, and the move from what he calls the pleasure principle to the reality principle. The infant's peace of mind is disturbed by peremptory inner needs, such as hunger. His first response is by hallucinatory wish fulfilment, an omnipotent phantasy of a need-satisfying object, a hallucination. His other response is by motor discharge, trying to rid himself of the experience by discharging it through muscular action. Eventually, however, he discovers that neither the hallucination nor the discharge satisfied the need. It was only the non-occurrence of the expected satisfaction, the disappointment experienced that led to the abandonment of this attempt at satisfaction by means of hallucination. Instead of it, the psychic apparatus had to decide to form a conception of the real circumstances in the external world and to endeavour to make a real alteration in them. The new principle of mental functioning was thus introduced. What was presented in the mind was no longer what was agreeable, but what was real, even if it happened to be disagreeable. This setting up of the reality principle proved to be a momentous step (ibid., p. 219). To form a conception of the real circumstances and to endeavour to make a real alteration in them could be called a first step in thinking. It takes the place of the mindless motor discharge. Freud says: "Restraint upon motor discharge (or an action) which would then become necessary, was provided by means of the process of thinking" (ibid., p. 221). According to Freud, it is thinking that makes it possible for the mental apparatus to tolerate an increased tension and to delay action. He calls it "essentially an experimental kind of acting". Thus, thinking evolves in the gap between the experience of the need and its satisfaction.

On this hypothesis there is a distinction between hallucination and thought. I shall come back to that. A further extension of this hypothesis on the origin and nature of thought emerges from the work of Melanie Klein, particularly with very young children, and that of Wilfred Bion, particularly with psychotics. In Klein's view, the response to hunger is a hallucination of an all-satisfying breast, as suggested by Freud, but she adds that when this cannot ward off the hunger, hunger itself is experienced also as the presence of an object, but a bad one, gnawing, tearing, attacking, a hallucinated bad object. According to Bion, such an experience, felt to be a bad object, can only be dealt with by expulsion. I think that the motor discharge, as described by Freud, may be a way of dealing with bad hallucinations, an attempt to expel them.

It is, I think, the realisation that this discharge does not relieve the need, that brings in the realisation that a need is not an object that can be got rid of, but is something intrinsic to oneself, something originating within oneself, not a bad object, but the need for an object that is absent. The hallucinations are recognised as the product of one's mind. A phantasy of an ideal object or a persecutory one is recognised as a phantasy. So long as a phantasy is omnipotent, it is not a thought because it is not recognised as such.

When a phantasy is recognised as a product of one's own mind, it moves into the realm of thought. One then can say: I phantasised this or that, or I thought such and such. In that, thought differs from hallucination, or delusion. Freud says that the reality principle is nothing but the pleasure principle subjected to reality testing. I would add that thinking evolves from omnipotent phantasy, and it is a phantasy recognised as such and one that can be subjected to reality testing.

Thinking first starts with, and then promotes, reality testing. It starts with the realisation, this is not what is, it is what I made it to be in my mind. But it also promotes reality testing, in that omnipotent phantasy cannot be used for reality testing. Its very aim is to deny the reality of the experience. Thinking is not only an experimental action, as described by Freud, it is also an experimental hypothesis about the nature of things, a constant checking of what one phantasised against the evidence. Primitive thought starts at the preverbal level and is eventually encompassed in a word or a phrase: "Mummy, Daddy, Mummy gone." A word or sentence encompasses a complex experience. Both the omnipotent phantasy, hallucination, and thinking enable one to bear the gap between need and satisfaction, the absence and the need for a satisfying object. But while omnipotent phantasy denies the experience of need, thought, which admits the need, can be used to explore external and internal realities and deal with them. But thought, because it springs from and admits frustration, can be attacked at its very inception.

This hatred of thought processes, deeply rooted in the unconscious, can be active throughout life. For example, I had a patient who was highly intelligent and articulate in some ways, but certain areas of his personality were functioning at a very primitive level. He had psychosomatic symptoms, a gastric ulcer, and at times of tension thinking was replaced by impulsive acting out. He had become aware in the course of his analysis of how he was obsessed with women's breasts. Towards the end of one session, he reported a dream in which a woman was giving the breast to a baby. They were so close to the patient that he could fondle the woman's breasts. Then the woman went away, but she left the breast with the baby and the patient, who continued the sucking and fondling. He added that the baby must also be himself, as it was so close to him. He started the next session with a great deal of irritation with himself. He said that he had plenty of important problems in his adult life which he wanted to talk about, but the moment he set eyes on the analyst he noticed she was wearing a white blouse and started thinking about her breasts and he said with exasperation: "I am not only obsessed with breasts, but I am also mad. I am obviously mad about breasts." He then spoke of how he was always sucking something, like his toes and his thumb in his childhood, and now sweets, chewing gum, cigarettes, anything that he could put into his mouth. As he was talking, he was getting more and more dreamy and remote. I drew his attention to this and reminded him of the dream in which the baby and he sucked and fondled the breast while the woman went away. He interrupted me angrily, saying: "Don't make me think. I don't want to think. I want to suck. I hate thoughts. When I have thoughts, it means I have nothing to suck."

My making the comment about his state of mind made him aware that what he was experiencing was a living-through of the dream that he had possession of the breast, and it made him aware of my presence. I was the woman with the white blouse, and there was a gap between us, necessitating speech for communication. The moment he became aware of that, he became aware that he was having thoughts, not a breast in his mouth, and he hated it. He hated the fact that he needed thinking to deal with this gap and with the problems he referred to at the beginning of the session, not the least of them being an impending psychoanalytic holiday break.

The nascent thought conflicts with the illusion that the infant is merged with, or in possession of, an ideal breast. And disillusion must be tolerated for thought to develop. An element of this disillusion persists in sophisticated thought.

Towards the end of his analysis, another patient brought the two following dreams. In the first dream he saw himself. He was slim, but otherwise unchanged, a balding middle-aged man. On waking from the dream, he thought that his dream meant that being slimmer did not actually make him be any younger. This patient, with a tendency to corpulence, used periodically to diet and to slim, and as he lost weight he used to become very manic. He had had a near-conscious phantasy that being slim made him again into an adolescent, young and beautiful. In his association to the dream, he recognised with a certain sadness that it was no longer so. He was still pleased at having lost weight in the last week, but he could not feel as he used to, that it had changed him. His belief in the magic rejuvenating power of slimming and the elation associated with it had gone.

The following day he brought a more complex dream. He was saying goodbye at the door to an adolescent. He felt very tender towards him and sad at parting. In the background stood X, the adolescent's father, a cripple, and still further in the background, the patient's parental family. He had many associations to the dream. The first one was that the adolescent was himself, and he was saying goodbye to his phantasies of being still an adolescent and goodbye to the picture of himself as still dependent on his original family. The associations to X were more complex. X was a rich, extremely mean, successful businessman, now crippled through a disease of the central nervous system. The patient himself had been a businessman, successful and ruthlessly greedy.

When he came to analysis, being successful in business was equated in his mind with being not only powerful, omnipotently so, but also very righteous. It was part of the culture he grew up in to believe that people were poor only because of their own fecklessness. Wealth was equated with godliness. Unconsciously, however, this greed and ruthlessness gave rise to a great deal of guilt, persecution, and feelings of emptiness, which eventually brought him to analysis. In the course of his analysis, he recognised how crippling to his mental development were those attitudes. The cripple in the dream represents his past self and an aspect of his father, who had the same set of values in a less extreme form. In the dream he says goodbye, not only to the adolescent self, but to the set of values and ideas that he can no longer entertain. Now he is no longer free to think that being rich is equivalent to being righteous. Nor can he think any more that that aspect of his father is admirable and to be emulated. So, while analysis freed his perceptions and thoughts from the rigid set of values he was brought up in and which also suited his own greed and envy, he felt regret and sadness at the loss of a set of thoughts and beliefs belonging to the past. He mourned the lost idealisation of his father and mostly of himself. Aspects of his personality, which he had used to think of as marvellous, he now thought of as crippling to his whole central nervous system. Certain ideas he could still think but could no longer believe.

I am aware that I seem to be confusing here belief with thought, but among its other functions, thinking has that of examining belief. He could still think about the ideas he used to have and sometimes regret that he could no longer hold them any more as true, but he could no longer use them in thinking about the world and base his action on them. Similarly, once we learned that the earth is a planet revolving around the sun, we are not quite free to think that it is flat. Or, rather, we can entertain such a thought as an intriguing phantasy, we can even, if we have the talent and inclination, write a science fiction novel about a flat world, but we have to recognise it as a phantasy thought.

If thinking, as I suggested, is related to matching phantasies with realities, phantasies lose their omnipotent character. The patient I referred to came to recognise that many of his views of himself and the world, and sometimes irrational actions that sprang from them, were based on omnipotent unconscious phantasies. For instance, he had a phantasy that his faeces had magic powers and were superior as food to mother's milk, and in potency to his father's penis. When this omnipotent phantasy had become a clear thought, he had to face his real feeling of helplessness and dependence as a child in relation to his parents and now, as a patient in relation to me. Freud links thinking with "forming a conception of the reality circumstances in the external world" (1911b, p. 219). This involves also forming a conception about oneself, one's needs, and one's impulses, that is to say, forming some conception of one's own internal world. The patient's belief in the magic of his faeces had been linked with another omnipotent phantasy. He had a phantasy, amply illustrated in many dreams, that he had swallowed me up (as in the past, he had phantasised about his mother) and inside himself had emptied me of all my supposed riches and attributes, physical and mental, so that in his manic state he felt the owner of all power and riches and contained me as an impoverished object full of greed and envy. This omnipotent phantasy underlay both his states of manic elation and those of persecution. This state of affairs was experienced, not as thoughts, but as a reality. Very schematically, one could say that there were three steps in his gaining of insight in that area:

1. My faeces are everything (omnipotent).
2. This is so because my internal parents are empty and I have it all, that is also why they persecute me.
3. This is so because I wished it so; in my mind I made it so by imagining that I had swallowed them up and emptied them.

This third step brings him in touch with the fact that the state of affairs he experiences is something he phantasised because he wished it. He begins to recognise that these are the thoughts he has, and he can no longer believe them as separating reality perceptions. The omnipotent phantasies turn into thoughts that can be expressed as: This is what I wished, or this is what I wish.

This is what I thought I had done or could do. At that point reality testing, "can I do it", begins to play a part, and it plays a part in two ways. One is a reality testing of the omnipotence of one's wishes, for instance, the realisation by that patient that it was a phantasy that he could possess himself of my attributes in that way. But another equally important element of reality comes into play, an internal reality testing in relation to other feelings and wishes that one may have, in the case of that patient, for instance, such feelings as love, gratitude, a wish to preserve inside himself a good perception of me, guilt about his greedy and envious thoughts and concern about what it was doing to his internal world, and how it was affecting his behaviour in the external world. All those feelings were in conflict with his omnipotent megalomania.

I have been led by this example to bring in several additional problems, awareness of impulses, sense of guilt, the problem of values. Are they relevant to my theme? I think I have to introduce here the concept of integration and its relation to thinking. An omnipotent phantasy can, and indeed must, be split off from certain perceptions, external and internal, that conflict with it. When a phantasy loses its omnipotent character and becomes thought, a hypothesis to be tested or a wish recognised as such, it becomes integrated with other thoughts and wishes. Thought allows conflict and seeks resolution. I cannot here go into the difference between having thoughts and thinking, suffice it to say that such an integration, comparing and matching and judging, is also a step from the state of having thoughts to the state of thinking. In the case of the patient, in a simplified way, a megalomanic phantasy, lived as a reality, began to give way to thoughts, to the appraising of himself, me, and the world and an appraisal of his contradictory wishes.

This was linked with a change in his sense of values, because a sense of values and thinking are inextricably bound up. The sense of values naturally influences all thinking, but conversely, too, the sense of values is determined by what we think. Money-Kyrle explored this theme in such works as "Psychoanalysis and ethics" (1952) and *Man's Picture of His World* (1961). My patient's view of the world was based on the phantasy that he had robbed his object and therefore feared that his object would rob and annihilate him; it led to a sense of values based on the idea: You have to kill if you are not to be killed. With the emergence of integration and thinking and a changed view of himself and the world, his sense of values unavoidably had to alter. A paradoxical and complex situation arises in relation to the superego. When integration begins and thinking takes the place of split-off omnipotent phantasies, guilt is in some way lessened and in others augmented. In my patient, the omnipotent phantasy of his superiority was linked with a terrifying superego, a parental figure, stripped of all positive assets and seething with greed and envy. His thinking was not only constricted by the infantile need to annihilate any thought that would conflict with his own omnipotence, it was also under continuous attack by an equally omnipotent envious and hostile superego, which did not allow him any real enrichment in feeling, thought, or knowledge.

When the phantasies are recognised as phantasies, they are allowed to exist in thought. The less the omnipotence, the more permissible a thought becomes, as it does not have the omnipotent power to change the object into a monster superego figure. On the other hand, however, this inner persecution by a monstrous superego is replaced by a feeling of responsibility for one's own thought and more conscious guilt, which I think is unavoidable, even if the thoughts are recognised as not omnipotent.

In the case of the last patient I wrote about, the megalomanic phantasy and the accompanying fears, both mutilating his capacity to think, were replaced by realisations that, for instance, there were people he depended on, that this often stimulated in him greedy, envious, and hostile thoughts and phantasies, and that the existence of those thoughts gave him some pain, both of guilt and of disillusionment in his view of himself.

What then is the freedom of thought? Nietzsche (1886) says: "The thought does not come when we want it, it comes when it wants." We could add: It is not what we want, it is what it wants. This, of course, is rather personifying thought, as though it were a being with a will of its own. There is such a category of thought, those attributed to and felt as emanating from an internal object, as an inspiration or a persecution. But more generally thought and thinking are the outcome of a complex interaction of our impulses, wishes, phantasies, and perceptions, and as such, they are not necessarily what we would wish them to be.

Freedom of thought, and at best I think we still have a very limited freedom in that respect, means the freedom to know our own thoughts, and that means knowing the unwelcome as well as the welcome, anxious thoughts, those felt as "bad" or "mad", as well as constructive thoughts and those felt as "good" or "sane", and being able to examine their validity in terms of external or internal realities. The freer we are to think, the better we can judge these realities, and the richer our experience. But like all freedoms, it is also felt as a bind in that it makes us feel responsible for our own thoughts.

And formidable forces, external and internal, militate against this freedom. The psychoanalyst sets himself the task of helping the patient first of all to recognise the immeasurable value of such freedom and the worthwhileness of struggling for it and then to achieve such freedom in a greater measure.

References

Freud, S. (1911b). Formulations on the two principles of mental functioning. *S. E., 12*: 213–226. London: Hogarth.

Freud, S. (1916–17). *Introductory Lectures on Psycho-Analysis. S. E., 15–16*. London: Hogarth.

Money-Kyrle, R. (1952). Psychoanalysis and ethics. *International Journal of Psychoanalysis, 33*: 387–393.

Money-Kyrle, R. (1961). *Man's Picture of His World: A Psychoanalytical Perspective*. London: Hogarth.

Nietzsche, F. (1886). *Beyond Good and Evil: Prelude to a Philosophy of the Future*. W. Kaufmann (Trans.). New York: Vintage, 1973.

Segal, H. (1987). *The Work of Hanna Segal: A Kleinian Approach to Clinical Practice*. London: Karnac.

Segal, H. (1989). Psychoanalysis and freedom of thought. In: J. Sandler (Ed.), *Dimensions of Psychoanalysis* (Chapter 4). London: Karnac.

CHAPTER 9

Illusion, disillusion, and irony in psychoanalysis*

John Steiner

Dual identities: Participant and observer

As we listen to our patients, it is important to be able to identify with them, to empathise with their situation, and to participate in their dramas. It is equally important, however, to be able to limit our participation and to be able to withdraw from the identification in order to function as an observer. We need to be able to engage in the patient's conflicts and also to retain a questioning attitude in which observation of the patient and trying to understand how his mind works is our primary aim.

Normally, we alternate between these two states, being emotionally engaged as participants on the one hand and becoming separate to be able to observe on the other, and to achieve this dual role requires a capacity to identify in a flexible and reversible manner. Keeping a proper balance is not always easy, and the analyst may behave

* This chapter was originally published as Steiner, J. (2016). Illusion, disillusion, and irony in psychoanalysis. *The Psychoanalytic Quarterly*, *85*(2): 427–447. https://doi.org/10.1002/psaq.12080,

inappropriately if he allows himself to get trapped in identifications with his patients or their objects. Equally, he will fail to understand his patient if he behaves only as a detached observer without feeling himself into the patient's experiences.

In thinking about the effect of a theatrical performance on an audience, I was struck by parallels between the role of the analyst when listening to his patient and that of the spectator of a classical drama. In her discussion of Aristotle's theory of catharsis, Turri (2015) summarises the classical view that the emotions of terror and pity are central to the experience of tragedy. Moreover, she explains that, according to Aristotle, terror involves a fear of something happening to ourselves, while pity, by contrast, is based on feelings for the person whom we are observing. I take this to mean that when we in the audience feel terror, we have identified with the hero of the drama and are feeling what we imagine he is feeling. However, when we feel pity, we have withdrawn from this identification and are observing the suffering as it is happening—not to us, but to someone we have come to care about.

To understand a play and the effect it has on us requires that we engage in both roles, and later in this chapter, I will utilise the ideas of Schafer (1970) and others (Lear, 2003, 2014; Stein, 1985; Walsh, 2011) to suggest that this dual identity as participant and observer is achieved through a capacity for irony. The two states are irreconcilable: we cannot be both involved and detached, but when we are involved, there is a lingering awareness of a capacity to observe, and when we are observers, we know that we have been, and again will become, involved. Because neither position is stable, this awareness leads to self-doubt, which is essential to irony and can serve as a reminder of our human frailties. Without irony, the situation can become so real that there is no gap between the drama and the audience, or so unreal that the drama seems to have nothing to do with us. The parallel with the psychoanalytic situation raises the possibility that we can learn something about the analytic attitude from a consideration of the impact of a theatrical performance on the audience.

Critics commonly use Sophocles' *Oedipus the King* (5th century BC) to illustrate irony in a situation in which the audience observes the tragedy from a position of knowledge that is not available to the protagonists in the drama. For example, Fowler, in his *A Dictionary of Modern English Usage* (1926), states:

> [Ironic] drama had the peculiarity of providing the double audience—one party in the secret & the other not .... All the spectators, that is, were in the secret beforehand of what would happen. But the characters, Pentheus & Oedipus & the rest, were in the dark, ... the dramatist working his effect by irony. (pp. 295–296)

I will suggest that this double attitude, one in ignorance and one in the know, reflects an internal situation in which we both know what is happening and at the same time deny that knowledge. I will explore this theme in *Oedipus the King*, but first I will look at a similar situation in *The Wild Duck* (Ibsen, 1884).

A central theme in both plays is the devastating impact of reality on lives that have been based on evasion of truth. These evasions have allowed an illusion of superiority to develop, which does not appear to be a problem until it collapses into catastrophe as the truth becomes known. This is a common if not universal theme in tragedy, and it is also a recurring if not universal experience in analysis, in which the impact of reality may be felt as a cruel expulsion from a period of blissful existence. To varying degrees, we all have a Garden of Eden fantasy of an idealised time when we were sole possessors of the breast, and this may support a belief that the idealisation can be recovered and does not have to be relinquished (Steiner, 2013, 2015). Our awareness of preteens, falsehood, and self-deception varies from the gross lying of the impostor to a dim awareness that all of us have something to hide because none of us can live up to the standards of the ideal (Deutsch, 1955; Greenacre, 1958; Steiner, 2011).

Both these plays deal with the growing impact of reality on the lives of protagonists who have been living under the spell of an illusion, and it is the sudden dramatic impact of reality as it shatters illusions that gives rise to the plays' tragic element. Examining this theme can remind us that illusions serve important functions, and that there are dangers if reality is forced onto an individual who is not equipped to deal with it. In both plays, we have a protagonist who is determined to expose the truth, and in both, the truth proves to be unbearable and the consequences tragic once it is revealed.

Henrik Ibsen's *The Wild Duck*: The brutality of truth

The drama in *The Wild Duck* (Ibsen, 1884) centres on a confrontation between truth and illusion that follows the reunion of two childhood friends, Hialmar Ekdal and Gregers Werle. They knew each other when their fathers were business partners prior to the disaster that struck Hialmar's father, Old Ekdal. He was convicted of a fraudulent forestry deal, imprisoned, and stripped of his army rank, while Gregers' father, Hakon Werle, was acquitted and went on to become a prosperous merchant.

The humiliated, lowly status of the Ekdal family compared to that of the Werles is evident when the play opens with a sumptuous dinner given by Hakon Werle for his son, who has accepted his father's invitation to return after some seventeen years of resentful absence following the death of his mother. In defiance of his father, Gregers invites his friend Hialmar to this dinner, in the course of which Hialmar gives an account of his recovery after his family's disgrace. Thanks to Gregers' father, Hakon, Hialmar has been able to establish a photographic studio and to meet the woman to whom he is now happily married. He adds that his wife, Gina, was once in service with the Werles, and Gregers is shocked when he realises that she was not only the person who kept house for them during the last year of his mother's illness, but also the one with whom he suspected his father had a relationship.

Hialmar's presence is an embarrassment to the gathering, and the awkwardness is even more painful when the shabby, doddering Old Ekdal walks through the company and is looked down on by everyone—even by his own son, who averts his gaze.

Hialmar leaves early, and Gregers then confronts his father and attacks him for allowing Old Ekdal to take the blame for the crime that both partners were guilty of. This Werle denies, and Gregers goes on to accuse him of helping the Ekdals with money to cover up his guilt. Moreover, he also accuses him of covering up his relationship with Gina by marrying her off to Hialmar. Hakon asks if it was Hialmar who has accused him of this, and Gregers tells him that it was his mother who told him about his liaison with Gina. Exasperated, Hakon responds by saying that Gregers sees everything through his mother's eyes and has ignored her clouded vision. Despite the long-standing animosity between father and son, Hakon is seeking a reconciliation with Gregers and has invited him to return home to join the business as a partner, so that Hakon himself can retire to the country and marry his present housekeeper.

Gregers sees this as an attempt to get him to collude with yet another cover-up by condoning his father's behaviour and concealing the family's ugly secrets, including rumours about his mistreatment of Gregers' mother. As the two argue, Gregers' idealisation of his mother and his hatred of his father clearly emerge, and their row ends with Gregers refusing to support his father and leaving, insisting that they will never meet again. When his father asks him what he will do if he does not join the business, Gregers proclaims that he has now found his mission in life. It is clear that this mission is to expose the lies of Hialmar's marriage, and we realise this has more to do with exposing his father than with helping his friend.

The remainder of the play takes place in Hialmar's studio, where we see the various illusions and self-deceptions that the Ekdal family lives by. Despite these, Hialmar and Gina manage to live a contented life and, albeit with hardships and tensions, they care for each other, so that Hialmar can say, "Our roof may be poor and humble, Gina; but it is home. And with all my heart I say: here dwells my happiness" (Ibsen, 1884, p. 35). They gain great comfort from their love for their daughter, Hedvig, now age fourteen, who is described as their greatest joy, but also as their deepest sorrow because she is going blind.

Hialmar and Gina each cope with their humiliation through enacting a pretence. Old Ekdal escapes to the attic, which contains a make-believe forest where rabbits and hens are kept, and where he can put on his old uniform and pretend he is still an officer shooting bears. Hialmar, instead of working in his studio, dreams of his great invention, which will restore the family name and allow him to rehabilitate his father. Gina supports these illusions, keeps the business going, economises to make ends meet, and pretends that it is Hialmar who is the breadwinner. Hedvig adores her father but like her mother, she treats him as a difficult child, and she continues to believe that she is loved despite the growing evidence of his selfishness and neglect.

Also in the attic, in a special basket, sits the wild duck, shot and wounded by Hakon and given to Hedvig, after being rescued from the "depths of the sea" by Hakon's dog. The wounded wild duck has many resonances—most obviously, perhaps, as a symbol of the objects damaged by Hakon and given to the family to look after.

Gregers becomes the Ekdals' lodger, and his passion for truth grows as he sees the make-believe world they inhabit. He invites his old friend Hialmar for a long walk, in the course of which he reveals Gina's secret liaison with his father and the dubious motives for his support of the family. He has embarked on his mission to rescue Hialmar from a life based on illusion to one founded on truth.

Gregers has always been an idealist, and he expects Hialmar to have identical views, which would lead him to embrace the truth, accept what has happened, and rebuild his marriage on a new, sound footing. However, Hialmar is nothing like Gregers, and when he discovers Gina's past and the support that Hakon has secretly provided, he reacts with righteous indignation: he is determined to leave the family and to return everything he has received from Hakon Werle. In his rejection of all he has been given, he even tells his daughter, Hedvig, that he would like to strangle the wild duck and that the only thing preventing him from doing so is that he knows how much it would upset her.

Another blow to Hialmar's pride takes the form of a letter from Hakon that contains a deed of gift, which Hialmar tears up in a rage when he learns that it provides a pension for Old Ekdal until his death, and after that for Hedvig. However, the final blow comes when he begins to recognise that Hedwig may not be his daughter. It becomes clear that Hakon is himself going blind, and this creates the conviction in Hialmar that Hedvig's blindness is hereditary, and that Gina was already pregnant when she married him. Gina confesses her affair and admits that she cannot be sure who Hedvig's father is. Hialmar's cruelty becomes most poignant when he rejects Hedvig and calls her an interloper.

Gradually, however, Hialmar allows himself to lean on Gina once more, and as he begins to feel less righteous and more needy, he glues together the fragments of the torn letter so that the legacy need not be rejected. When he hears that Hedwig intends to sacrifice her precious wild duck to demonstrate her love for him, his rejection of her also softens—but it is too late, because the drama comes to its tragically fatal conclusion when Hedvig, instead of shooting the wild duck, shoots herself. She has come to believe that it is she who is the burden on her family, having been damaged by Hakon Werle and shunned by Hialmar.

A voice of reason appears in the form of Dr Relling, who explains that in his view, it is Gregers who is disturbed, saying, "But one disease he has certainly got in his system ... He is suffering from an acute attack of integrity" (Ibsen, 1884, pp. 71–72). Dr Relling has been trying to support Hialmar despite his illusions because of his belief that: "Rob the average man of his life-illusions and you take away his happiness at the same stroke" (p. 100). Gregers has failed to recognise that Hialmar is an average man, and he has no understanding of his feelings. Moreover, Gregers' motivation for revealing what he did had less to do with Hialmar's happiness than with the wish to expose the alleged wrongdoing of his father. Gregers' hatred arises in part from his idealisation of his mother and his denial of her paranoia and alcoholism, which led to her husband's alienation and hastened her death. This means that the truth Gregers wants to impose does not take into account the wider picture and is equally based on illusion.

The role of irony

In *The Wild Duck*, Ibsen forcefully reminds us that truth can be cruel and that we can become blind to the tragic consequences of its impact. The tragedy raises the importance of feelings such as pity and kindness as they are evoked in the audience, who are made aware of Gregers' inability to feel them.

The need for kindness is a theme pursued by E. M. Forster, an admirer of Ibsen (Forster, 1936) who argued that kindness is as important as truth—not only to mitigate the harshness of truth, but also to make it more true. In *A Passage to India* (1924), his heroine, like Gregers, felt only "cold justice and honesty" and "no passion of love for those whom she had wronged" (p. 217). Forster asserted that: "Truth is not truth in that exacting land unless there go with it kindness and more kindness and kindness again" (ibid.).

Forster's point is not simply that truth without kindness can be cruel, but that truth without kindness is not fully true. Nevertheless, we also know that truth is essential for our mental health and that pursuing truth is one of the basic goals of psychoanalysis. We find ourselves in agreement with Freud when he asserts that "We must not forget that the analytic relationship is based on a love of truth—that is, on a recognition of reality—and that it precludes any kind of sham or deceit" (1937c, p. 248).

Moreover, in *The Wild Duck*, Gregers' view of the benefits of truthfulness is close to that held by psychoanalysts in their model of healthy development. We argue that facing the reality of loss allows us to mourn our lost objects, to recognise our guilt, and to repair the damage we have done. What we sometimes forget is that in order for guilt to be accepted and to motivate us towards reparation, it has to be bearable—and this is often the critical factor, as it proves to be for Hialmar. As we relinquish and mourn our illusions, we must also relinquish and mourn our omnipotence; paradoxically, this means that facing reality includes an acceptance of our limitations, including the limits to the reality we can accept.

Freud recognised that a love of truth is not the same as an idealisation of truth. He was very aware that we all need defences and that neurotic compromises are part of ordinary existence. In his words:

> It is not his [the analyst's] business to restrict himself in every situation in life to being a fanatic in favour of health ... We must allow that in some cases that flight [into illness] is fully justified, and a physician who has recognized how the situation lies will silently and solicitously withdraw. (1916–17, p. 382)

Freud was a great admirer of Ibsen, and in relating one of his own dreams, he described a sentence "written in a positively norekdal style" (1900a, p. 296). He concluded that "norekdal" was a condensation of Nora and Ekdal—the first a character in *A Doll's House* (Ibsen, 1879) and the second in *The Wild Duck* (Ibsen, 1884). In discussing this dream, Anthi (1990) suggests that, at the time, Freud was beginning to become aware that his studies in hysteria were exposing him to criticism from his colleagues, and that, in identification with Old Ekdal, he feared humiliation and disgrace. Anthi also suggests that Freud's partnership with Fliess was coming to an end, and that the imprisonment of Old Ekdal reminded him of his guilt about their dangerous collaboration in the case of Emma Eckstein (Masson, 1984). I suspect, however, that Freud was also becoming aware that, in his treatment of hysterical patients, he had been exerting pressure on them to accept the truth, and that the portrayal of Gregers in *The Wild Duck* may have alerted him to the harm that can be done by overzealous idealists.

Freud could recognise both the value of truth and the dangers of an insensitive imposition of it on others, and this capacity is essential to irony. By contrast, Gregers' concrete solution to the problem shows that he is completely without a capacity for irony, and he cannot extricate himself from identification with Hialmar; hence he cannot observe what he has done or feel pity for those whom he has exposed. He cannot feel tolerance or kindness towards them and is intent only on taking action that is unrestrained by thought or self-doubt.

Oedipus the King: Collusions to avoid reality

In *Oedipus the King* (Sophocles, 5th century BC, a), we have a similar though even more dramatic example of a determination to expose the truth that results in tragedy. This time it is Oedipus who pursues the truth without realising where it will lead, and we identify with him as he gradually discovers what a disaster this exposure will be. If we emerge from our identification, however, and temporarily become sufficiently detached, we can also observe how the collusions and evasions among the drama's participants led to a denial of the truth for so many years. Having triumphed over the Sphinx, Oedipus, along with his family and indeed the whole city of Thebes, lived under an illusion of stable prosperity until a plague disturbed the status quo.

Other analysts have recognised the importance of *The Wild Duck* in understanding the complex relationship we have with reality. Anthi (1990), Killingmo (1994), and Szalita (1970–71) have contributed interesting papers on the play's relevance to psychoanalysis, and Zachrisson (2013) explored the search for truth and the need for illusion in both *The Wild Duck* and *Oedipus the King*.

Like the original Greek audience, we are familiar with the story, but we do not always recognise that each of the main characters had his or her own reasons for evading reality, and how this led them to collude in establishing and sustaining their ignorance of the facts. At the beginning of the play, Oedipus is confronted with the crisis of the plague, which leads him to embark on a quest to determine its cause. Seventeen years previously, he had entered Thebes as a homeless fugitive from the court of Corinth, to be welcomed in triumph because he had solved the riddle of the Sphinx. He was made king of Thebes in place of Laius, who had been killed a few days earlier, and accepted Jocasta, the former queen, as his wife. However, in order to enjoy his good fortune, he had to evade a number of facts that, had he pursued them, would have led him to discover the truth and to avoid the false premises on which his good fortune was based.

Moreover, the other characters in the drama—Jocasta and Creon in particular, but also the elders of the city—found it expedient to turn a blind eye in order to ignore events that would have enabled the truth to emerge (Steiner, 1985). It was this unconscious collusion that established Oedipus as an upright king and a respected father in what turned out to be an illusion of normality. Furthermore, it was an illusion that has enabled the family and the city to survive until it is shattered as the facts emerge in the course of the play.

In an earlier paper (Steiner, 1985), I use the term to turn a blind eye to denote a situation in which we have access to reality but choose to ignore it because it proves convenient to do so. This mechanism involves a degree of ambiguity as to how conscious or unconscious the knowledge is; most often, we are vaguely aware that we are choosing not to look at the facts, but without being conscious of what it is we are evading. These views of Sophocles' play are based on the work of Philip Vellacott, an idiosyncratic classicist who is known for his translations of Aeschylus and Euripides but whose views on Oedipus (Vellacott, 1971) have not been generally accepted.

When the tragedy's disillusion arrives, we in the audience are moved to terror and pity as we witness the unfolding events. In identification with Oedipus, we share in his determination to discover the truth, and we are terrified as each new discovery implicates him more certainly as the source of the corruption. However, we are also able to disidentify with the hero and observe the total situation, and this allows us to acknowledge the facts that Oedipus has been evading, as well as the complex involvements of all the characters in the cover-up. As we withdraw from the identification and stop to observe and think, we are bound to ask: "If these things can be brought to light now, why were they not discovered seventeen years ago when Oedipus first entered Thebes?"

The attitude of Oedipus

We can begin by imagining the thoughts going through the mind of Oedipus when he first entered Thebes to be acclaimed as a hero. He has left Corinth determined to avoid the prophecy at the centre of the play, and he has just killed an older man with a retinue outside the city. He has married the widow of the king, a woman old enough to be his mother, and he did this within a very short time of being told by the oracle that he was destined to kill his father and marry his mother.

We know the fateful history, but we watch attentively as it becomes clear that Oedipus failed to make the crucial connections. The city must have been buzzing with news of the recent murder of King Laius, but Oedipus had not asked where the king had been killed, by whom he was attended, or what he looked like. Instead of pursuing the obvious enquiries, Oedipus has erected a plausible facade to cover up the truth, which he persuaded himself and others to accept. He felt safe in Thebes because he convinced himself that the one thing he feared was a return to Corinth, where he might kill King Polybus and marry Merope, the couple he believed to be his parents. He overlooked the fact that he had gone to Delphi expressly to ask about his parentage because doubts had been cast on it, and the oracle had failed to provide the answer. He accepted his new situation without qualm because, as Green (1987) suggested, the desire to enjoy Laius' throne and Jocasta's bed made him a poor logician.

The testimony of Teiresias

One of the remarkable moments of the play occurs quite near the beginning when Oedipus swears to find and banish the killer of Laius, and the ancient soothsayer Teiresias is sent for. At first he refuses to identify the guilty man, but when Oedipus becomes childishly abusive, Teiresias gets angry and tells him in plain terms first that the killer Oedipus is seeking is himself, and then that it is he who is "the cursed polluter of this land … living in sinful union with the one you love" (Watling, 1947, p. 36).

Creon, the elders, and Oedipus all hear this, and all go on to act as if they have not heard it. The remarkable thing is that we in the audience also hear it and, while knowing it to be true and witnessing the wholesale denial, we identify with Oedipus and join in the collusion, apprehensively waiting for the denouement as the play gradually and with many diversions leads inexorably towards the truth.

Jocasta's attitude

Jocasta must have been told of the death of her husband, and she knew of the prediction that led him to fear that his son would murder him. Despite this she agreed to the marriage and repeatedly expressed her contempt of prophecy. In the play, she reassures Oedipus by insisting that guilt is inappropriate because all lives are ruled by chance. Marriage to the youthful Oedipus offered her the opportunity to remain queen of Thebes and once again to bear children. It is not difficult to suppose that these advantages led her to turn a blind eye to the truth and to collude in the cover-up.

As psychoanalysts, we recognise that the oedipal illusion is universal and includes a fantasy of mutual love between mother and child, irrespective of differences in age. Jocasta's fate, however, reminds us of the tragic consequences if these illusions remain untouched by reality.

Creon's attitude

Jocasta's brother, Creon, was responsible for ruling the city after Laius was killed. He explains that he had no ambition to rule and was content to retain an influence in the background. He shows no surprise when told of Teiresias' accusations, despite their terrible import, saying only, "If he did so, you know best" (Watling, 1947, p. 40). Earlier, when Oedipus asks what stopped them from tracking down the king's killer there and then, Creon replies, "The Sphinx with her riddles forced us to turn our attention from insoluble mysteries to more immediate matters" (Watling, 1947, p. 29).

Oedipus asks why Teiresias was not summoned to identify the murderer at that time, only to be told that he had been summoned but had remained silent. When Oedipus asks why he has now spoken after staying silent for so long, Creon answers simply, "I do not presume to say more than I know" (Watling, 1947, p. 41). It makes sense for Creon to deny his complicity; Oedipus cannot be saved, but Creon can—and in fact he comes out of the drama unscathed.

The attitude of the elders

Finally, the chorus of elders, on stage throughout the unfolding of the drama, are shown to be concerned with their own interests as they begin to suspect that all is not well with Oedipus. When Oedipus proclaims that he will find the guilty party, they deny having had anything to do with it and indicate they prefer divine knowledge to that arrived at by investigating reality.

Even though the elders heard Teiresias make clear that it is Oedipus who is the killer of Laius and the polluter of the land, they avoid all reference to these accusations. Instead, they speak of an unknown robber with bloodstained hands who has committed the most unspeakable of crimes and refer to him roaming the countryside at large. Eventually, they admit that Teiresias' testimony is disturbing, but they affirm their compliance and decline to take sides. They are terrified of the chaos that they think will arise if their king is dethroned, and they are also playing it safe while there is a chance that he might survive.

The cover-up

A cover-up requires conspirators who agree either overtly or tacitly to collaborate. If Creon had called for a proper inquiry, the witness would have been interrogated, and the truth would have come out. If Jocasta had not ignored the oracle that she so hated, she might not have turned a blind eye to her young husband's resemblance to Laius, to the fact that his age was precisely that of her son had he lived, or to the scars on his feet that must have puzzled her. If the elders, too, had been more vigilant and not so concerned about backing the winning party, they might have demanded an inquiry, or at least asked about their new king's background.

The cover-up could only take place because it suited several parties at the same time and thus enabled the participants to be of mutual service to each other. We in the audience also collude in the cover-up because we empathically identify with everyone's need to do so.

Oedipus' remarkable pursuit of truth and the horrible denouement

If we recognise the only-too-human evasions of truth that led to the massive cover-up in *Oedipus the King*, then the determination and courage shown by Oedipus as he faces reality is even more remarkable. We see him vacillating and struggling with his ambivalence, but this only makes his final achievement so impressive.

The climax of the play occurs when the shepherd who took Oedipus away as a baby makes the whole truth clear, and Oedipus accepts it with great courage and without prevarication or excuse. He admits everything, saying simply, "Alas, all out! All is known! No more concealment! Oh light! May I never look on you again, revealed as I am, sinful in my begetting, sinful in marriage, sinful in the shedding of blood" (Watling, 1947, p. 56).

At this point, the truth, although awful, seems to be accepted by Oedipus, but the next event in the tragedy—the final blow of Jocasta's death—seems to make the situation unbearable. A messenger announces the suicide of the queen and describes what happens next: when Oedipus sees her suspended body, he cuts her down and then puts out his own eyes with her brooches. We are moved with horror and pity as we recognise that his guilt has led to this tragic self-mutilation, which seems to indicate that looking at the truth became impossible when it included responsibility for Jocasta's death. Her death was unexpected and doubly shocking. The murder of his father and his marriage to his mother were part of the prophecy, but nowhere was Oedipus warned that his crime would devastate and destroy his mother as well.

Moreover, the hero is now alone, with neither parent able to serve as a good object to make tragedy and guilt more bearable. After his determined pursuit of the truth and his courageous acceptance of responsibility, his self-blinding initiates a move away from truth, which deepens in *Oedipus at Colonus* (Sophocles, 5th century BC, b), where Oedipus adopts a godlike status and emphatically denies his guilt (Steiner, 1990, 1993).

Sophocles highlights the conflict between the wish to face the truth and the wish to evade it, surely one of the deepest of human conflicts, and one that every patient who embarks on an analysis has to wrestle with. We can identify with the hero who espouses such devotion to truth, but I believe that looking again at *Oedipus the King* and *The Wild Duck* can lead us to temper our love for truth with a recognition of its cruelty and an acceptance of the need for evasions that can make life bearable. This means that the acceptance of reality is more complex than a simple facing of facts, and that different visions of reality are required to enrich our understanding and to make it more true. To support the patient as he embarks on developments in accord with reality requires the analyst to appreciate how complex, multilayered, and rich our relationship with reality is. The analyst needs to accept that reality can be cruel, that evasions and illusions are universal, and that understanding them is often possible only in a wider context, where the total situation can be taken into account.

Comic, romantic, tragic, and ironic visions of reality

I have used *The Wild Duck* and *Oedipus the King* to argue that the discovery and acceptance of reality is complex, and that the history, circumstances, and personalities of the participants must be taken into account to gain a broader and truer view of the total situation. In an important contribution, Schafer (1970) explored some of these complexities and put forward the view that the apperception of reality depends on the attitude or state of mind of the perceiver. He considers four different attitudes to reality, which he discusses under the headings of the comic, romantic, tragic, and ironic visions. His thinking is based in literary criticism (Frye, 1957), and these visions have a relevance beyond the psychoanalytic setting, dealing as they do with basic human understanding and the definition of what it means to be human (Lear, 2003, 2014). The relevance for the psychoanalyst is partly that these visions may help him better recognise attitudes and states of mind in his patients, but also that they may lead him to a clearer view of his own approach to reality.

In Schafer's comic and romantic visions, a hero is driven to recover an idealised state and to achieve the desired outcome by overcoming obstacles, rather than by trying to understand them. In this sense, these two visions support illusion and invoke the pursuit of success rather than the acceptance of truth. In analysis, they can be thought of as antithetical to prioritising truth, and yet they play an important role in enhancing the patient's quality of life and they contribute to a liveliness that adds to the pleasures of living. Eventually, when attempts are made to face reality, a critical issue is whether or not the resultant experience of disillusion is bearable.

In contrast to the optimism of the comic and romantic visions, the tragic vision involves an acceptance of reality and a suffering of both the pain and the pleasures that reality bestows. The tragic vision gives depth to experience and makes a simplistic goal of avoidance of pain seem superficial. To give an example, Klein (1936) described how a deeper and more enduring meaning of love can arise only after we have suffered the pain and depression that follow attacks on our good objects (Steiner, in press). We do not fully appreciate people or things that we value until we face their loss.

Perhaps most significant is the fact that the tragic vision moves us because it maps the often-catastrophic meeting of evasions of reality in confrontation with the truth. This means that the terrible pain and disappointment of the loss of idealised fantasies is part of the tragic vision and is, I think, an essential feature of it (Steiner, 2013, 2015).

It seems to me that in both *The Wild Duck* and *Oedipus the King*, it is catastrophic disillusionment that gives the tragedy its bite. We witness how the people who have come to matter to us are crushed by the impact of reality, and we are moved to feel terror and pity that enriches our lives.

The ironic vision

A consideration of the tragic vision helps us to recognise that a gap has emerged between the protagonist in the throes of relinquishment of his illusion and the audience aware of the reality he has so energetically been avoiding. Moreover, this gap exists in all of us as we alternate between participation and observation in the dramas of others, but also in our own dramas, which we both live through and reflect on. The ironic vision involves an awareness of this gap and a willingness to tolerate both points of view. We realise that all along we have known something of the truth; we feel pity for the blindness of the protagonists, and we shudder as collusions and seductions are exposed.

Because these attitudes are contradictory, they cannot be resolved, and the conflict has to be recognised as inevitable and permanent. It is part of the human condition that we wish both to deny and to accept reality. I think it is a sense of irony that allows us to live with this contradiction and also with other contradictions, such as that between subjective and objective, symbolic and concrete, actual and ideal.

Irony as an attitude to life

We have considered irony to arise in the relationship between illusion and reality, and this includes a recognition of illusions we have about ourselves that affect our attitude to reality in general. This is the view of Lear (2003, 2014), who provides an extended discussion of the topic from a philosophical point of view that makes extensive links with psychoanalysis. He suggests, for example, that we all live a pretence in the sense that we make a claim to be something or someone, and that, to varying degrees, these claims are illusory. At the same time, we are concerned with the impact of reality on these claims, and the coexistence of the two gives rise to the ironic view.

The gap between pretence and reality is another version of that between illusion and reality, and one that is relevant to our identity and our aspirations and goals. In this way, irony can arise when there is a discrepancy between different views—for example, between the self as an active participant and a self that is self-reflective and sceptical.

The subjective and the objective

Lear also considers the relationship between subjective and objective knowledge, especially in relation to the psychoanalytic attitude. If we consider the subjective to arise from an experiencing self, we can link it with the feelings and thoughts that we have as we participate in our own or in other people's dramas. The objective view, by contrast, arises from our position as observer, self-reflective in our own dramas and experiencing those of others from the outside. The fact that we are human beings means that neither the position of the involved participant nor that of the detached observer is stable, and we alternate between them as we are pulled into and out of either position.

Sometimes the detached position as an observer is thought to be scientific and is pursued in attempts to make psychoanalysis respectable. Such attempts are valuable and important, but only if they are tempered by an ironic vision that recognises that we can only transiently extricate ourselves from subjective involvement. This does not mean that objectivity is impossible, but rather that it is always suspect and open to self-doubt. An ironic view that recognises the value of both the subjective and the objective can in this sense be more truthful than a simplistic objectivity.

Since it aims at detachment, irony may be used defensively to lessen the impact of tragedy. Fowler speaks of the delight of irony in a "secret intimacy" (1926, p. 296) with those in the know, and it is these delights that may lead to feelings of superiority as we disengage from the tragedy and look down on those suffering it. This relief may contribute to the humorous element in irony, which causes us to smile as we see the discrepancy between the tragic struggles of the protagonists on stage and our own apparently deeper knowledge. Irony may then descend into sarcasm and mockery if self-observation gives way to action and condescension. The distinction is important; in true irony, the smile is always tinged with pain since we are simultaneously laughing at ourselves and identifying with the protagonists of the tragedy.

It seems to me that the ironic view allows us to appreciate the importance of both sides in the conflict between reality and illusion. It encompasses both the comic and the tragic, the subjective and the objective, the concrete and the symbolic. If we are able to experience each of these states in turn, we can become aware of the conflict and contradictions in our complex relationship with reality. We can also recognise how easily the ironic view can collapse into a concrete certainty with the potential for insensitivity and cruelty.

Irony in psychoanalysis

Having looked at the complexity of our responses to the characters portrayed in *The Wild Duck* and *Oedipus the King*, we can see a similar complexity as we listen to and try to understand our patients. I have stressed the fact that the ironic stance is also relevant to an intrapsychic conflict within ourselves. We can become keenly involved in our beliefs and actions if we are also able to stand back from them to observe what we have done and what the consequences of our actions have been. This sequence of action followed by observation and reflection repeats over and over as the analytic session proceeds, and we can observe the patient's responses to our interpretations and use them in part to understand the patient better, and in part to detect flaws within ourselves and to correct errors in our constructions.

In her unpublished lectures on technique of 1936, Klein suggests that a good analytic attitude involves a "rather curious state of mind, eager and at the same time patient, detached from its subject and at the same time fully absorbed in it". She says this requires a "balance between different and partly conflicting tendencies and psychological drives, and ... a good co-operation between several different parts of our mind" (Steiner, in press).

These characteristics seem to me to be part of an ironic stance that, when it is functioning well, can allow an eager involvement with our patients, while a capacity to laugh at ourselves protects us from dangerous overinvolvement with passionate beliefs.

References

Anthi, P. R. (1990). Freud's dream in Norekdal style. *Scandinavian Psychoanalytic Review, 13*: 138–160.

Deutsch, H. (1955). The impostor—Contribution to ego psychology of a type of psychopath. *Psychoanalytic Quarterly, 24*: 483–505.

Forster, E. M. (1924). *A Passage to India*. London: Edward Arnold.

Forster, E. M. (1936). Ibsen the romantic. In: H. Ibsen, *The Wild Duck* (pp. 143–146). D. B. Christiani (Trans.). New York: W. W. Norton, 1968.

Fowler, H. W. (1926). *A Dictionary of Modern English Usage*. Oxford: Clarendon, 1937.

Freud, S. (1900a). *The Interpretation of Dreams. S. E., 4–5*. London: Hogarth.

Freud, S. (1916–17). *Introductory Lectures on Psycho-Analysis. S. E., 15–16*. London: Hogarth.

Freud, S. (1937c). Analysis terminable and interminable. *S. E., 23*: 211–253. London: Hogarth.

Frye, N. (1957). *Anatomy of Criticism*. New York: Atheneum, 1967.

Green, A. (1987). Oedipus, Freud, and us. In: M. Charney, J. Reppen, & J. A. Flieger (Eds.), *Psychoanalytic Approaches to Literature and Film* (pp. 215–237). London: Associated Press.

Greenacre, P. (1958). The impostor. *Psychoanalytic Quarterly, 27*: 359–382.

Ibsen, H. (1879). *A Doll's House*. Clayton, DE: Prestwick House, 2005.

Ibsen, H. (1884). *The Wild Duck*. E. M. Aveling (Trans.). CreateSpace Independent Publishing Platform, 2015. (Reprinted from the 1890 version, W. H. Baker, Boston, MA.)

Killingmo, B. (1994). Ibsen's *The Wild Duck*. *Scandinavian Psychoanalytic Review, 17:* 145–158.

Klein, M. (1936). *Lectures on Technique: Their Relevance for Contemporary Psychoanalysis.* Includes transcripts of her seminars of 1952. Edited with critical review by J. Steiner. London: Routledge, 2017.

Lear, J. (2003). *Therapeutic Action: An Earnest Plea for Irony.* London: Karnac.

Lear, J. (2014). *A Case for Irony.* Cambridge, MA: Harvard University Press.

Masson, J. M. (1984). *The Assault on Truth.* New York: Farrar, Straus & Giroux.

Schafer, R. (1970). The psychoanalytic vision of reality. *International Journal of Psychoanalysis, 51:* 279–297.

Sophocles (5th century BC, a). *Oedipus the King.* In: R. C. Jebb (Trans.), *The Complete Works of Sophocles* (1904). New York: Bantam, 1982.

Sophocles (5th century BC, b). *Oedipus at Colonus.* In: R. Fagles (Trans.), *The Three Theban Plays: Antigone, Oedipus the King, Oedipus at Colonus.* New York: Penguin, 1984.

Stein, M. (1985). Irony in psychoanalysis. *Journal of the American Psychoanalytic Association, 33:* 35–57.

Steiner, J. (1985). Turning a blind eye: The cover up for Oedipus. *International Review of Psycho-Analysis, 12:* 161–172.

Steiner, J. (1990). The retreat from truth to omnipotence in *Oedipus at Colonus. International Review of Psycho-Analysis, 17:* 227–237.

Steiner, J. (1993). *Psychic Retreats: Pathological Organisations of the Personality in Psychotic, Neurotic and Borderline Patients.* London: Routledge.

Steiner, J. (2011). The impostor revisited. *Psychoanalytic Quarterly, 80:* 1061–1071.

Steiner, J. (2013). The ideal and the real in Klein and Milton: Some observations on reading *Paradise Lost. Psychoanalytic Quarterly, 82:* 897–923.

Steiner, J. (2015). The use and abuse of omnipotence in the journey of the hero. *Psychoanalytic Quarterly, 84:* 695–718.

Steiner, J. (Ed.) (in press). *Melanie Klein's 1936 Lectures on Technique, Seminar Transcripts, and Contributions by E. Spillius and J. Steiner.* London: Routledge.

Szalita, A. B. (1970–71). Some questions for psychoanalysts: Reflections on Ibsen's *The Wild Duck. Psychoanalytic Review, 57:* 587–598.

Turri, M. G. (2015). Transference and katharsis, Freud to Aristotle. *International Journal of Psychoanalysis, 96:* 369–387.

Vellacott, P. (1971). *Sophocles and Oedipus: A Study of Oedipus Tyrannus with a New Translation.* Ann Arbor, MI: University of Michigan Press.

Walsh, J. (2011). Unconscious dissemblance: The place of irony in psychoanalytic thought. *Pivot Journal, 1:* 143–158.

Watling, E. F. (1947). *The Theban Plays.* London: Penguin.

Zachrisson, A. (2013). Oedipus the King: Quest for self-knowledge—Denial of reality: Sophocles' vision of man and psychoanalytic concept formation. *International Journal of Psychoanalysis, 94:* 313–331.

CHAPTER 10

Symbolisation, representation, and the role of narration in overcoming traumatic experience: The many faces of psychic truth

Elias M. da Rocha Barros

Proust, quoted by Benjamin (1955), posits that the past resides:

> somewhere beyond the reach of the intellect and unmistakably present in some material object (or in the sensation which such an object arouses in us), though we have no idea which one it is. As for that object, it depends entirely on chance whether we come upon it before we die or whether we never encounter it. (1955, p. 158)

This poetic reflection brings to mind moments when something—be it an object, a memory, an affection, or even a phrase—evokes within us a sensation of authenticity, of intimate truth. It is a sudden impact, like a flash of lightning, striking us viscerally, emanating from the deepest strata of our being, and altering our very mode of existence. It may or may not occur. The analytical setting precisely aims to foster the conditions for such an experience to emerge. What is evoked is felt as real, as a psychic truth.

Herein, I do not intend to delve into the philosophical concept of truth, or to dwell on the inherent complexity of the notion of psychic truth, a term as elusive as it is multifaceted. Truth is not a single concept but a spectrum of views that reflect the complexity of human perception, thought, and mental functioning and also the complexity of reality.

In some ways the world as we see it is not the world that is (Rovelli, 2017). In psychoanalysis, psychic truth refers to the emotional life of the internal world, which is perceived with the same intensity and conviction as we perceive the external world, as if this internal perception asserted itself as objective reality. It is a manifestly experiential phenomenon, generating an explosion of feelings, opening new affective chains, and expanding our very notion of being. Moreover, it is an experience that inherently carries the imperative to be transformed into a narrative, in the profound sense, implied in all of Hannah Arendt's work, which teaches us that a life that cannot be narrated is also a life not worth living. The brain is a storyteller, as Antonio Damásio (2018, p. 106) tells us.

For Bion—in my interpretation of his work—psychic truth entails the profound, and often painful, recognition of one's own internal emotional state. It involves the capacity to embrace painful and contradictory feelings without immediately expelling them from the mind or distorting them to the point of becoming unrecognisable.

Psychic truth constitutes an emotional experience that allows for the broadening of perspectives and the authentic experiencing of feelings, endowed with internal coherence and generating a concomitant sense of I-ness in dialectical relation with Me-ness, thereby fostering a profound atmosphere of intimacy. The relational field has shifted further in recent years to We-ness, as discussed by Civitarese (2024).

Elizabeth Rocha Barros (2024, p. 107), in attempting to define what constitutes an emotional experience, observes:

> Under these circumstances, I have chosen to employ the term "emotional experience" in but one of its many acceptations, namely, as "direct, intuitive, immediate knowledge we possess of facts or phenomena" (Lalande, 1960), with some authors contending that a true experience only exists when, and solely when, it is associated with the apprehension of meaning and situated within a relational context.

For Jorge Ahumada (2011), psychic truth results from what he terms ostensive insight, an experience of direct contact with the unconscious at the very moment of "being", when a perception asserts itself as true and genuine, a living transition between self-recognition as a subject and the acquisition of an identity. This becoming a subject through a state of being is, as a rule, unknown to both the patient and the common individual in crucial moments of their lives. The idea of the ostensiveness of truth derives from the notion of knowledge by acquaintance, originally proposed by Bertrand Russell (1911).

I contend, therefore, that in clinical practice, we encounter various levels of psychic truths, each plausible within its respective field of experience. It is not a singular moment, but rather a process, a movement, a "being". In Bion's (1965) conception, in our words, psychic truth is thus the experience of approaching "O"—not knowing but being transformed by the attempt to be in contact with what is real. "O" is the unknowable ultimate reality or truth-in-itself.

Segal, cited by Hunter (1993), observes:

> What is new about analysis is that it is the only discipline which considers that the search for truth is in itself therapeutic. Not a truth with capital "T" because you can't find that, and it changes. But the fact is that the search for truth, for psychic truth, is the therapeutic factor. (1993, pp. 9–10)

To illustrate this conception, I propose to examine, through two patients, the nature and quality of traumatic experiences across their varying levels of meaning, as they can be understood from their existence in both the repressed unconscious, the dynamic unconscious, and the unstructured unconscious (Levine, 2013, 2023). I include this last term as a recently proposed concept by Levine (2013) because I believe that a certain layer of psychic truth can be experienced even at levels not yet represented in the psychoanalytic sense. The narration of experience, in its various registers, performs an integrative function and serves to tame anxiety.

Trauma

In the traumatic experience, both the event itself—lived as a violent expulsion from the known world—and the various layers of meaning it evokes, hold psychic truth value. Which of them leads to "O", to ultimate truth? The ultimate psychic truth does not reside in a single layer, but, in my view, in the living sum of all possible truths. It is a movement towards expansion.

Trauma, as Alberto Rocha Barros Neto and Elias da Rocha Barros (2021) observe, can be likened to a tumour that spreads through the psychic apparatus: on one hand, destroying tissues; on the other, creating pathological connections—the so-called "metastases"—between different layers of the mind.

Roussillon (2011, p. 12) describes trauma, once established as a mental experience, as generating a radical impasse. The subject plunges into a state of existential despair and feels "shame for merely being alive". Subjectivity is threatened with disintegration, and the mental apparatus finds itself disorganised in its structure and functionality.

The central premise of this essay is that, precisely because it is not representable—in the psychoanalytic sense that we will discuss further on—trauma becomes a constant presence as a psychic register, operating outside time, like a recurring mental colic, with no foreseeable cessation.

A detailed analysis of traumatic situations allows us to reflect upon and relativise the concept of psychic truth, understanding that it always remains a partial truth, assuming distinct forms, all genuine at the time of their emergence. Truth, with a capital "T", can only constitute itself as such through the living sum of smaller truths, even if partial. Psychic truth, therefore, is linked to hope, embeds suffering within temporality—and invariably fulfils a liberating function.

The term "trauma" is, in itself, slippery and labyrinthine. It encompasses both the original injury and its psychic repercussions, including acute manifestations and delayed effects. Nevertheless, not all intense pain necessarily transmutes into trauma. At times, a seemingly banal event may, due to its resonances, become traumatic. Traumas are processes, not isolated events. They develop over time, in layers, commencing with an injury—whether physical or psychic—that frequently acquires new contours through successive re-significations.

Over the decades, the focus of psychoanalytic works has shifted from the traumatic event itself to the transitional space between the mental injury and its manifestations. That is to say, the focus has moved towards attempting to comprehend how a trauma remains alive and active in its various manifestations, not merely as a memory, but as an organising—and paralysing—structure of psychic functioning. Contemporary studies on mental states that do not reach symbolic representation have led to this shift in perspective. It is not uncommon for a traumatic process to manifest as a reduction in the feeling of being alive, as a kind of non-conscious somnolence that robs the injured party of their sense of vitality, even if the traumatic event itself is not present in memory, or alternatively, as a hypochondriacal manifestation.

In clinical practice, it is common to hear lengthy accounts of injurious experiences—almost invariably accompanied by resentment, hurt, or indignation. Yet these accounts, often meticulous, belong more to the injurious fact than to the trauma proper. Trauma, as a living structure, extends like a shadow throughout the victim's life, a pervasive mist. It can be disconnected from the original event and frequently operates through the symptoms of metastases, affecting areas of psychic life that, at first glance, appear unscathed. Its effects may manifest as unsettling dreams or nightmares, a chronic and undefined malaise, a constant complaint, a psychosomatic symptom, fear of an impending heart attack, or a pervasive feeling of incompleteness. There is a state of "lack", of "less"—an absence of something the individual themselves cannot name, yet which persistently troubles their existence.

Trauma often requires gaining new significations throughout life. It does not vanish—unless it is symbolised at understood levels, containing multiple meanings and determinations, and thus mentally metabolised through complex psychic processes that allow for deep reflection, a contextualisation within time and the trajectory of life. To illustrate, I adopt as a metaphor the delayed effects of sepsis. The victim, though recovered and seemingly healthy, remains vulnerable: organs previously affected become fragile zones, susceptible to future infections. Trauma leaves behind "holes of vulnerability".

In a seminar, a participant summarised an article by Alfred Margulies (2025) as follows: "The sensation of 'being at home in the world' is intrinsically linked to immersion in the everyday life." Heidegger (1956) termed this condition as *being-in-the-world*—an *un-self-conscious* mode of inhabiting existence, wherein all flows seamlessly. However, trauma erupts as a collapse of this mode of being. It shatters the continuity of the quotidian, akin to an abyss rending open, compelling the subject to confront finitude, the erosion of meaning, and the sheer weight of their own existence.

Margulies (2025) evokes the Holocaust survivors, whose capacity to feel "at home in the world" was irremediably shattered. This radical loss can precipitate a schism within the lived body, manifesting as compulsions, addictive behaviours, a desperate attempt to reclaim vitality, a life longing for being alive again.

Trauma destabilises the world. What was solid liquefies. Routines, once sources of comfort, become precarious. Certainties crumble. Trust yields to suspicion. A fog shrouds the path. Yet, despite this, the individual persists in living as though everything were normal. It is a life diminished. Those brutally wounded—by betrayals, disloyalties, guilt, torture, or repression—are torn from what they once called their "psychic home". They lose the very ground of belonging. One who has lived something akin to the dilemma of *Sophie's Choice*, depicted by William Styron (1979), may have awakened what Winnicott termed "primitive agony", a concept re-examined by Roussillon (2011). The new trauma activates prior traumas, becoming the harbinger of a continuous—at times silent—suffering.

In this essay, I shall endeavour to explore the inherent difficulties in the symbolisation—and consequently, the psychoanalytical representation—of traumatic states. I will seek to elaborate upon what it signifies to "be capable of representing" such suffering. To render this reflection more concrete, Viñar (2004, p. 18) precisely synthesises the perspective embraced herein, writing:

> [Today I would call it] trauma or a traumatic situation the fact that the perpetual metabolism of self-construction can be invaded, inundated, or overwhelmed by a situation in which the psyche ceases to be able to signify, or cannot modify the meaning of experience, and either breaks down or interrupts its symbolic production that founds and grounds psychic existence, creating, temporarily or definitively, a hole, a tearing that demands mending.

Viñar thus points to the temporary—or indeed, enduring—collapses of the mentalization function in severely wounded individuals. The mind forfeits its capacity to make sense, to affectively organise lived experience, thereby suspending its ability to symbolise. Mankind, as Merleau-Ponty (mentioned by Skidelsky, 2008) observed, is condemned to signify, to find or build meaning for their experiences. When this access to meaning is disrupted, a profound psychic isolation sets in. The subject finds themselves trapped in an eternal present, divested of a "before" and an "after". Only an agonising, unending "now" is experienced. There is no prospect of relief from suffering. The very capacity for imagination diminishes and vanishes. The victim becomes hostage to a continuous nightmare, awake, yet without access to psychic death—nor, for that matter, to full life. Their creativity is affected; a certain mental inertia sets in, although these manifestations are often only perceived *a posteriori* once the traumatic experience has been psychically metabolised.

A patient described this state with the following words: "I could only walk forward, not aiming to reach anywhere, I just couldn't stop, and I wept silently. Everything ached—but it wasn't the body, it wasn't something physical, it was the spirit. There was nowhere to go, nowhere to return. The world became an endless continuity, nothing mattered, only pain existed, but even this was part of being."

This unceasing walk lasted half a day. Upon reaching the urban limits, skirting a plantation, he turned back—without direction, without purpose. On other occasions, this same patient would go to airports merely to observe, for hours, the arrival and departure of people and flights. As if the movement of others were an attempt to reconnect with his own life, which remained suspended within him. Trauma, then, becomes a model—a structuring structure—that colours and contaminates all subsequent experience, reverberating perpetually in the spirit, even when not directly related to the original injury. In such moments, there is no perception of psychic truth in the Bionian sense—as a movement in pursuit of "O". There is only suffering, malaise, an indistinct psychic agony.

I insist that, when speaking of trauma, it is essential to distinguish the catastrophic event itself from the subsequent attempt to figure it out. It is in this latter moment that mechanisms of refusal—often in the form of *foreclosure* or *disavowal*—come into play to deny or invalidate the pain, as astutely observed by Chrein (2025). In many cases, trauma only constitutes itself as such in this second stage when it fails to acquire meaning due to a refusal or disavowal and thus cannot be represented. Trauma only begins to be metabolised when the injury acquires one or more meanings and then begins to be consciously and unconsciously represented.

To symbolically represent an experience—and thereby engage with a psychic truth that shapes a person's inner world—implies activating mental operations that regulate anxiety, such as contextualising, historicising, subjectivising, and objectifying within a frame of reference. Each of these functions, whether isolated or conjoined, contributes to the transformation of the experience. Symbolising a lived experience permits its elaboration and its inscription within the subject's internal history. At this juncture, narration—and empathic listening—become central instruments of psychic work.

It is crucial to underscore that the symbolic function not only regulates anxiety but expands the capacity for experience to be understood and comprehended in its broader meanings and impacts. It generates availability for thought, permits the evocation and connection of new affects and affective networks, and promotes emotional digestion. By expanding the imaginative field, it allows for the transcendence of the sterile repetition of pain, a characteristic of traumatic states. Psychic suffering, when unsymbolised, constricts the mental field, inhibits the creation of new symbols, and can even paralyse the representative function, given that the feeling of being alive is affected. "Less life" is imperceptibly reflected across all levels of existence until it acquires sense and meaning. It is not uncommon for this to occur many years after the event, and even after the conclusion of a successful analysis.

Symbols are not mere receptacles of meanings: they are living organs of thought. It is they that enable freedom from fixation on traumatic pain. It is these metabolic capacities that, in clinical practice, we strive to restore.

Clinical example 1: Marcela

Marcela sought analysis upon her psychiatrist's recommendation. Her complaint was precise and disquieting: she claimed to have never lived a life of her own, but merely a borrowed existence. She described her family as insensitive—or, more trenchantly, as tormenting—due to her parents' and relatives' systematic blindness to her needs and even to the life unfolding around them. She recounted never having felt seen, understood, or respected in her most fundamental desires. As an example, she mentioned the disregard for her schooling continuity: her parents would transfer her from school—or even from city and country—at any point in the academic year, without warning or explanation. The family operated as if no one, including she herself, truly existed. In her words, they were "frightening zombies".

Her discourse during sessions was fluent, articulate, and continuous, yet populated by dozens of characters whose roles in her life remained unclear. I felt lost, unable to discern who was who. She did not sound depressed, or lethargic. There was an energy in the session, a kind of agitated background noise, which nonetheless produced an unusual effect in me: I was overcome by an uncontrollable urge to sleep, entirely uncharacteristic of my life. It was as if the session's atmosphere, despite variations in verbal pace, was laden with an emptiness. Gradually, I came to understand that behind her abundant narrative lay an absence of identifiable connections. The individuals mentioned had names, but no identities. From me, the patient seemed to expect only constant affirmation, session by session, that she was improving.

Frequently, I had the impression of being amid a noisy crowd of strangers wandering aimlessly. At other times, I envisioned someone adrift in a desert. These images were accompanied by an intense sensation of futility. On one occasion, I recalled the moment before a surgery: the instant I was anaesthetised. On that occasion, I was suddenly overcome by an irreversible drowsiness during a session with Marcela. And then, in a sudden reverie, during the session, I found myself in an anaesthetic recovery room where someone—perhaps her, or someone without identity—was agonising, while doctors and nurses rushed about. These images and sensations constituted, I believe, a *reverie*—a subject upon which I have written with Elizabeth Rocha Barros (Rocha Barros & Rocha Barros, 2019). At a certain point, Marcela remarked: "I believe you were asleep. I noticed it from your breathing." I was startled. I looked at her and wondered if her shirt was orange. It was. The colour orange brought to mind an expression used in ICUs, when machines beep, indicating that a person is in life-threatening danger. The ensuing mobilisation is referred to as "code orange". My association between the colour of the patient's sweater and the ICU expression signalled: danger to life!

I responded almost immediately: "I have the impression that if I were to insist on interrupting your stories about the people you met during this week and tried to redirect your attention to consider what you wish to communicate, you would be terrified. If you were to take me seriously, you might even feel as if you were dying."

There was a silence. Then, her voice choked, she said: "So-and-so [a close relative] killed herself on the floor above I was in in my house while I was watching a cartoon. The sound of the gunshot startled me. But I continued watching the cartoon. I didn't move. I remained inert."

At this instant, a conscious memory was activated. We do not know if the evoked recollection generated an unconscious representation at that moment—but it is possible it did not, and the memory only emerged due to the overcoming of a refusal (*Verleugnung*)—as formulated by Chrein (2025)—and as a result of the emotional resonance generated by my words. It is plausible that, in a minimal span of time, she intuited the gravity of what had transpired, became terrified, perhaps even identified with the relative's despair who shot herself. Yet she remained motionless, continuing to watch the cartoon, while the house was consumed by the commotion of the staff followed by the arrival of police.

Monique Schneider (1974, quoted by Ulhoa Cintra, 2023) distinguishes between "the acquisition of awareness" and "the admission of consciousness". The acquisition of awareness implies a distancing—not impersonal, but necessary—followed by a subjective appropriation. Only this appropriation inaugurates a new understanding, capable of reorganising affective life.

I believe my intervention—which did not bear the more precise character of an interpretation—served to unfreeze affects. It generated in me an insight into the meaning of my drowsiness and allowed me to formulate a hypothesis regarding Marcela's mental functioning: she was projecting into me, through projective identifications, expressive aspects of her experience of a world populated by beings without identity. A deadly world, where I, as the analyst, was also depersonalised and dying to the living affects of her narrative. It was her way of objectifying affect.

When I told her that she might feel as though she were dying if confronted with the futility of her accounts, something shifted. She connected the suicide episode to her own emotional paralysis—a dissociation that had, until then, protected against the advent of painful awareness. Such an evocation, at that moment, served a liberating function. A fragment of herself re-emerged. For the first time, it became possible to reflect upon the impact of her experiences both in the session and in life. We were faced with an experience of contact with a psychic truth: a shock that unleashed new affective chains or network, the product, I believe, of a profound intuition that something central to her *being* was being denied. Here, we can speak of the formation of an unconscious representation.

In another work, I noted that it was Rocha Barros Neto (2015) who elucidated for us that it was the pre-Socratics who made the crucial leap in characterising the notion of representation, highlighting that we are not merely interested in what presents itself to us as a subjective image in itself or as representative in the parliamentary sense of something, but in identifying and understanding its *arché*, its principle or foundation. This quest for what is now better known as the *arché* leads us to a radical abstraction. Here, the *arché*, the organising principle, was the identification with a world of zombies, devoid of identity, yet all constituting a deadly object, a destroyer of life's traces, akin to a flesh-eating bacterium. In psychoanalysis, it is not the image itself or a form, the conductor of this *arché*, but the process that figurability unleashes in drive terms that is central to the constitution of subjectivity grounded in mental representations in the psychoanalytic sense. The essence captured by representation functions as a formative mould for experiences and a generator of new lived experiences.

From that point onwards, we began to talk in her sessions about how, in that traumatic moment of the suicide of her relative, something within her had also died, having been devoured by her childhood experiences, by the infantile (as an instance) of her personality. By being moved, by confronting the idea of her own psychic death, Marcela began a process of signifying her loss. She began, at last, to elaborate the pain of being who she was. And with that, she felt more alive, more real, more subjective. In this context, we can speak of the constitution of a representation that actively functions as an unconscious fantasy, consisting of picturing a world of characters without identity, including her parents who, even when present, were experienced as absent and, therefore, incapable of helping her in a moment of psychic suffering.

Clinical example 2: Paulo

A patient, whom I shall call Paulo, recounted feeling devastated upon discovering, by chance, that he had been systematically defrauded for years by his partner, associate, and intimate friend. The revelation left him utterly stunned. This associate, a friend since primary school, had been a constant presence in his life: frequenting his home, vacationing with his family, treating his children as if they were his own nephews. Furthermore, he was a man of considerable wealth, hailing from a rich family, who already received a substantial share of the profits from their shared enterprise.

The discovery occurred when their mutual accountant casually mentioned having booked part of the profits "into your advertising company". Paulo, astonished, retorted: "What company? I don't have any advertising company with Júlio!" Thus, the existence of a phantom company came to light, used by the associate to divert funds for more than twenty years. What most ravaged him, however, was not the financial loss, as we shall see.

The analyst, attuned to the nuance of Paulo's distress, observed that his pain did not stem from the theft itself, but from the collapse of an essential affective bond, a deep loving bond. What devastated him was the perception that, for his friend and partner, he was not as significant as he had imagined. The betrayal was not merely financial—it was the rupture of loyalty, affection, and trust devoted to his partner and friend, of a bond hitherto deemed unbreakable. Paulo did not feel merely disappointment—nor even anger. He felt bereft of value, impoverished, a nobody incapable of eliciting love. It was as if the diversion of money (felt as a treason) revealed that he himself "was worth nothing", that he did not inspire genuine affection. His identity wavered, and his internal world crumbled.

He was touched by the analyst's interpretation of these feelings, yet his anguish did not subside. That night, he could not sleep. He described feeling as though he were being boiled alive in a cauldron. An insight had occurred, but it was nascent. The pain remained, as did the awareness of the wound.

What was missing, however, was the symbolisation—in the psychoanalytic sense—that would enable him to elaborate on his mental suffering. His mind was formed at the beginning only by a constellation of icons (Peirce, 1958), still far removed from the status of a symbol. Icons, a category within the family of representative devices, denote the similarity of phenomena, experiences, or memory, representing their quality through resemblance. At this stage, we cannot yet speak of symbols, psychic instruments that transcend mere resemblance, for instance, words indicating relations. Symbols, above all, carry within them something that Duarte (2025, p. 199), drawing from Peirce's philosophy, termed "logical interpretants". The expression indicates that a proper symbol, especially when it carries a high degree of abstraction (united by an *arché*), bears an interpretive function, that is, a reference to a pregnant meaning.

I now believe that, at this first stage, it was an icon, in Peirce's terms, as highlighted by Duarte (2025): a link of contiguity and resemblance between affect and fact, but not yet a symbol with a wider interpretive capacity. There was contact with psychic pain, but in a rudimentary form. The experience had struck him, but it had not yet become a subject of reflection.

I interrupt the session's sequence to present a dream, which occurred on another occasion, and which, in my view, marks the beginning of a deeper and qualitatively different symbolisation process. In the dream, someone—perhaps he himself—was driving a car with another passenger: a relative? A girlfriend? The car skidded, and the passenger died. The forensic analysis indicated that chewing gum stuck to the tyre was the cause of the accident. Paulo imagined that he himself had thrown the chewing gum onto the road. The logical content of the dream was contradictory: if he was driving, he could not have thrown the chewing gum earlier, before skidding. But dreams, as we know, do not submit to ordinary logic. They operate through condensations, displacements, metaphors.

Upon recounting the dream, Paulo commented that something as mundane as chewing gum had caused a tragedy. He then recalled a childhood episode: he had been unjustly accused of sticking chewing gum in his sister's hair. He received a humiliating reprimand from his father and, for a time, was nicknamed "chewing gum". Later, it was discovered that his sister herself had put the chewing gum in her hair.

The word "irrelevant" insistently recurred in his discourse and resonated to the analyst's ears. Paulo stated that both the chewing gum and the motive for his partner's betrayal were irrelevant. The partner did not need money. The unbearable aspect was that the collapse of his affective world had occurred for a trivial reason. The chewing gum, a symbol of something chewed until it loses its taste, represented the traumatic banality—the insignificant gesture that destabilised an entire life. He hypothesised that the betrayal might have been the result of Júlio's depressive state, of a humiliation or emptiness experienced at the time the ethically unacceptable act of treason began. Júlio was wealthy, competent, yet fragile.

This dream started a movement towards a deeper level of symbolisation. Previously dispersed affective fragments began to connect childhood experiences of injustice, the fear of not existing in his parents' minds, pain, humiliation, and the recent narcissistic wound of betrayal. This articulation does not occur in a single act. It is what Bion would call learning from experience, that which allows for the emergence of a transformative psychic truth.

Paulo's case illustrates how pain, even when recognised, can remain broadly unsymbolised, and how the constitution of symbols becomes the basis for more abstract and integrative thought. The experience of betrayal lacked a representational symbolic form that would enable emotional metabolisation. The pain was recognised but not transformed—a pain still incapable of being thought. For it to become tolerable, it must be inserted into a broader narrative of the vicissitudes of human life, with its contradictions, beauties, and mysteries. As Riobaldo, Guimarães Rosa's character, said: faced with a narration, "We enter a labyrinth of doubts from which neither wisdom nor traditional norms are of any avail. For to learn to live is indeed to live itself" (Arrigucci, 2019, p. 491; my translation).

The dream offered a condensed image of the emotional experience: a precursor to more complex symbolisation, a proto symbolisation. The chewing gum—mundane, irrelevant, infantile—became an index of a tragic destiny. The memory of paternal injustice, the humiliation of the nickname, the powerlessness in the face of betrayal, the inability to dissolve the partnership, the lack of courage to do so: elements that, through a chain of associations, began to constitute the germ of a psychic truth. It was the beginning of a representational construction in the psychoanalytic sense.

It is in this field that analytical work is inscribed: not in the pursuit of an objective and definitive truth, but in the cultivation of forms of truth that emerge when the subject manages to affectively appropriate their history. Psychic truth is something in process, ever expanding, whose therapeutic function lies not in certainty, but in the capacity to generate new meanings.

The analyst commented that Paulo perceived himself as a victim of a life accident, the discovery of disloyalty, which left him emotionally in agony: something worse than being dead, for he maintained awareness of the slow deterioration of his affects. This state awakened in him feelings of being irrelevant to everyone: to his partner, to his parents, to his wife. This experience caused him to slip into a lack of meaning in life and even desire death, even to contemplate suicide. Everything he had lived through with his friend, his partner, had been irrelevant as an affective bond, a lie. It was as if life, until then, had been false.

I now wish to reflect on the process of symbolisation implicated in this analysis. The "chewing gum", after its meaning was unveiled, gained a broader and more complex symbolic power: it evoked feelings and reflections, much like in shamanic healings where a hidden meaning is invoked. The chewing gum—which was also himself, for he had been so called—did not represent merely an external object; it became associated with injustice, humiliation, with something sticky and tasteless, chewed out of habit, a symbol of his ruminated mental suffering. In agony, he was the chewing gum: a being kept out of habit in the lives of others, not out of love. This was the true agony, the agony was him, not merely something he felt. This constitutes an unconscious psychic representation, perhaps the central unconscious fantasy: the belief of never having elicited a love solid enough to ensure true care. To realise this plunged him into agony: a state without future, without prospect.

Here is the question: what psychic truth, what emotional experience, could supervene this agony and rescue him from this state? Awareness of the fantasy is not enough. He could reflect on the implications of feeling agonising, he could create beliefs about how to seek loyal love, but this would only be possible upon emerging from the agony.

My hypothesis, to be tested in future sessions and in life, is that only a profound feeling of shared experience with the analyst, one who genuinely recognised having disappointed the patient by implicitly promising a cure and a better life, could generate this change. A true love, an authentic *caritas*. The analyst would have failed the patient and himself. The genuineness of this awareness would need to be communicated, though it is not easy to articulate how this occurs. Only an object capable of self-disappointment for having betrayed the object of care and capable of conveying this to the patient, could overcome the state of agony.

To support this thought, I turn to the reflection of Luiz Claudio Figueiredo and colleagues Marina Ribeiro and Gina Tamburino (2025):

> Bion introduces the contrast between transformations *in* O and transformations *of* O, governed by the K-link. The expression "growth in becoming" seems to demand a translation such as an expansion of the capacity to embrace O in its imminence, that is to say, growth in the psychic capacity of being, understanding this being not as a substantive state, but as potentiality, as a verb.

This idea, though complex, illuminates the process of psychic change and contact with "O", ultimate truth. Agonising suffering can be transformed by a constitutive experience of being that supervenes—in this case, the mutual commiseration (the feeling of being moved together) between the victimised object and the object of disaffection—and by a new experiential perspective, implanted not merely through knowledge, but through being.

Only an interpretive comment, wherein the analyst acknowledged having failed Paulo by implicitly promising to help him live better and suffer less, could generate such a transformation. The analyst and psychoanalysis itself appeared, then, as a disappointment, just as Júlio had become one for Paulo by revealing his lack of significant affection in betraying Paulo's trust. Something that, at first, generated overwhelming dismay, a staggering astonishment.

In a subsequent session, still obsessed with the betrayal, Paulo commented that, throughout their lives, he and his partner played squash and, at times, basketball, usually on opposing teams. Now, recalling these situations, he said he perceived something he had not given importance to before: his friend was extremely competitive and hit the ball with anger—not merely anger, but with hatred—when they played squash. He could understand the rivalry, even the resentment for always being victorious in their encounters, but the hatred, conscious or not, seemed incomprehensible to him. He felt that this hatred, perhaps unknown to his friend, had undermined his capacity to like him, to respect him, to maintain a bond of loyalty. His friend had felt capable of betraying his trust, stealing from him, almost emotionally destroying him.

Paulo added that he wished he could enter his friend's mind to understand what he was thinking when he betrayed him, when he misappropriated the money, when he lived harmoniously with him and his family while deceiving him. He wanted to know what had become of the affection he deemed true in their conviviality. This statement indicated that, through symbolic representations of what had occurred, affects began to acquire the force of an unconscious mental representation, capable of generating a dream, of containing associations born of significant reflection.

The analyst observed that Paulo remained stuck to the situation, like chewing gum to which he compared himself, because he could not understand part of what had transpired. He understood the fraternal rivalry, but he could not figure what transpired in his friend's mind while the latter betrayed him and it was precisely this that seemed central to the installation of the trauma. What caused him much suffering was being unable to imagine what went through his partner's mind when acting thus.

The analyst commented that, without understanding how his friend had thought when almost mortally wounding him, Paulo would not be able to free himself from the pain. It was not enough for Júlio to apologise. For Paulo, it was essential to understand what transpired in his friend's mind while he was stealing from him, betraying his trust, and simultaneously maintaining such close conviviality. There was an omnipotent fantasy there that caused him even more suffering: the desire that the analyst could become Júlio and provide him with the explanation that would alleviate his pain.

For a qualitative change in his suffering, it would be necessary to transform this concrete and omnipotent expectation. An analyst's comment might be: "Only if I were Júlio and could explain how I thought when betraying you, might that perhaps help to diminish your pain. But I have the impression that your suffering is so profound that only if Júlio himself explained to you, and if he knew, why and how he betrayed you, could you feel some relief. And we have no power over Júlio to induce him to do so."

The analyst added: "I imagine you must have felt anger towards yourself for having trusted him all these years. You might feel foolish, and that does not help in recovering self-esteem. It is possible that you fear being deceived again—and that would be devastating." This comment, though formulated somewhat differently in the session, brought some immediate, but fleeting, relief. Paulo had not yet developed sufficient affective maturity or mental expansion to free him from the concrete need for explanation.

The interpretation regarding the analyst acknowledging having disappointed Paulo partially addressed the agonising experience and opened space for reflection. But this was captured by the concreteness of the expectation. As long as this need persisted, there could be no deeper change in the unconscious belief of not having generated enough love to merit care, respect, and consideration. It is not merely a matter of not being loved, but of not being loved enough to prevent the rupture of fidelity and loyalty.

Symbolisation is not reduced to the ordering of metaphors representing the injury. It is a creative gesture that renders pain tolerable, allowing one to inhabit suffering without being destroyed by it. To symbolise is to give form to pain without denying it, broadening the perspective on what hurts in the present, the past, and even the future of the present. All associated with interpretive meanings of the flow of life, what Winnicott termed "going on being". It is to inscribe the catastrophic event into the history of human living for an individual within a culture pregnant with values constituting a cultural superego. Sometimes, life hurts. A symbol needs to have a broad reach to contain a truth, an "auratic" psychic truth (Benjamin, 1936), that is, an experience imbued with authenticity, resonance, and ethical authority.

As Bion formulated, thinking is the fruit of tolerated frustration, of unevaluated suffering. It is in the space between the incomprehensible and what one attempts to think that insight is born—not an intellectual solution, but a transformative movement of being. When the patient manages to name what was once merely a kind of mental noise, there is a moment of K, of emotional knowledge. Insight, here, is a crossing, an opening, a possibility of integration and, perhaps, of experiencing.

The analyst's function is not to transmit a truth, but to help construct it: to participate with the patient in the symbolic edifice of experience. This truth is not fully pre-existent; it forms in the intersubjectivity of the analytical field, in the intertwining of voices, in shared listening, in the containing silence.

Revisiting Proust, psychic truth conceals itself like the taste of a madeleine steeped in tea: we can live an entire life without encountering it again, but when it emerges, even for an instant, it reconnects us to something essential—a fragment of being, an affective tonality, a form of presence, an entire life lived in an instant, an aura, using a term dear to Benjamin (1936).

Narration, in this context, is not a simple recounting of something already transpired; it is the fruit of a complex form of symbolisation, an act imbued with aura (Benjamin, 1955). The aura elevates the world beyond the facticity of the everyday. To narrate is to insert the lacerating fact into a broader perspective of existence, to deepen the understanding of the human, to place reality within its magical dimension, where the unreal can occur as illusion. And to narrate, often, is the first step to continue being ("going on being"). To narrate is, among other things, to insert the historical individual into a broader narrative, bestowing upon them the status of a character whose nature and actions are co-determined by their surrounding environment, both familial and cultural. Pain, transformed into a tale, becomes amenable to examination from a certain distance and can thus (though not always) become milder and more comprehensible. Understandable by associating feelings and acts within the perplexity of living. Arendt (1958, p. 8) impacts me by stating that "Our existence is indefinitely renewable by the extraordinary." I would further say that the narration transforms the past into the future, and we know that a happy life is always in the past, even if in a past of the present, as Saint Augustine teaches.

As Hannah Arendt suggested, a life that cannot be narrated is a life that empties itself of meaning by not allowing for examination from a certain distance, in which the historical individual transforms into a character in a complex plot full of multiple determinations. The capacity to recount one's own story, to give it structure, to recognise within its rhythm, affective logic, a before and an after, a possible future, is the capacity to restore oneself to time, to reoccupy the internal and external world with subjective dignity and even a certain refined humour. To identify oneself as a character in a story is a way to reclaim the sense of dignity lost in humiliation. This holds true for individuals, cultures, nations.

Psychic truth is not merely that which is found, but that which is constructed from fragments, in the labour of the mental pottery that also produces new bricks or Lego pieces, and with the same elements erects new structures. Each step taken on this path, however faint, is an expression of something fragile yet true: a possibility of living with greater authenticity, internal coherence, and freedom, fruits of the recovery of dignity and self-respect. It is when we can observe that an unconscious representation has been revealed, born of an *arché* that extracted the essence of each evoked experience.

Acknowledgements

I am deeply in debt to Professor Luiz Carlos Figueiredo for his comments and corrections and to Vanessa Chrein for her careful reading and suggestions.

References

Ahumada, J. L. (2011). *Insight: Essays on Psychoanalytic Knowing.* London: Routledge.

Arendt, H. (1958). *The Human Condition.* Chicago, IL: University of Chicago Press, 2002.

Arrigucci, D. (2019). O mundo misturado: Romance e experiência em Guimarães Rosa [*The Mixed World: Novel and Experience in Guimarães Rosa*]. In: *Grande Sertão Veredas.* São Paulo, Brazil: Companhia das Letras.

Benjamin, W. (1936). A obra de arte na era da reprodutividade técnica [The work of art in the age of mechanical reproduction]. In: *Magia, técnica, arte e política* [*Magic, Technique, Art and Politics*]. S. P. Rouanet (Trans.). São Paulo, Brazil: Brasiliense, 1982.

Benjamin, W. (1955). On some motifs in Baudelaire. In: *Illuminations: Essays and Reflections* (pp. 155–200). H. Zohn (Trans.). New York: Schocken, 1969.

Bion, W. R. (1965). *Transformations.* New York: Jason Aronson, 1983.

Chrein, V. (2025). *Novas dimensões da recusa* [*New Dimensions of Refusal*]. São Paulo, Brazil: Blucher.

Civitarese, G. (2024). Intuition and we-ness in Bion and post-Bionian field theory. *International Journal of Psychoanalysis, 105*(1): 13–39.

Damásio, A. (2018). *A estranha ordem das coisas: As origens biológicas dos sentimentos e da cultura* [*The Strange Order of Things: The Biological Origins of Feelings and Culture*]. São Paulo, Brazil: Companhia das Letras.

Duarte, P. (2025). O uso de elementos da filosofia de Peirce por quatro reconhecidos autores psicanalíticos [The use of elements of Peirce's philosophy by four renowned psychoanalytic authors]. *Livro anual de psicanálise, 39*: 195–214.

Figueiredo, L. C., Ribeiro, M., & Tamburino, G. (2025). *Reading Bion's Transformations*. London: Routledge.

Heidegger, M. (1956). *Was ist das—die Philosophie?* [*What Is Philosophy?*] (3rd edn). J. Stambaugh (Trans.). New York: Twayne, 1969.

Hunter, V. (1993). An interview with Hanna Segal. *Psychoanalytic Review, 80*: 1–28.

Lalande, P. (Ed.) (1960). *Vocabulaire technique et critique de la philosophie* [*Technical and Critical Vocabulary of Philosophy*] (12th edn). Paris: Presses Universitaires de France.

Levine, H. B. (2013). *Unrepresented States and the Construction of Meaning*. London: Karnac.

Levine, H. B. (2023). Mea culpa? In response to Richard Simpson's article, "Questioning the Unrepresented: The Essential and Accidental in Psychoanalysis, Part 2." *Psychoanalytic Quarterly, 92*(3): 527–537.

Margulies, A. (2025). Future tense: Permacrisis, falling out of the world and our existential moment. *International Journal of Psychoanalysis, 106*(5): 1038–10655.

Peirce, C. S. (1958). *Collected Papers of Charles Sanders Peirce (Vols. I–VIII)*. C. Hartshorne, P. Weiss, & A. Burks (Eds.). Cambridge, MA: Harvard University Press.

Rocha Barros, E. L. (2024). Experiência emocional no campo analítico: Teoria e clínica [Emotional experience in the analytical field: Theory and clinic]. *Revista Brasileira de Psicanálise, 58*(1): 105–116.

Rocha Barros, E. M., & Rocha Barros, E. L. (2019). Una ri-fondazione del concetto di controtransfert-reverie [A re-foundation of the concept of countertransference-reverie]. *Rivista di Psicoanalisi, 3*: 595–614.

Rocha Barros Neto, A. M. (2015). Sobre o que falamos quando falamos de representação: Ensaio de historiografia filosófica [What we talk about when we talk about representation: An essay on philosophical historiography]. In: T. Candi (Ed.), *Diálogos psicanalíticos contemporâneos*. São Paulo, Brazil: Escuta.

Rocha Barros Neto, A. M., & Rocha Barros, E. M. (2021). Landscapes of mental life under Covid-19. In: H. B. Levine & A. de Staal (Eds.), *Covidian Life: Common Distress, Individual Experience*. London: Phoenix.

Roussillon, R. (2011). *Primitive Agony and Symbolization*. London: Karnac.

Rovelli, C. (2017). *A realidade não é o que parece* [*Reality Is Not What It Seems*]. São Paulo, Brazil: Editora Objetiva.

Russell, B. (1911). Knowledge by acquaintance and knowledge by description. In: *Mysticism and Logic*. London: Unwin Paperbacks, 1989.

Schneider, M. (1974). Afeto e representação na metapsicologia [Affect and representation in metapsychology]. Paper presented 4 November 1991,

São Paulo. Cited in Cintra (2021), in Campos, Bocchi & Loffredo (Eds.), *Psicanálise em face ao desamparo e seus destinos* [*Psychoanalysis in the Face of Helplessness and Its Consequences*] (pp. 189–190). Bauru: Unesp, 1991.

Skidelsky, E. (2008). *Ernst Cassirer: The Last Philosopher of Culture*. Princeton, NJ: Princeton University Press.

Styron, W. (1979). *Sophie's Choice*. New York: Random House.

Ulhoa Cintra, E. M. de (2023). A questão do ódio à realidade em Bion [The question of hatred of reality in Bion]. In: M. F. R. Ribeiro & E. M. de Ulhoa Cintra (Eds.), *Vastas emoções e pensamentos imperfeitos*. São Paulo, Brazil: Blucher.

Viñar, M. (2004). Noción de trauma en psicoanálisis y campos afines [The notion of trauma in psychoanalysis and related fields]. *Boletín de la Asociación Psicoanalítica Argentina*, *72*: 89.

CHAPTER 11

Freud's "probability of truth": Construction and reconstruction

Sara Collins

[O]ne has to remember that the probable need not necessarily be the truth and the truth not always probable
—Freud, 1939b, p. 1.

This enigmatic statement was made by Freud towards the end of his life. While emphasising that truth is important, it cannot always be guaranteed to be certain, or universally applicable. It reflects his later recognition of the limitations of human capacity for ultimate certainty, and his growing appreciation of the subjective nature of truth in psychoanalysis. He was revisiting his cornerstone notion of construction (1937d), hitherto his main therapeutic tool, and contemplated its relation to truth. His own rigorous scientific approach required that claims for truth could not just be made; they had to be substantiated by some form of proof. Therefore, he was looking for corroboration of his assertions on construction from other fields or research, as well as using metaphors and analogies. In this discourse Freud engaged with other disciplines such as archaeology, history, and literature, through which he explored tools for proving objective truths.

Freud's metaphor for "truth": Construction

Looking for proof of the scientific validity of construction, Freud explained it by drawing an analogy with archaeology, an area in which he was profoundly interested: "The analyst's work of construction, or, if it is preferred, of reconstruction, resembles to a great extent an archaeologist's excavation of some dwelling-place that has been destroyed and buried ..." (1937d, p. 259). The vividly evoked scene of an archaeologist at an excavation site serves as a metaphor for analytic reconstruction.

According to this metaphor, when fragments of a work of art, say a vase, are found under layers of earth, these fragments testify to the pre-existence of a whole vase, a real and concrete artefact that could have been seen and touched, before it broke. The pieces that are dug out—these too can be seen and touched. The archaeologist wishes to know what the whole vase looked like, and he or she goes about it by putting together the fragments raised from the debris, in order to reconstruct the actual original vase. In the work of construction, Freud saw his project as that of uncovering, by the lifting of repression, an accurate account of what actually happened in childhood, which he called "the probable historical truth" (1937d, p. 261). In a manner analogous to that of the archaeologist who uses pieces of pottery, Freud used shards of memory, associations, and symptoms with which to piece together a historical truth; and he believed, at this stage of his work, that it was a real and truthful experience that he had recovered.

When presenting a reconstruction to the patient, it was essential to determine the time at which the experience occurred. The aspect of deciding the stage at which a relevant event took place was also explained in terms of the archaeological metaphor. It was the idea of levels in an archaeological dig, and how various levels correspond to different historical periods, a clear reference to Freud's theory of developmental phases and how they can impinge on one another. If an object makes its appearance in some particular developmental level, it often remains to be decided whether it belongs to that level or whether it was carried down to that level owing to some subsequent disturbance. It is easy to imagine the corresponding doubts that arise in the case of analytic constructions.

A main point in using this metaphoric device was to drive home his theory, of which he was convinced at the time, that it was possible to get down to the real objective truth of childhood events in a manner as indisputable as a piece of pottery is a piece of pottery. The technique he derived from this theory was equally, seemingly, straightforward. After the initial stage of removing the layers of rubble, that is, the lifting of the repression, the pieces of earthenware are revealed, and memory is recovered. The next stage is to put together the broken pieces so that the whole artefact can be reconstituted. That is, putting together the patient's shards of recovered memory enables the reconstruction of a childhood event. And that, in essence, was what led to the patient's recovery from symptoms, for "if the analysis is carried out correctly, we produce in him an assured conviction of the truth of the construction which achieves the same therapeutic result as a recaptured memory" (Freud, 1937d, pp. 265–266).

The project of *Moses and Monotheism*, one of his latest works, brought the critical problem of truth in construction into sharp focus, not least because it evoked great controversy. In this case Freud addressed his ideas through a dialectical engagement with Egyptology and history. Still, he could not assert that his ideas about Moses were the undisputed truth. By his own accounts, his assertion that Moses was an Egyptian rather than of Jewish descendance delayed the publication of *Moses and Monotheism* (Freud, 1939b). He stated that "I was not prepared to uphold them publicly, since they were based only on psychological probabilities and lacked objective proof" (Freud, 1937e, p. 1). In the end he gave up hope of finding objective proof that would seal claims of undisputed truthfulness in constructions. Abandoning that, he instead evoked the notion of psychological probabilities.

The notion of probability provided a bridge for what was for Freud a troubling gap between historical facts on the one hand, and supposition on the other. This has become accentuated in relation to reconstruction, since talking to patients about their past, in which only they and not the analyst had participated, is an area that greatly depends on the reliability of memory. Probability of reconstruction, then, connotes a sense of likelihood and only a degree of confidence in one's conclusions that something is likely to have occurred in the precise way it has been described.

Moreover, the improbability of truth in reconstruction represents the widely held contemporary view in psychoanalysis. Namely, that the past cannot be objectively verified once we consider the subjective, the internal, and the emotive nuances of remembrance. However, it is important to note that discussions about memory of the past primarily relate to experiences and emotions. For example, "I had a wonderful childhood," or "My father was always kind to me, but my mother was angry all the time." It excludes historical statements relating to basic facts like "My sister was born six years after me": or "My grandfather passed away in New York."

The contemporary view on narrating the past further asserts the past as being determined by the present. This view is by no means unique to psychoanalytic theory and has been amply supported by existential philosophers. May (1958) further privileges the present in her thinking that present temporality also encompasses the future: "It has often been said that one's past determines one's present and future. Let it be underlined that one's present and future—how he commits himself to existence at the moment—also determines his past" (p. 88).

Reconstruction post Freud

In one of the earlier indications of the problematic nature of reconstruction, when conceived as a factual reflection of historical truth, Kris (1956) highlighted difficulties in getting to the truth in reconstruction as patients develop myths about childhood events. This was especially so with regard to emerging knowledge at the time on screen memories. He observed that: "Individuals use their autobiographical memories … as a protective screen …." (p. 653), by which "The autobiographical self-image has become heir to important early fantasies, which it preserves" (ibid.). In other words, history as told by patients operates as a defence, rather than as a straightforward recollection of facts. The significance of Kris' writing is not only in revealing cracks in Freud's use of an archaeological model for reconstruction earlier on, but also in pointing out that the source of its difficulty is in the inevitable intrusion of fantasy and wishful thinking into any attempt at historical reconstruction.

What followed in Melanie Klein's work on unconscious fantasy resulted in a clear departure from Freud's archaeological construction model (Klein, 1927, 1975). She firmly located the recollection of early life within internal rather than external reality, which, by its very nature, is subjective and susceptible to unconscious influence.

However, Feldman (2007) later provides a discussion on the value of links between the present and past history and its implication for truth. His focus is on "the role of reconstruction in bringing about *psychic change*" (p. 609, my italics). He suggests that this may be done by way of the analyst holding in mind aspects of the patient's history. Although "links with the past can be enriching, giving the patient a greater sense of integration and meaningful continuity ..." (p. 616), his clear view is that there is no need to investigate the patient's early childhood extensively, since historical objects are available for immediate examination in the live transference, which reveals unconscious early phantasies in relation to internal objects. Internally, infantile history is being revised and reconstructed as early internal object relationships mutate through life, by processes of projection and introjection, until they appear in a contemporary interaction between patient and analyst.

On the question of historical truth in reconstruction, Feldman's emphasis is firmly on the capacity of the present to provide clues about truths in relation to the patient's history. The live exchanges in the here and now and their analysis provide the vital evidence as to whether a claim about the past is true or false. Therefore, it is from the examination of what is at hand and immediate "out of which *a different* historical perspective may emerge" (p. 609, my italics). In short, the present effects and transforms notions of the past that hitherto were held as "truths". In this, Feldman concurs with Kris' (1956) ideas on screen memories and their potential for distortion. Feldman and others also believe that the analyst's own emotional responses in the countertransference inform the formulation of interpretations, and this view inevitably adds a further dimension of subjectivity to the formulation of reconstruction.

In contemporary psychoanalysis discussions over "truth" have moved across considerable ground. Gabbard (1997), among other contemporary authors, acknowledged the impossibility of objectivity in the consulting room, and has therefore recognised the impracticality of retrieving a true historical past. Consequently, its use as a therapeutic tool has declined.

Ogden (1999) and others (e.g. Renik, 1996, 1998, 2004) portray the patient and therapist as creating a story of the patient's life, together remoulding their own Freudian vase between them, so to speak, in the context of a current and unique relationship. This then is a far cry from the depiction of a scientifically oriented analyst, on an assignment to unearth an objective reality from the past, and to reconstruct a pre-existing vase—a picture conjured up in Freud's (1937d) original notion of reconstruction.

In the modern era "reconstruction" is set in motion through a present affective state in the patient, combining both explicitly conscious and unconscious elements. A unique present moment in the analytic situation triggers the act of recollecting. Or, in the context of Freud's metaphor, rather the act of reassembling fragments of memory into a new shape of the past, for the present moment. Since the moment of recollection is in the present, it is therefore fundamentally bound by the present, and is being reshaped for a present psychic purpose. Ogden (1999) writes: "The analytic experience occurs on the cusp of the past and the present and involves a 'past' that is being created anew (for both analyst and analysand) by means of an experience generated between analyst and analysand ..." (p. 471).

Case material—John

A male patient in his late twenties, of Scottish background, was suffering from severe anxiety associated with a long-standing habit of dressing up to look like an attractive woman. Married to a woman and a father of six, he had led a divided life, keeping what he called his "cross dressing" underground. His marriage came under strain when his wife became aware of his secretive "second life" and they separated. He also feared discovery and dismissal by his overseas multinational employers at the time.

He had felt compelled to put on women's vintage stockings and shoes since the age of nine, when he secretly took items of clothing from his mother's wardrobe. He kept the two parts of his life strictly separate and had taken major decisions in his life with his dressing up compulsive habit in mind. This was also charged with excitement, fear, and sexual arousal.

In the initial stages of the analysis, he talked about dressing up in detail, describing it as a meaningful and enhancing experience, essential to his existence. Yet, he sought help for the great anxiety it evoked in him and the complications of keeping two separate streams of life going in tandem, one called male, the other female. Frequently he elaborated on the paradox experiencing anxiety bordering on panic as set against the exquisite sensations that being in female garb afforded him.

Reconstructing onset

John talked about the onset of his fetishism on two separate occasions. The first time was at the beginning of treatment, and the second time was about eighteen months into it.

The first time, he talked about how, aged about nine, he was with a school friend, at his house. Walking up the stairs, they passed by the friend's older sister's room, where on the floor were scattered high-heeled shoes. He felt enormously intrigued by and attracted to those shoes. From then on whenever he encountered girls he was focused on their leg wear, wishing he had those shoes for himself. He categorically stated he was sure this was when "it all began" as he put it, and sought to validate this point of onset by recounting other events that took place at that time. He began secretly putting on his mother's shoes and underwear.

On the second occasion, John again recounted his memory of the onset of his dressing habit, with the same assured conviction of its historical truth. He happened to be looking at an article in the newspaper that was on the kitchen table. It was about the harmful effects of high-heeled shoes on women's legs and backs. He immediately felt concern for his mother, who wore high stilettos. He vividly recalled going to her bedroom to look at her shoes, and found himself stepping into them, while rummaging through her underwear drawers, lingering for a long time. At the time of telling he seemed immersed in the memory, including the scent of his mother's clothes, and convinced by it being "the first time".

The patient's accounts of onset were spontaneous. He was curious to narrate his life with me and was focused on establishing the history of his difficulties. He thought it would help him find an explanation for what had suddenly changed his life for good.

The two reported instances of "onset", reported on separate occasions, one at a friend's house and one at his home, were distinctly different from each other, though they were both told with an equal conviction in their historical "truth". When the patient told me the second version of onset, he was not consciously aware of his first account.

A few questions might be asked here. Are either of these two versions real historical events, and if so, which is the correct account of it being "the first time"? However, for this discussion the important question is why the versions changed, and what was the analytic context that facilitated it. The analyst cannot give a definitive answer to the question of which of the two versions was true. However, it is possible to understand the contextual framework of the analytic relationship in each instance, in terms of the contemporary transference within which those early memories were recounted.

I suggest that in each case the contemporary context of the transference affected the patient's historical construction regarding the onset of his symptoms, as will be shown below.

The context of the transference

In the first, earlier account the patient is at a friend's house; he is going up a staircase. As he passes, he peers into his friend's sister's room, where he sees high-heeled shoes. According to the patient, this is the initial encounter with the object that was to become an obsessional preoccupation, highly significant to his sexual identity and development. I see this description not as an account of an undisputed telling of reality. Rather, I approach it as a dream, or as a symbolic representation of an internal psychic state where the place and its objects represent an important communication about the transference situation at the time. My consulting room is a few floors up, and the patient needs to climb stairs to reach the waiting room next to my office. There are several closed doors as he passes, until he reaches my office area.

The patient's telling of this first onset account took place during the early stages of treatment. His mother had been significant in her absence during this phase. She was described as ineffectual and powerless, and the material focused on a sadistic father who expected great things from his son. The analyst was equally dismissed as a person. In the countertransference she experienced herself as being made a bystander, with no mind of her own, except for providing focused emotional relief. There seemed to be a link between a sharp part-object (stiletto shoes) and the role responsiveness (Sandler, 1976) unconsciously imposed on the analyst at the time, as follows. The patient expressed his dread (conflicted with an unconscious wish) that I would suggest that he has a full sex change, which would resolve his tormented divided life. He therefore remained aloof and distant, as if metaphorically placing himself "out in the corridor", afraid to properly come in.

Before the second account of onset the patient began talking about his mother at some length. He was surprised at having omitted her from his memory and tearfully experienced some regret and grief at her loss, for the first time since her death.

At this stage the patient was beginning to look less frightened when he came into the room. As he took on board that I was not going to suggest any form of physical operation, nor impose any sex change, he began to feel safer with me. Accordingly, the patient's story of onset was remarkably changed, shifting the context of the surrounding scenes from an external to an internal location, thus reflecting the transference situation at the time. In summary, John's construction of his past fitted his evolving contemporary present. The change was in the kind of internal object the analyst represented for the patient at both stages. Initially the transference was dominated by projections of a castrating and denigrating father, who presented himself to his child as knowing what was best for him, albeit through imposing punishing routines. This was associated with the belief that the analyst was going to impose a sex change operation on him. The presentation later gave way to a transference in which a more benign, though seemingly ineffective maternal figure featured in the material. It is representing his mother whom he saw as accepting and kind: this was a change that mirrored the developing transference relationship with the analyst. Neither version could be said to be the "undisputed truth", while both narrations were correct and authentic for the time of telling.

Construction and belated memory

In 1895 Freud (1950a) wrote about the phenomenon of "retroactive temporality", which he called *Nachträglichkeit* (translated as "afterwardness", "deferred action", and "*après coup*"). This occurs when an initial event, not experienced as traumatic at the time, gains emotional, sexual, or traumatic meaning retroactively at a later stage. It happens because of a trigger by a new event, due to reaching a different development stage, or gaining a new understanding in the process of analysis. In the case of Emma (Freud, 1950a), an initial study that prompted the outline of the *Nachträglichkeit* notion, Freud stated in its conclusion that it was a case of "a memory arousing an affect which it did not arouse as an [initial] experience" (p. 356).

The essence of the concept, also later referred to as *après coup* and "deferred action", is that the original memory and affect associated with trauma could not be experienced at the time it occurred, nor were they available to conscious memory. The belated affective experience, taking place at a later point in time, was essentially therefore a retroactive emotional event, felt as though something was being experienced not just afresh but as if it were for the first time. This called into question the truthfulness and reliability of memory and its reporting, especially in the case of trauma. This then had implications for the construction of what might have been forgotten.

Faimberg (2005, 2007) greatly broadened our understanding of afterwardness in the psychoanalytic situation. She ascribed to it aspects of unconscious narcissistic identification, which required an active interpretive approach, in which a meaning is presented by the analyst in the form of a construction, which then leads to a radical revision of the patient's historical narrative. Faimberg's expansion rests not only on the broadening of the contents of *Nachträglichkeit* beyond the sexual dimension. It also locates this evolving clinical event in the relationship between analyst and patient. It takes place, as she stresses, by an interpretation which offers a new and retroactive meaning the patient has been unaware of. This is a result of the presence of the analyst, who helps to reshape and remould the memory.

Therefore, Faimberg's broadening of *Nachträglichkeit* with an intersubjective focus provides a helpful framework for thinking about the nature of truthfulness in the formation of construction and interpretation.

Clinical material—Jayne

A female patient in her early thirties was suffering from acute anxiety and recurrent panic attacks (Collins, 2024). She described feeling compelled to secretly follow her boyfriend's activities on social media. Things came to a head when she began physically stalking him. Desperate to see him, she would stand outside his house, feeding her imagination with what was going on, which made her acutely jealous. It resulted in furious rows and a threat to the relationship.

Jayne was the second of two girls. Her father was an engineer who travelled a great deal for work. The mother was a teacher. When Jayne was four and a half years old, her mother travelled to meet the father and was fatally injured in a road traffic accident. She was taken to a hospital in another town, where she later died.

Jayne's acting-out activities in relation to her boyfriend were intensified around analytic breaks. It was understood in the transference as a panicked reaction to the analytic separation. She was unconsciously convinced the break would spell the death of the analyst. This was projected onto the boyfriend, accompanied by an omnipotent fantasy she could control him and secure her connection with him by forcing his presence by means of stalking.

The dream and the transference

Three years into the analysis Jayne had to go abroad for a period of several months due to a work assignment, which meant she was taking an improved leadership role in her profession. She asked to be seen periodically online, and this was agreed.

Shortly after her departure to another country, Jayne brought a dream: She was looking at a world atlas in which each country had a different, bright colour and each had a string attached to it. Her association to the dream was that this reminded her of a children's activity book where elements can be manipulated and moved around. A hand appeared flashing, pointing to a string, inviting her to pull it. This was like visual advertisements on the internet, she said. In the dream she was amazed she could easily move countries around and rearrange them as she wished, and they could glide around at a touch. It made her feel powerful, and she alluded to moving countries around the globe as being child's play. An older man appeared in the dream, at first vaguely, then his image moved to the fore. He stood in front of the atlas like a teacher in front of a board. He warned her that moving the countries around would unsettle the fish in the oceans, as it would make the water too hot. The scene again changed, and she saw a giant whale lying stranded on a remote shore. She thought it was a female whale. Her association to this part of the dream was about climate change, which, she said, was due to human interference. If ignored, it could result in a catastrophe.

In further associations to the dream, she remembered that when she was a child, she was shown pictures of the city where her mother was taken into hospital after the accident, and where she died. She remembered believing the city was far away, wishing it was nearby, and she felt regret that she hadn't seen her mother before she died, though the hospital was actually close.

The dream pointed to the changing frame of the analysis in that it moved from in-person to online, and, with lesser frequency, it also changed the nature of the transference at the time. This was experienced as a dangerous interference with what had been a stable order in the rhythm and safety of the frame. The patient's belief that the move to another country would be easy (gliding countries around the globe was child's play) turned out to be dangerous: either she or the analyst could be stranded and in danger of dying. The analyst was unconsciously seen as responsible for the significant change in the analytic setting; since she agreed to it in the first place, she was seen as colluding in it. The analyst needed to be alerted to the patient's anxieties over the change to distance analysis, potentially a scenario in which there would be a repetition of her relationship with her mother—a death.

In a dynamic *après coup*—described above as an expression of retroactive temporality in Freud's concept of *Nachträglichkeit*—Jayne recovered memory fragments of traumatic experiences following her mother's death which had not hitherto been fully available to her or previously experienced as painful. This happened during the work on the dream, and in the context of the changing setting, After the death of her mother, Jayne was told that her mother had gone to heaven and was looking after her from up there. She strongly believed her mother would come down soon to be with her and kept asking whether she would come down to take her to school, and "Why is she not coming to my birthday?" She was met with a nod or a "maybe next time" and each time a hoped-for event passed, it was another devastating disappointment. Eventually, she asked questions only in silence, as she understood they would upset her bereaved father if she voiced them.

In time, her dead mother was consigned to an ephemeral and mythical space in her mind, neither present nor totally absent, though Jayne's longings to reach her did not abate. For example, the patient remembered and recounted how she nurtured fantasies of reaching out to the sky and touching the clouds, where she believed her mother lived. These were especially acute whenever she was flying a kite or sitting on a swing. Then she would strain and stretch her body up as much as she could only to find herself drawn back down again. In a moving moment, Jayne quietly murmured a childhood rhyme: "Swing, swing, take me up, take me higher and higher. Take me up to the sky, where I can see my mother. My mother who had gone and never returned."

Jayne's emerging new memories in the context of the work on the dream led to new interpretations within the development of the transference and a new construction in the *après coup*. It also led to a reconsideration of the dynamic origins of her symptoms, primarily her desperate need for omnipotent control of her objects.

Construction or reconstruction

A close analysis of the text reveals that Freud used construction with the prefix "re" only consistently in the section of the paper that discussed the archaeological analogy. By introducing this prefix, Freud seemed to have in mind that he was adding something to what was already (seemingly undisputedly) present in the material. There is both a gathering together and an adding of elements. "Both of them have an undisputed right to *construct* by means of *supplementing* and combining the surviving remains" (Freud, 1937d, p. 259, my italics).

Throughout the rest of the paper Freud uses the original term contained in the paper's title, namely "construction", even when he would appear to mean "reconstruction". However, this seemingly "dancing on a pin's head" Talmudic type argumentation about wording is only relevant in that it points to the heart of the debate over what is historically and factually true, and what is narrated in an imaginative, storytelling fashion, and therefore "untrue" in an objective sense, within psychoanalysis. Chianese (2008) for example, considering constructions in relation to the analytic field, revisits the twin usages by Freud of construction and reconstruction, and assigns to them the opposite meanings to what is discussed above. According to him, "construction" would stand for the creatively narrated story, compounded by fantasy, whereas "reconstruction" would be closer to what is historically and factually correct, and therefore true.

Spence (1982) altogether opposes post-Freudian attempts at distinctions between "construction" and "reconstruction". His writings are aimed at blurring differences between the two. Spence's thesis is that whether or not there might be a disparity between construction and reconstruction, in both cases imaginative input and fantasy on the part of the patient and on that of the analyst play an important part.

It would seem that Freud (1937d) concurred with and foreshadowed the modernist view when he stated that, "the analyst's work is one of *construction, or, if it is preferred, of reconstruction …*" (p. 259, my italics). Here he recognised an ambiguity of usage he was quite happy to leave alone, which links the argumentation back to Freud's later terminology of the "improbability of truth".

Truth, probability, and authenticity

During Freud's era, probability was an emerging field within mathematics, whereas other mathematical disciplines have origins tracing back to ancient Greece. In the post-Freudian era scientific thinking on probability exponentially developed into a mainstream scientific discipline, which explores theories of the coalescence between the probable with the improbable, uncertainty with certainty. It could be argued that some underpinnings of probability concepts match Freud's nascent thinking at the end of his life's work. These are anchored in the particular terrain between knowing and not knowing, predictability and the inability to predict exactitude of events. Probability science therefore provides a framework for understanding and even quantifying uncertainty, including in the context of human behaviour.

Kahneman and Tversky (1979), whose scientific base was psychology, developed the "prospect theory" about human judgement and decision-making, in which one of the foundational principles is anchored in probability. Further, Tuckett's (2018, 2024) research work on uncertainty in decision-making integrated complementing insights from psychoanalysis. The notion of probability therefore bridges what for Freud is a troubling gap between historical facts, on the one hand, and supposition, on the other. Probability in reconstruction, then, connotes likelihood and a degree of confidence in one's conclusions about historical events—but only to a degree that something is likely to have occurred. A conclusion about the past is reached after weighing up a ratio of favourability of one possibility against the others, in a subliminal mathematical manner.

Elsewhere (Collins, 2011), I proposed linking Freud's late notion on probability in reconstruction with "authenticity". Morris maintained that: "the use of criteria like 'authenticity' and 'genuineness' … extends only up to a point" (1993, p. 51). But I hold that the use of the term "authenticity" can be extended further and linked with Freud's late notion of "probability".

I suggest that authenticity in psychoanalysis also differs from truth. The analyst searches for genuineness and trustworthiness of an historical account within the context of the transference and countertransference relationship. The analyst's observations are anchored in the present, and his or her thoughts about the past originate in the context of a contemporary relationship with the patient. In that way "authenticity" in reconstruction denotes a genuineness of origin that is both sourced from and is faithful to a unique and current stage of an analytic encounter. Like Freud's use of "probability", authenticity in reconstruction differs from truth in that it lays no claim to undisputed certainty. Both probability and authenticity are distinguishable from truth in that neither seeks to demonstrate a sole objective certainty.

Authenticity, therefore, is proposed as a helpful concept in the debates over the question of "truth" in psychoanalysis. At times these discussions seem as though they might have reached an impasse. The improbability of truth in reconstruction represents the general view that the past cannot be objectively verified once we consider the subjective, the internal, and the emotive colouring of historical facts.

Moreover, the concept of "authenticity" in psychoanalysis rests on the assumption that past experiences are reconstructed in the immediacy of the present. The contemporary transference and countertransference experiences offer the emotive prism through which the past will be refracted. Thus, there can only be an approximation towards an objective historical claim for "truth" about childhood; and a reconstruction can be deemed "authentic" rather than "true". Authenticity in reconstruction, then, is a particular form of dependability and trustworthiness of historical accounts, given within the analytic discourse. These are validated through the transferential experiences in the sessions themselves from which a reconstruction emerges. The origins, genuineness, and dependability of what is being reconstructed are sourced from within a present transference and countertransference experience.

Conclusion

Freud's passing comment on the "probability of truth" seems to have foreshadowed significant developments in psychoanalysis leading to a new contemporary meaning of "truth", as did his concept of "construction". In clinical practice it is an interpretation or set of interpretations leading to an authentic moment of truth. That is, when past and present coalesce and together come into focus. The intersubjective analytic work is in the present which carries with it the knowledge of the patient's past history. The history is in the form of a certain pattern or a particular configuration of object relation that explains something essential for the patient regarding current dilemmas and obstacles to development. This leads to a psychic change, thus achieving the analytic aim. Therefore, the truth is a psychic truth. It is a psychoanalytic truth that analysts can know about also through their own countertransference with the patient.

Therefore, in that kind of truth there are no absolutes. There are only probable truths, and truths invested with affect as well as logic and intellect. Something revealed and hitherto unknown "feels" true, and "feels" correct. Therefore, it is a moment when mind and affect combine to arrive at a new discovery that can lead to transformative developments.

References

Chianese, D. (2008). Constructions and the analytic field. D. Birksted-Breen (Ed.). New Library of Psychoanalysis. New York: Routledge.

Collins, S. (2011). On authenticity: The question of truth in construction and autobiography. *International Journal of Psychoanalysis, 92*: 1391–1409.

Collins, S. (2024). On the belatedness of psychoanalytic clinical writing. *Psychoanalytic Quarterly, 93*(1): 157–181.

Faimberg, H. (2005). Après-coup. *International Journal of Psychoanalysis, 86*: 1–6.

Faimberg, H. (2007). A plea for a broader concept of *Nachträglichkeit. Psychoanalytic Quarterly, 76*(4): 1221–1240.

Feldman, M. (2007). The illumination of history. *International Journal of Psychoanalysis, 88*: 609–625.

Freud, S. (1937d). Constructions in analysis. *S. E., 23*: 255–269. London: Hogarth.

Freud, S. (1937e). If Moses was an Egyptian … *S. E., 23*: 1–32. London: Hogarth.

Freud, S. (1939b). *Moses and Monotheism. S. E., 23*: 3–137. London: Hogarth.

Freud, S. (1950a). A project for a scientific psychology. *S. E., 1*. London: Hogarth.

Gabbard, G. O. (1997). A reconsideration of objectivity in the analyst. *International Journal of Psychoanalysis, 78*: 15–26.

Kahneman, D., & Tversky, A. (1979). Prospect theory: An analysis of decision under risk. *Econometrica, 47*(2): 263–291.

Klein, M. (1927). The psychological principles of infant analysis. *International Journal of Psychoanalysis, 8*: 25–37.

Klein, M. (1975). *Love, Guilt and Reparation and Other Works 1921–1945*. London: Hogarth.

Kris, E. (1956). The personal myth: A problem in psychoanalytic technique. *Journal of the American Psychoanalytic Association, 4*: 653–668.

May, R. (1958). Contributions of existential psychotherapy. In: R. May (Ed.), *Existence: A New Dimension in Psychiatry and Psychology* (pp. 37–91). New York: Simon & Schuster, 1967.

Morris, H. (1993). Narrative representation, narrative enactment, and the psychoanalytic construction of history. *International Journal of Psychoanalysis, 74*: 33–52.

Ogden, T. H. (1999). The analytic third: Working with intersubjective clinical facts. In: S. A. Mitchell & A. Lewis (Eds.), *Relational Psychoanalysis: The Emergence of a Tradition* (pp. 459–492). London: Analytic Press.

Renik, O. (1996). The perils of neutrality. *Psychoanalytic Quarterly, 65*: 495–517.

Renik, O. (1998). The analyst's subjectivity and the analyst's objectivity. *International Journal of Psychoanalysis, 79*: 487–497.

Renik, O. (2004). Intersubjectivity in psychoanalysis. *International Journal of Psychoanalysis, 85*: 1053–1064.

Sandler, J. (1976). Countertransference and role-responsiveness. *International Review of Psycho-Analysis*, 3: 43–47.

Spence, D. P. (1982). *Narrative Truth and Historical Truth*. Toronto, Canada: George J. McLeod.

Tuckett, D. (2018). Conviction narrative theory and understanding decision-making in economics and finance. In: J. Beckert & R. Bronk (Eds.), *Uncertain Futures: Imaginaries, Narratives, and Calculation in the Economy* (pp. 62–82). Oxford: Oxford University Press.

Tuckett, D. (2024). *Seizing Uncertainty* (HSBC global research study on decision-making in an era of radical uncertainty, explicitly building on Conviction Narrative Theory).

Part III

The particularity of truth

CHAPTER 12

On Bion's concept of truth in an extra-moral sense*

Giuseppe Civitarese

Anyone who starts to familiarise themselves with Bion eventually realises that he is an author who employs an idiosyncratic concept of truth, and correspondingly, of the concept of lies or falsehoods. At the beginning, it is nearly impossible to resist a sense of scepticism. We hear the word "truth" invoked daily by people of the worst kind. The most fanatical among humans love to utter this word. In philosophy, things are no better. Every author has a personal conception of it. Just as one begins to accept a certain relativism, someone else immediately advocates a return to the (presumed) true reality to save us from the misery of so-called absolute relativism, the famous or infamous "anything goes". And in psychoanalysis? We are more or less in the same situation. Otherwise, we wouldn't speak of the Tower of Babel of languages, which is an image that refers to different psychoanalytic orientations that don't recognise each other as legitimate. Hence the reason for a sense of annoyance at merely hearing the word mentioned.

* This chapter was originally published as Civitarese, G. (2023). On Bion's concept of truth in an extra-moral sense. *American Journal of Psychoanalysis*, 83: 495–519. https://doi.org/10.1057/s11231-023-09430-w. It is reproduced with the kind permission of the editors of the journal.

But there's no escape. If we want to understand Bion and those who draw inspiration from his thinking, we cannot avoid the task of grasping the way he uses this easily abused word. The concept of truth is central: a) for Grotstein (2004), the only instinct Bion speaks of is the instinct for truth (Civitarese, 2013, 2016); b) Bion himself writes (1962) that truth is the nourishment that feeds and grows the mind, placing it at the heart of therapeutic action—as if to say: if you have no idea about it, change your path; c) he makes it an essential element of the Grid (Bion, 1977) in Column 2 (lies/falsehoods); d) he establishes a close connection between lies and the thinker, but not between truth and the thinker; e) he believes that liars can be treated because the definition of truth and lies changes; and finally f) the novelties introduced by Bion are taken up and developed in the post-Bionian theory of the analytic field (BFT), also in light of the ontologies of intersubjectivity elaborated in the last century by philosophy, starting from Husserl onwards, which allow us an approach that is as detached as possible from moralistic views.

I address the following points in order: the meaning of the concept of truth in Bion's theory of thought; then, in his conception of clinical work; finally, from the perspective of BFT.

The factor of truth in the theory of thought

Thoughts without a thinker

For Bion, addressing the matters of truth and lies is also a way to expand his theory of thought. An aspect of lies is that they require an audience. For the analyst to accept being this audience, she must attribute enough importance to the patient's false constructions, essentially considering them *true*. One way to achieve this is, of course, to interpret them, not merely adhering to their apparent meaning. Transitioning from lies to their hidden meaning is like moving from PS to D.

Furthermore, Bion introduces a contrast between thought based on falsehood and authentic thought. According to him, falsehood necessitates an active effort from the thinker to create and maintain a deceptive narrative. Conversely, true thought, or truth, exists independently of the presence of a thinker. In other words, truth is not dependent on the subject thinking it.

However, things are not so straightforward, because if we assume the subject unconsciously speaks the truth while lying, it means that, just as they determine truth, the infinity of language and sociality, or the Other, they also contribute to determining falsehood, albeit at different levels of consensus. Nonetheless, there is a crack in the notion of falsehood, and Bion's original, and somehow also "wild", thought about the link between lie and truth helps us to sense how the harmony of an individual's life could be expressed in gradients of intersubjectivity or consensuality. In my view, a thinker is not only necessary for falsehood but also for truth; otherwise, it would negate the very idea of a subject, which would be nonsensical. And still, what might appear as an odd idea, that is, the fact that it inevitably requires a group or is inherently intersubjective, actually helps us approach a concept of truth as communion with the entirety or the totality of what is, a concept traditionally associated with religions, but not with the logical-rational discourse that psychoanalysis is part of.

If thought doesn't need to be thought by the thinker, it means thoughts do not belong exclusively to the thinker. It's as if, for any idea, the idiomatic expression *embracing an idea* applies—a metaphorical image that also implies an element of passion. This is a way of saying that the unconscious is *transindividual*. On the other hand, if the thinker is necessary to formulate a lie, then the lie is classified as -T (minus-thought), meaning it deviates from sociality. We might even think, considering that C2 is represented in the Grid by Ψ (the symbol for psyche) (see Figure 12. 1), that being subjects means having multiple systems of *lies*. Don't we often say that the moment a child discovers they can lie is important, and that "lying" and *mens* (Latin for *mind*) share the same etymological root? In fact, the discovery of the possibility of lying, in addition to the attainment of other cognitive skills, marks the moment when the child becomes aware that he or she has an inner world that is not an open book to others, but has its own boundaries.

On the level of technique, Bion's weird assertion seems to be another way of stating the principle of negative capability/faith, which plays a significant role in his thought. Saying that "Nobody need think the true thought: it awaits the advent of the thinker who achieves significance through the true thought" (Bion, 1970, p. 103), reminds the analyst that they must avoid all forms of activity and instead actively position themselves in passive

THE GRID

	Defini-tory Hypo-theses **1**	ψ **2**	Nota-tion **3**	Atten-tion **4**	Inquiry **5**	Action **6**	**...n**
A β-elements	A1	A2				A6	
B α-elements	B1	B2	B3	B4	B5	B6	. . . Bn
C Dream Thoughts Dreams, Myths	C1	C2	C3	C4	C5	C6	. . . Cn
D Pre-conception	D1	D2	D3	D4	D5	D6	. . . Dn
E Conception	E1	E2	E3	E4	E5	E6	. . . En
F Concept	F1	F2	F3	F4	F5	F6	. . . Fn
G Scientific Deductive System		G2					
H Algebraic Calculus							

Figure 12. 1 The Grid

Used by permission of the Marsh Agency Ltd., on behalf of the estate of W. R. Bion.

receptivity to the dream. In this regard, Grotstein (2007, p. 142) offers an amusing metaphor: "It is as if the unconscious works like a Hollywood producer who might characteristically say to an actor auditioning for a part: 'Don't call us; we'll call you!'"

Nonetheless, it's a remarkably ironic effect that Bion has conferred a uniquely suggestive force on the concept of "thoughts without thinker", that couldn't be more anti-Cartesian. A typical way to misunderstand it is illustrated by Hanna Segal (1998, p. 212) when she writes, concerning this concept, that it would be an example of "a rather mystical kind of philosophy". While she does grasp the reference to Descartes, Segal fails entirely to realise that it's a way, deliberately ambiguous and somewhat provocative, if you will, of alluding to a psychology where the split between subject/object no longer prevails. Merleau-Ponty (1945, p. 473) expresses it differently, for instance, "I am a field, an experience" and it would amount to saying the same thing. What do I mean? That Bion's idea of thoughts without a thinker is merely a way to infer that, ontologically, intersubjectivity is a constitutive element of the subject. The relationship between the thinker and thoughts without a thinker is akin to that between *being* and *beings*, which Heidegger (1927) summarises in the concept of ontological difference. So, while it's an oversimplification, because it's true that the subject is spoken by the Other but also produces it, nonetheless, like many of his other provocations, Bion's bizarre idea that links only the lie to the thinker urges us to look deeper into something known but often not truly understood, that is, the radical social nature of subjectivity.

To be or to be a lie

When "O" impacts the personality, it can give rise to thoughts (true) or lies. If lies are produced, the relationship between them and the individual is parasitic; a link is formed, much like that between a parasite and its host. In other cases, there can be commensal or symbiotic relationships.

Something similar, the birth of a bond marked by envy and hatred occurs when an individual expresses the truth in a group which instead is lying. Two individuals whose linking rests on lies are destined to mutually destroy each other. The concept of lies should not be restricted to the content of thought. Someone can live as if they *were* (that is, embodying in their being) the lie. Bion writes: "it is possible to be a lie and being so precludes at-one-ment in O" (1970, p. 104). Let's recall that one of the definitions of "O" is "absolute truth" (Bion, 1970, p. 26).

This annotation significantly broadens the sense of Bion's reflection on these themes, as it immediately brings to mind the theme of authentic life—from Heidegger (1927) to Jullien (2020); furthermore, it promotes a view of lying in non-moralistic terms. From a certain perspective, following Bion we come to conceptualise lying as an excess of absolute, ultimate, impersonal, infinite truth or "O", which the individual cannot receive as personal (finite) truth without suffering a disastrous disintegration. Each person can hold only a certain amount of truth, after which it becomes excessive, as the sun's light for the retina when looked at directly.

Bion transcends the divide or the caesura between lie/truth. No longer dichotomous terms, they appear as opposite elements of a continuum. The "quest for truth", the "regard for truth", the *truth function*, that is, the ability to distinguish between the two terms, for the personality, becomes a function like others, such as alpha function or the function of intuition, etc. Like any function, it depends on factors that express its variables. For instance, as Grotstein (1997a, 1997b) suggests, one variable is "faith". Faith promotes the type of non-split truth that is characteristic of dreaming (dream + waking). The problem is perhaps that one cannot give oneself faith; it is itself a reflection of numerous past experiences of being recognised by the other, thus nourishing trust in the object. Depending on the vertex chosen, this process can be conceptualised as uni- or bidirectional. Sometimes presenting it as unidirectional, even from a radically intersubjective point of view, serves only to break down a complex process in order to explain it more clearly. For example, if we say that the mother contains the child's anxieties transmitted through projective identification, this account is still too unidirectional; it should be supplemented by the notion that the child also "contains" the mother's anxieties, trivially by showing healthy responses to stimuli.

Curiosity and envy

Bion (1958) dedicates a significant amount of space to curiosity. Mostly, he underscores its negative character when it is accompanied by arrogance and stupidity. On the other hand, it's easy to recognise that a certain level of curiosity indicates intelligence, openness, faith, and a positive tone of mood. However, it can turn into arrogance when it doesn't respect the inherent limits of the intellect. Excessive curiosity pursues lies in the form of a split truth. In this sense, it's also stupid. In my view, it is the same *stupidity* expressed by proponents of a *scientific* psychoanalysis modelled after exact sciences. Psychoanalysis is a hermeneutic discipline with an empirical field of application, with its own strict rules of consistency and logic. It could never be an exact science, because the phenomena it deals with are beyond the grasp of the senses, and therefore certainly cannot be the subject of laboratory experiments.

It's worth reiterating here that Bion reverses the assumption regarding the contents of truth. For him, truth is a concept that pertains to emotional truth, and thus inevitably to a social bond. Furthermore, he asserts that it doesn't make sense to talk about an emotion outside of a relationship or linking. Emotion—think of a newborn grappling with the immense task of emerging from the chaos of sensations it experiences in the process of constructing its world—represents the first concept or *abstraction* in the sense of a schema or simplification of a multidimensional perceptual field. This initial abstraction, which as such can only sediment from the repetition of similar positive experiences, could it ever, precisely due to its *schematic* nature, operate outside of an infant's interaction with the mother?

Emotions are psychic qualities or "perceptions" focused on internal time and space, not the external realm where objects are observed. They yield a sense of truth when consistent. Bion's example (1962) is the processing of emotional ambivalence towards an object. It establishes correlation among diverse aspects of the object known from varied experiences. Following Melanie Klein, Bion links conscious perception of psychic qualities to a positive relationship with the breast. This suggests that the coherence of perceptual and internal experience depends on the consensual truth of primary relations with the object, which are themselves embedded in a broader social context.

Bion's theory of truth-as-food-for-the-mind is rooted in affectivity. In this manner, he effectively reimagines the quandary explored by Freud (1911b) regarding the establishment of the reality principle. According to Bion, a "sense of truth is experienced" when a fact, appearing in the form of "[unmistakable] reality" emerges from a positive "shared emotional perspective" (Bion, 1962, p. 310). This perspective encompasses not only conscious awareness but also the unconscious, or more precisely, the binocular vision that operates as a unified system of both conscious and unconscious.

If correlated data seem coherent among themselves, then "the sensation accompanying this fact is that of being in the truth" (Bion, 1962, p. 182). If this doesn't happen, Bion suggests that there is a "state of debilitation: this fact suggests that the lack of truth is something very similar to a lack of nourishment" (p. 182). Deprivation of truth takes on various names: arrogance, envy, jealousy.

This is another reason to free the concept of truth from arrogant claims, that is, to remove it from the naive view that makes it something dictated by morality. The truth of which Bion speaks, precisely the nourishment that fuels psychic development, has nothing directly to do (or not yet) with true propositions about reality. Instead, it has to do with embodied patterns of behaviour, initially in pre-reflective phases of life, and then increasingly in contexts where an ego is present.

The essential elements to grasp are these: First, if we consider that the mother does know how to speak, the cultural factor indirectly influences the accumulation of emotional knowledge in her body and in the body of the infant in the form of implicit or procedural memory traces. Second, equally counter-intuitive, there is no truth in the form of a true or scientific proposition that doesn't rest on the terrain of this initial mutual understanding, which is based on the innate capacity of two individuals to resonate and emotionally influence each other. Instead of criticising psychoanalysis for not being *scientific*, those in the field of experimental sciences should be grateful. With its tools, psychoanalysis offers an intersubjective foundation for truth, which scientists often simplistically believe to be "rock-solid", which in fact is the result of human agreements in which shared emotional truth is a *fact.*

Would it be conceivable for a scientist to solve complex equations without having first constituted themselves as a subject within a primary (i.e. mother–infant) relationship? Would it be conceivable to think that this initial constitution of the ego ceases to operate at a certain point? That it can be discarded like an old garment to leave only the purely rational or abstract dimension of thinking? What would we then say about Poincaré (1952) and all those who have emphasised the deeply intuitive aspect of scientific creativity?

Truth and falsehood in the primary relationship

Bion argues that the model of the therapeutic relationship is the mother–infant bond. This is like saying that the problem to be solved is how to transmit to a thinker, who at birth is not a true thinker as he is "all-conscious" but has no unconscious (a system of explicit and implicit or procedural memories of interactions with objects and the environment that will serve as a filter for intuiting analogies and new patterns and thus "reading" reality), the thoughts circulating in the group to which he belongs. In other words, how to get him to "embrace" ideas and thus become a thinker himself.

However, if everyone has passed through this stage, it implies that no one has ever thought their own thoughts and that everyone has merely received them. If this seems illogical, let's ask ourselves: who then is the thinker who thinks the thoughts that an individual can select and embrace to become themselves? I suggest that the thinker who thinks the thoughts *is the group, is the community, is sociality*. Thought itself and the thought of an individual thinker would be a contradiction in terms, unless we envision a group identity within the individual and acknowledge that the individual possesses an intersubjective or trans-individual constitution.

We could then say that *to exist is to lie*, because from the very beginning any possibility of total and mere coincidence with oneself is excluded, precisely as being oneself means being the Other, as in the famous Rimbaud's sentence "*I* is someone else [*Je est un autre*]"(1966, p. 305). As Morin writes, Merleau-Ponty does insist on the fact that there is no coincidence between one side of the chiasm and the other, and hence that each remains heterogeneous to the other. At the same time, the fact that one encroaches on the other also means that there is a minimal zone of transgression or overlapping ... where the two are confused or blurred (Morin, 2022, pp. 123, 218, 248).

The field angle (Ferro, 2021, pp. 354, 357–358) ventures more decisively to focus attention on the intersubjective dimension of the therapeutic relationship: the invisible, infinite realm of the unconscious. BFT (Ferro & Civitarese, 2015) primarily chooses to deal with the third superordinate and independent subject that emerges from the analytic relationship, which is the price we pay (subjugation) to become subjects. This subjugation isn't a limit, rather a precondition of subjectivity. Freud's depiction of psychic development suggests an *internal* path within the individual subject. However, in reality, a subject can become one only when they move out of themselves, transferring into the Other and seeing themselves reflected in the Other, and vice versa. (Only another subject can recognise me.) In this circularity, in which it "agrees" (i.e. obeying an innate impulse for linking) to decentralise itself or to alienate itself in the other, that is, to alienate or "falsify" itself from the self it was a second before the process of reflection began, in order to become (partially) what is reflected in the eyes of the Other; this is how a relational bond is structured.

Bonding is the commonality of seeing each other. In fact, this applies to every form of sensibility, not just the visual. What is reflected is one's own body in the body of the other; or rather, the series of innumerable bodies that the subject is with the infinite series of other bodies. The first glimmer of a sense of reality (objectivity, consensus, truth, meaning, etc.) is established through this cycle of sensibility in which the subject moves into the Other and back to itself and vice versa, thus establishing elements of identity (seeing certain things in the same way) within a general framework of difference. If we consider that *ek-stasis* or the desire for recognition—for Lacan (1966), desire for the desire of the Other—is reciprocal and simultaneous, it is easy to imagine a process of mutual adaptation, like two atoms combining with shared bonds or the exchange of electrons.

Of course, the prerequisite for recognition is the ability to communicate. But this capacity, starting from a virtual state, must become actualised. Bion writes that the greater or lesser capacity for reverie in the mother will transform into specific psychic qualities (emotions), which will give their colour to the "channels of communication, the *links* with the child" (1962, p. 34, emphasis mine). Defining the bond as a channel of communication is Bion's original, potent thought. Usually, when we think of a bond, the first thing that comes to mind is the heritage of shared memories and affections, not, so to speak, roads, bridges, or railways. However, between Romeo and Juliet, there's a Los Angeles-style freeway with many lanes. Between Tybalt and Mercutio, trenches have been dug between the rival families of the Montagues and Capulets. And sometimes, just as in the case of the two most famous lovers in literature, when an incident blocks communication, the consequences can be fatal.

In the case of atoms, it's made possible by "valence" (Bion, 1961), the availability of a certain number of electrons that can be shared or exchanged between different atoms. Between alienation in the Other that establishes the subject and alienation that disestablishes the subject, the balance is delicate. The reconciliation "in which the two Egos renounce their opposing existence, is [that] it's the existence of the Ego that has expanded into duality" (Hegel, 1807, p. 444). Or we could say that the "we" is always at risk of failure.

Column 2 of the Grid

We all know how important the Grid is in Bion's theory of mind and in the practice of psychoanalysis. There's scarcely a page where he doesn't mention it or a significant book that doesn't reproduce it, despite it being heartily disliked by almost everyone who studies Bion and loves him. Column 2 of the Grid is the column of falsehood (W). With the exception of algebraic calculations, any element of the genetic axis, from beta to scientific deductive systems, can be used to lie, to avoid emotions, to feel pain but not suffer it, etc.—all ways of inauthentic existence.

No sooner do we formulate a defining hypothesis of something than the column of falsehood is lurking nearby. Moreover, as we said, the column of falsehood is indicated by the symbol that signifies the psyche, W! What on earth can this mean? As previously mentioned, the fact that *mind* and *to lie* in Latin have the same root. Or a way to emphasise that evading emotion is always the shortest path? And what does it mean that Grotstein (2007, p. 284) has renamed Column 2 the *column of dreams*?

The Grid is a powerful synthesis of Bion's theory of thought. Structured like a Cartesian diagram with its coordinates along the "y" (vertical) axis and "x" (horizontal) axis, it places the genetic column on the ordinate, representing the axis along which, going from 0[6] upwards, we have progressively less sophisticated expressions of thought, from the capacity for deductive thought, passing through the intermediate stages of dream and myth (row C), to concepts and images which are the alpha elements, to raw sensory experience, which Bion calls beta elements drawing upon Kant's concept of the thing-in-itself. "Beta elements, by contrast, are like the Kantian thing-in-itself" (Kant, 1781). "The datum of the experience in its crude state, not thought because the subject does not have the tools for metabolizing it" (Ferro, 2021, p. 357).

To the horizontal axis Bion assigns the task of representing the different uses to which any expression of thought can be subjected. Thus, for example, a concept—let's take the concept of a cat—can serve to gather certain elements in a constant conjunction and bind them with a name in order to lie, to remember something, to direct attention to a given object or situation, to act, etc.

The Grid should be imagined, like thought itself, as extremely dynamic and traversed by infinite movements, both progressive (south-east) and regressive (north-west). At every instant, we will have one or more outcomes of these movements, hence also contradictory ones. What is missing in the Grid is an adequate codification of emotion and affectivity. This isn't surprising because it extends beyond the Kantian thing-in-itself dimension of representability. Perhaps only beta elements, as mediums for projective identifications, bear the weight of representing them on the Grid. It might be for this reason, as it appears cold and cerebral, that the Grid has always had a bad reputation. However, there is one key aspect worth reflecting on. By showing us that the same psychic content can be used in various ways and for different purposes, the Grid obliges us to consider a principle of relativism or contextualisation. Nothing is absolute, that is, disconnected from the context in which it appears. For instance, it's a principle that should also facilitate dialogue between different models. This is significant for our discipline.

Normally, we see thought as an ascent towards abstraction. However, Bion reverses the direction, just as he reverses the concept of falsehood. Indeed, after a long and tortuous journey, we realise that C2 exists to remind us that no one can be entirely in O, in absolute reality, *except perhaps in death*. Parenthetically, this might be a way to re-evaluate Freud's (1920g) concept of the death instinct—when one merges back into the whole. So, truly, to exist means to deviate from the second law of thermodynamics, to take from the infinite, to tear something from it, to become finite. In this sense, again, *lying becomes a prerequisite for becoming a subject*. The term *persona* in Latin means mask. The mask isn't glued to the skin of the face, it's not the face, it can be removed and changed (Esposito, 2014). With respect to the face it covers, the essence of which belongs to O, the mask "lies" (In Italian, *mente*, from the verb *mentire*, but written in the third singular present tense as the substantive *mente*, meaning *mind*), just as the clothes we wear can lie, as can the idea we embrace or formulate, and yet we can only be ourselves because of these necessary lies.

But what then is the difference between falsehood, for example, in literary fiction and mythology that aids living, and falsehood, for example, in religious fanaticism that can be violent and destructive? The question is rhetorical, and the answer lies in the word *fiction*. The *awareness* of fiction can be salvific. One can reside in fiction while knowing that it is fiction and understanding that fiction doesn't mean *not true* but *true in a way that I cannot fully realise*. In turn, how much *fiction* one can bear, I think, stems from the fear we all have of various internal and external *enemies* and how well equipped we are to tolerate this primal emotion.

Thus, Grotstein's (2007) proposal to rename Column 2 in the Grid from the "column of falsehood" to the "column of dreams" seems to me a good solution. I've always had the impression that Grotstein, like me, struggled to accept the bitter truth of the necessity of falsehood. Bearing this truth, I realise that perhaps this term should be reserved for the conscious lie and not the broader category of falsehood. However, this is precisely what Bion does, by broadening the scope of what is meant by the *lie* in order to free the word and extract it from the iron grip of arrogance and moralism.

However, I remind myself, this is inadequate unless we confront the ambiguity of the concept of truth/falsehood. Perhaps we should stop talking about truth *tout court*—too luminous, beautiful, isolated—and speak of truth/falsehood not with a *slash*, but rather with a hyphen to make clear that no one possesses truth while others don't; that we all grope about with half-truths and half-falsehoods and that, depending on the vertex, a truth can be used to tell a falsehood and vice versa. For instance, from the psychoanalytic point of view, a lie on the factual level can very well unconsciously communicate an emotional truth, and all the more so if we consider a truth of the analytic couple or of the small group formed by it. In psychoanalysis, on the other hand, the greatest lie is to keep to the factual level of the conversation, a real betrayal of the method invented by Freud. Another example would be when someone says something that is true in itself but is meant to hurt the other, or simply says something that the other cannot contain, for example, a parent to a little child: only in the abstract can we hold as true a content that fragments the other's psychic container. At least this is Bion's view. A truth is not such if it is not shared.

Seen in this light, Grotstein's solution seems to de-intensify Bion's concept, to strip it of its provocative power, which urges us to think on our own. That is, if it's true that thinking equals lying and there's no content that doesn't go through Column 2, and if dreaming equals thinking, then the distinction between dreams and nightmares disappears. However, it's also true that Grotstein's reimagining Column 2 helps us to appreciate the inherent falsity of metaphor, but also of the power of language in which one thing always stands for another.

Truth as nourishment for the mind

In Bion, the concept of truth as food for the mind is one of his most important ideas and implies not a positivist or metaphysical view of truth, but a consensualist, pragmatic, and intersubjective view. That is, something is true only if it is true for both. Such a principle, which we can agree on, is difficult to see at work in the clinical accounts of Bion's Kleinian period, where he reads the patient's protests as confirmation of envy emanating from individual subjectivity.

Once again there is the problem of orienting ourselves in the different phases of Bion's thought. Moreover, there is the problem of orienting ourselves in relation to insights that we can find in his work, but which Bion did not develop, and which point to a completely new way of conducting psychoanalysis. This new approach no longer focuses on content, but on the development of the container, that is, the psychic function; no longer on knowing, but on *becoming* and *being*. Then there are insights that we can only glimpse afterwards. In other words, insights that are revealed only in the light of new theories. Bion thinks about the concept of truth in light of projective identification theory and the content/container model. Developed from the Kleinian (1946) concept of projective identification, this is an example of an original concept endowed with great versatility of use. Compared with the concept of projective identification, it becomes more evident when we consider how Bion thinks about truth that no content can be forced into an inadequate container on pain of its destruction. The notion of content/container expresses much better a certain reciprocity between subject and object and presents itself as the mechanism underlying truth creation and, consequently, psychic growth.

So, when we speak of emotional truth as food that nourishes the mind, we are talking about the dialectic of identity and difference that is expressed in the process of *at-one-ment* or, in other language, through the process of mutual recognition and reconciliation. The two key words in the *Phenomenology* with which Hegel tells the story of how we come to be subjects endowed with self-consciousness are *recognition* and *reconciliation*. In English, *atonement* means reconciliation with divinity, and Bion writes that "atonement with ultimate reality, or O … is essential to harmonious mental growth … Disturbance in capacity for atonement is associated with megalomanic attitudes" (1967, p. 145). It is from this word that Bion derives his term "at-one-ment". At the same time, I think of another English word, which expresses the sense of surprise and bears a relationship to Bion's term, namely **A**s**TON**ish**MENT** (I have capitalised and bolded the letters in common).

Bion believes, and I agree, that recognition must be not only conscious but also unconscious, not only verbally expressed but also embodied in deep affective disposition. This is essential. Recognition can be facilitated but not intentionally brought about. Thus, recognition equates to establishing a bond of love or a similar structure. The patient desires the analyst's love, and the analyst desires the patient's gratitude (love). Both desire recognition. Recognition encompasses what is referred to as "political correctness", that is, using language and behaviour that is considered respectful and sensitive to individuals or groups who may have been historically marginalised or discriminated against because of their race, gender, sexual orientation, disability, religion, or other characteristics, but it is much more than that. As I said, recognition is the mutual or dialectical negation between two individuals that makes them "subjects", as illustrated in Hegel's *Phenomenology* and especially emphasised in Kojève's (1947) reading of this brilliant text. That's why it seems ridiculously naive to me to interpret the concept of recognition as merely intentional or conscious, cases in which it often translates an excessive desire to be good or an iatrogenic degradation of empathy to empathysm.

That recognition should be not only conscious but also unconscious; not only expressed but also embodied in a deep affective disposition is an essential point. One can create the premises for it to occur, but one cannot deliberately determine it. I repeat, in essence, recognition is equivalent to a bond of love, or, at any rate, has a similar structure.

As Grotstein (2004) points out, the truth drive is the only one we find in Bion's metapsychology, and we must understand it as an innate tendency of the subject to differentiate itself by being subjected to the pressure of the environment and the group to which it belongs. As Nietzsche (1873) says, becoming who we are is an achievement that the subject can only acquire socially by expanding the area of co-being and co-belonging or the common transcendental space that we call the unconscious. I can fulfil my human possibilities only if I accept being partly alienated by the Other and vice versa. The various expressions that Bion employs to convey the meaning of at-one-ment, such as *being with* or *unison*, are ways of reformulating the essential Hegelian insight based on the dialectic of recognition and the emergence of the subject as one who knows that he thinks his own thoughts.

This aspect can be better grasped if we keep in mind Bion's definition of thinking: "Thinking is the activity by which the individual abstracts the meaning of phenomena" (Bion, 1961, p. 21). We always circle around the same point, namely, the dialectic of identity and difference. What can be gained from difference in relation to identity is in the order of a concept that enables development of mind and the possibility of inter-human communication. What is the emergence of a pattern, that is, the "crystallization of a Selected Fact" (Mawson, 2014, p. 7) if not the identification of what is common to different terms and ultimately common to the judgement of multiple observers?

Can lies be cured?

I use Chapter 11 of *Attention and Interpretation* (1970) as a starting point because, in my view, it represents the most advanced stage of Bion's theoretical elaboration on the issue of truth.

Bion thinks that psychoanalysis has something to say to philosophy about truth and lies, because it deals with them not only from a theoretical but also from a clinical point of view. He begins with a key question: *Can a patient who lies be treated in analysis?* Some analysts would say you cannot; others that lying is not a problem if it is seen as a symptom, especially if the analyst treats it as if it were dream material from which to deduce not the factual or nonfactual truth quotient of the patient's assertion, but the basic assumption that pervades the analytic couple at a given stage of analysis. Ultimately, they would sustain that the best way to solve the problem of the lie as a symptom is to avoid the question of truth framed in this way and instead grasp the emotional truth of the relational field. From this perspective, lying is just one of the ways in which accumulations of undigested beta elements, or, from another perspective, suffering rooted in a deep split in the personality, manifest themselves.

Thus, the way one approaches the truth/lie question is influenced by the analyst's theoretical choices. For example, from a radical intersubjective angle, it would not, strictly speaking, be the patient (who lies) or the analyst. Rather, it would be the couple, in their oneness, who can or cannot come into contact with the truth of the emotions they feel. This is the vision of a radical intersubjective theory and not simply to the interaction between its members (Civitarese, 2021a, 2021b, 2023).

Although Bion moves in this direction, lays its premises, and anticipates some of its themes, this is not his perspective. His perspective remains that of a Kleinian analyst who, while innovating the theory of psychological functioning of groups, in the clinical situation operates within an I/you separate subjectivity framework. According to Bion, the liar is by definition the patient. Lying, however, is not only consciously telling a lie. To lie is to avoid emotions; it is to deprive oneself out of fear of something that is essential to psychic life. This is the first surprising shot, as Bion shifts the lie from the content to the container understood as a function of the personality deputed to manage emotions. It follows that for the subject, emotions must be of enormous importance. From this angle, one must write "lying" or "telling lies" in quotation marks. One who lies is lying first and foremost to himself, as well as to others.

"Lying" can take many forms, such as distorting facts, denying one's feelings, or creating alternative narratives to avoid emotional reality. Lying is a defence that hinders the process of learning and emotional growth. The person who lies avoids exploring her authentic feelings and thoughts and retreats into a world of fictions and illusions. This hinders the ability to understand oneself and others more deeply and authentically. However, if lying in this sense arises from the inability to supply herself with truth, and if truth coincides with at-one-ment, with the creation of a bond that can only be symmetrical on the unconscious and affective level, then *there are always two who are at stake here.*

For Bion, it is a truism that if one comes to analysis, it is because one is lying and consequently risks "exposure of the lie" (1970, p. 98); that the analyst will point it out to him or her, with the attendant risk of appearing self-righteous and judgemental. For this reason, Bion suggests that categorising the lie with Column 2 on the Grid has the advantage of avoiding negative connotations. For the analyst to think "The patient is lying to me" is not the same as thinking "The patient is making an assertion that falls into Column 2 of the Grid".

Bion gives the practical example of a patient who is always late but somehow denies the fact because he apologises each time yet repeats the behaviour. From my point of view, which is to consider the "we" of the analytic couple, the patient would have every right to do so. In fact, this could mean that it is not *he* but *they* who are always late; or even that they are not late at all, because it is an event that can be thought of as reverie in action, and therefore still improvisation in the theatre of analysis and not a resistance to the process. But, again, this is not Bion's view. His view is that the analyst is at a crossroads. If he accepts the patient's excuses, the analyst falls into the lie; if he does not accept them, the analyst plays the role of critical consciousness. Another complication arises: one must understand the purpose for which the false statement is made. If the function is evocative or provocative, it would not be correct to assign it to Column 2 (dream/lie). Rather, it would be Column 6 (action), since it is designed to cause emotional upheaval, and should be initialled with –L (–Love) or –K (–Knowledge).

The consequence of what has been said so far is that in psychoanalysis we cannot use the term "lie" unambiguously because it can mean different things in different contexts. What the lie draws attention to is not an invariant because it changes from time to time. In the aforementioned example, the same lie may have the precise aim of producing emotional turmoil (Column 6 dream/action) in one case, and of avoiding it (Column 2 dream/lie) in another. What the patient is avoiding is a catastrophic change. Such a risk causes him to experience intense emotions related to the presence of an outraged moralistic system.

This is the conflict experienced by the patient. What about the analyst? The analyst experiences a conflict as well. On the one hand, she assigns a central role to truth, as is the tradition in psychoanalysis, and thus values her own sense of integrity. On the other hand, she can be seduced by the patient into accepting that lying is a defence of a more sophisticated kind. Sometimes lying seems to be motivated by the desire and pleasure the liar derives from it. Often these are "believable" lies, but they test the analyst who takes a "scientific" approach, that is, one who gives importance to experiences captured by the senses; they test her far more than an analyst who approaches the session without memory or desire. For the former, truth and rational explanation come first. It is obvious that Bion considers such an assertion arrogant and false; that is, a lie in itself. For Bion, clarifying the patient's problems goes hand in hand with clarifying the problems of those who are supposed to treat him and those of the discipline (psychoanalysis itself) she uses. This is a way of reformulating the idea that the analyst's desire to know is sometimes expressed in the desire to know the truth at all costs, as he explains in his commentary to the essay "On arrogance" (Bion, 1967, p. 161).

A fable

To introduce what could be an opposing argument to the one given above, Bion (1970) tells a fable or phantasy. Implicitly this is a way to introduce a further level from which to explore the theme of truth and lies: the nature of writing in psychoanalysis (Civitarese, 2024a).

The liars showed courage and resolution in their opposition to the scientists who with their pernicious doctrines bid fair to strip every shred of self-deception from their dupes leaving them without any of the natural protection necessary for the preservation of their mental health against the impact of truth. Some, knowing full well the risks that they ran, nevertheless laid down their lives in affirmations of lies so that the weak and doubtful would be convinced by the ardour of their conviction of the truth of even the most preposterous statements. It is not too much to say that the human race owes its salvation to that small band of gifted liars who were prepared even in the face of indubitable facts to maintain the truth of their falsehoods. Even death was denied and the most ingenious arguments were educed to support obviously ridiculous statements that the dead lived on in bliss. These martyrs to untruth were often of humble origin whose very names have perished. But for them and the witness borne by their obvious sincerity the sanity of the race must have perished under the load placed on it. By laying down their lives they carry the morals of the world on their shoulders. Their lives and the lives of their followers were devoted to the elaboration of systems of great intricacy and beauty in which the logical structure was preserved by the exercise of a powerful intellect and faultless reasoning. By contrast the feeble processes by which the scientists again and again attempted to support their hypotheses made it easy for the liars to show the hollowness of the pretensions of the upstarts and thus to delay, if not to prevent, the spread of doctrines whose effect could only have been to induce a sense of helplessness and unimportance in the liars and their beneficiaries (Bion, 1970, pp. 100–101).

As readers can sense, Bion's fable is an endorsement of all those mythical, religious, or philosophical formations that, despite the absolute claims of science, have shown mercy towards the fragility of human beings and in this way preserved them. It is also praise for illusion as a protective shield for mental health—consider, for example, how essential it is for individual development in Winnicott's (1971) psychoanalysis. Significantly, Bion depicts truth not only as a shared truth and food for the mind, but as something that, though true in itself or *scientific*, can have a destructive impact. It is also a way of saying that a truth that doesn't respect individuals' capacity to accept it, is not truth. And we know why. Considering the truths of philosophy or religion as *lies* is a gross misunderstanding. Obviously, they have allegorical, metaphorical, mythical, or dream-like value, in other words, they belong to row C (dream/myth) of the Grid.

What we see again at play in Bion's *phantasy* text is his bewildering methodological principle, drawn from Descartes, of questioning everything, transcending divisions, and creatively using reversible perspective (Civitarese, 2008). Ostensibly, Bion is poking fun at scientists—and note, the target is also presumed "scientific" psychoanalysis. In reality, he is conducting a sophisticated discourse that can be read on multiple levels. In prosaic terms, it would be "Scientists cannot say anything about human experiences that are not of a sensory order."

The realities with which psychoanalysis deals, for example fear, panic, love, anxiety, passion, have no sensuous background, though there is a sensuous background (respiratory rate, pain, touch, etc.) that is often identified with them and then treated, supposedly scientifically. It must be a science of at-one-ment. It must have a mathematics of at-one-ment, not identification. There can be no geometry of "similar", "identical", "equal", only of analogy (Bion, 1970, p. 89).

The way to connect with these truths of a non-sensory nature is not through the five senses, but through our inner sense of intuition: "For convenience, I propose to use the term 'intuit' as a parallel in the psychoanalyst's domain to the physician's use of 'see', 'touch', 'smell', and 'hear'" (Bion, 1970, p. 7; also see Civitarese, 2024b).

It's always a matter of viewpoints, attitudes, and perspectives. The psychoanalytic viewpoint is not the scientific one (of exact sciences), nor the religious, philosophical, aesthetic, etc. Anticipating objections, Bion admits that it's easy to believe in facts! For instance, if someone jumps off a cliff and dies, it means that reality painfully refutes their belief in being able to fly. The example is paradoxical because it's the kind that is usually used to support objectivistic theses. On the contrary, Bion illustrates how irrational or mistaken convictions can influence people's choices, even when they are completely divorced from reality. Even if someone sincerely believes something, it doesn't change the objectivity of certain facts or the consequences of their actions.

If we denote the ultimate and unknowable reality with O, which pertains to any belief, deciding which to follow can only depend on the viewpoint assumed by the individual at a given moment.

The concept of truth in the post-Bionian theory of the analytic field

The truth of the intersubjective "we"

Building on Bion's work, BFT has also developed its own original concept of truth (Civitarese, 2022). For instance, in relation to the shift from a perspective oriented by "I/you" to a perspective oriented by "we". I have written several times that if we listen to the unconscious meaning of what is said in the analytic conversation as a text jointly written by the analyst and the patient, or rather, by the couple or small group, we can no longer be suspicious and question whether or not the patient is lying.

Strictly speaking, this also applies when I tune in to the unconscious discourse of the patient. It could be that they are intentionally lying, but since they don't control their unconscious speech, it means that from another viewpoint, they are telling the truth. So, there's no substantial difference or contradiction. The difference emerges when we think of the unconscious as the digestive function of the mind—no longer as a cauldron of dirty secrets. This is where the emotional attitude of the analyst changes, no longer focused on confronting the patient; rather using the truth expressed, even if it involves telling lies, to draw their attention to the fact that the patient lies to everyone, including themselves.

In analysis, not in a court of law, from the perspective of field theory, the point is to curtail this viewpoint. In the productions of the unconscious, there are no more truths to uncover, individual or group, but only *functions to develop*. I would never say that a poem *lies*. I would rather say that the dream of the session does or doesn't work. Truth changes its residence. It no longer pertains to content, but to the emotional bond between analyst and patient. What we are witnessing is the repetition in a different context of the same theoretical movement through which Bion brings the content-truth back to the truth of *at-one-ment*, but with technical consequences that go well beyond his theories.

If I were to answer the question of why the narratives of analysis reveal the truth about the quality of the bond at a certain moment, I would say that it's because there's no longer any issue of *content* truth, but only processes of matching/coupling that are more or less successful. I realise that when I've previously said that because it's a joint truth, it *must* be true, I haven't been precise enough. I should have said that considering *a priori* true (solely from this viewpoint) what is expressed in the psychoanalytic dialogue is just a way of saying that I'm no longer listening from the truth/lie perspective, but rather, as if I were listening to a musical piece to determine whether it *works* or not. Thus, there's no true or false way to ski, only different modes, and degrees of skill in sliding on snow.

In short, it's about revising *the very concept of truth*. It could be that from the viewpoint of an external observer, the couple is *lying* to themselves, and the issue of consensus should eventually be considered. But for the time being, I am suggesting there is significant value in focusing on the *we*. The analyst isn't suspicious anymore, and the risk of establishing relationships of dominance are eliminated or reduced.

The focus here is not on investigating causes, but on providing a *weather report* of the analytic situation. The analytic goal is to determine how to mitigate or eliminate negative effects. Abandoning the causal paradigm linked to lying is therapeutic in itself. What's achieved is contributing to the restoration of trust in the analytic relationship. Remember that for the patient, the empathetic understanding of their pain and the validation of their emotional experience are of primary importance.

If I assume as a postulate that any narrative reflects shared emotions, regardless of the emotional links L (Love), H (Hate), or K (Knowledge) characteristics, I have the possibility to hypothesise that a given emotion or affect is not just mine or the patient's, but both mine *and* theirs (Civitarese, 2021c). In addition to the fact that it automatically occurs by shifting to the "we" perspective, by increasing emotional investment and vitality, we also aim for more information from which to intuit the truth of what is unfolding between us. Does this mean I ignore the negative? Not at all. On the contrary, I see more clearly how it's rooted in the analytic relationship.

For the analyst, taking responsibility, for example, for an emotional atmosphere poisoned by hatred, jealousy, and envy doesn't so much mean questioning the causes, which would risk plunging analyst and patient unwittingly back into a diffident attitude, as it means listening from the viewpoint imbued with the "faith of we" and attempting to change a negative analytic atmosphere. On the one hand, listening without mistrust facilitates renouncing an ideal of perfection that would be omnipotent and perverse, and therefore renouncing blame; on the other hand, if "two are wrong", for however bad it is, it's shared, so neither member of the couple can judge the other or themselves anymore, as they could in an "I/you" split perspective. The overall movement that results is a shift towards the depressive position or "security" (Bion, 1970). This aspect of integration is more likely to occur if the analyst abandons the role of the detective who must interpret the distortions produced by the analyst's or the patient's transference.

Conclusions

Based on what has been discussed so far, it is clear that for Bion, the theme of truth must be addressed on three distinct but inseparable levels: epistemological, metapsychological, and clinical. On the epistemological level, Bion's denunciation of the positivism that pervades the criticism of psychoanalysis by advocates of the exact sciences or by psychoanalysts inclined to scientism is effective and is expressed in a vividly sarcastic tone. The remarks in this regard are distributed throughout his work, and if one were to gather them, it would compose a specific volume.

On the metapsychological level, Bion addresses the theme of truth primarily in relation to the aspirations of psychoanalysis and analysts to speak what they consider to be the truth *at any cost*. Bion shows us that when we have this pretence, we are like certain patients in a psychotic state of mind who we'd like to cure, but in vain, since we suffer from the same illness—namely the triad of curiosity, arrogance, and stupidity. Furthermore, he revolutionises the very way of dealing with truth as an emotional syntonisation and food for the mind, *à la* Nietzsche (1873) in the extra-moral sense, not of content but of function. However, in my opinion, this revolution is only achieved in the radically intersubjective development of his thought.

On the clinical level, in relation to his conception of truth, Bion introduces a series of concepts and techniques (at-one-ment, negative capability, faith, evolution, transformation, "O", the oscillation patience–security, etc.) that are extremely innovative. These are collected and developed along lines that are both faithful and original in BFT, which in my opinion is a devotedly authentic and fertile interpreter of his thought.

References

Bion, W. R. (1958). On arrogance. *International Journal of Psychoanalysis, 39*: 144–146.

Bion, W. R. (1961). The conception of man. In: C. Mawson (Ed.), *The Complete Works of W. R. Bion (Vol. XVI)* (pp. 9–27). London: Karnac, 2014.

Bion, W. R. (1962). *Learning from Experience*. London: Tavistock.

Bion, W. R. (1967). *Second Thoughts*. London: Heinemann.

Bion, W. R. (1970). *Attention and Interpretation*. London: Karnac, 1984.

Bion, W. R. (1977). The grid. In: *Two Papers: The Grid and Caesura* (pp. 1–34). London: Karnac, 1989.

Civitarese, G. (2008). "Caesura" as Bion's discourse on the method. *International Journal of Psychoanalysis, 89*: 1123–1143.

Civitarese, G. (2013). The grid and the truth drive. *Italian Psychoanalytic Annual, 7*: 91–114.

Civitarese, G. (2016). Truth as immediacy and unison: A new common ground in psychoanalysis? Commentary on essays addressing "Is truth relevant?" *Psychoanalytic Quarterly, 85*: 449–501.

Civitarese, G. (2021a). Intersubjectivity and the analytic field. *Journal of the American Psychoanalytic Association, 69*(5): 853–893.

Civitarese, G. (2021b). Symmetry and asymmetry in the analytic process: Reply to commentaries. *Journal of the American Psychoanalytic Association, 69*(5): 921–935.

Civitarese, G. (2021c). Bion's graph of "In search of existence." *American Journal of Psychoanalysis, 81*: 326–350.

Civitarese, G. (2022). *Psychoanalytic Field Theory: A Contemporary Introduction*. London: Routledge.

Civitarese, G. (2023). Sul concetto di intersoggettività in psicoanalisi. *Psicoterapia e Scienze Umane, 57*(3): 375–398.

Civitarese, G. (2024a). Does it "appear" to resemble reality? On the ethics of psychoanalytic writing. *Psychoanalytic Quarterly, 93*(1): 105–134.

Civitarese, G. (2024b). Intuition and we-ness in Bion and post-Bionian field theory. *International Journal of Psychoanalysis, 105*(1): 13–39.

Esposito, R. (2014). *Persons and Things: From the Body's Point of View*. Cambridge: Polity, 2015.

Ferro, A. (2021). Negative capabilities, play and the negative. *American Journal of Psychoanalysis, 81*: 351–360.

Ferro, A., & Civitarese, G. (2015). *The Analytic Field and Its Transformations*. London: Routledge.

Freud, S. (1911b). Formulations on the two principles of mental functioning. *S. E., 12*: 213–226. London: Hogarth.

Freud, S. (1920g). *Beyond the Pleasure Principle. S. E., 18*: 1–64. London: Hogarth.

Grotstein, J. S. (1997a). Why Oedipus and not Christ? Part I: Innocence, spirituality, and human sacrifice. *American Journal of Psychoanalysis, 57*: 193–220.

Grotstein, J. S. (1997b). Why Oedipus and not Christ? Part II: The numinous and spiritual dimension. *American Journal of Psychoanalysis, 57*: 317–335.

Grotstein, J. S. (2004). The seventh servant: The implications of a truth drive in Bion's theory of "O". *International Journal of Psychoanalysis, 85*: 1081–1101.

Grotstein, J. S. (2007). *A Beam of Intense Darkness: Wilfred Bion's Legacy to Psychoanalysis*. London: Karnac.

Hegel, G. W. F. (1807). *The Phenomenology of Spirit*. Cambridge: Cambridge University Press, 2018.

Heidegger, M. (1927). *Being and Time*. J. Stambaugh (Trans.). Albany, NY: SUNY Press, 1996.

Jullien, F. (2020). *De la vraie vie*. Paris: Éditions de l'Observatoire.

Kant, I. (1781). *Critique of Pure Reason*. F. M. Müller (Trans.). London: Penguin.

Klein, M. (1946). Notes on some schizoid mechanisms. *International Journal of Psychoanalysis*, *27*: 99–110.

Kojève, A. (1947). *Introduction to the Reading of Hegel: Lectures on the Phenomenology of Spirit*. Ithaca, NY: Cornell University Press, 1980.

Lacan, J. (1966). *Écrits*. New York: W. W. Norton, 2002.

Mawson, C. (Ed.) (2014). *The Complete Works of W. R. Bion*, Vol. 6. London: Karnac.

Merleau-Ponty, M. (1945). *Phenomenology of Perception*. London: Routledge & Kegan Paul, 2002.

Morin, M.-E. (2022). *Merleau-Ponty and Nancy on Sense and Being at the Limits of Phenomenology*. Edinburgh, UK: Edinburgh University Press.

Nietzsche, F. (1873). On truth and lies in a nonmoral sense. *JSTOR*, *49*: 58–72.

Poincaré, H. (1952). *Science and Method*. New York: Dover.

Rimbaud, A. (1966). *Rimbaud: Complete Works, Selected Letters*. W. Fowlie (Trans.). Chicago, IL: University of Chicago Press.

Segal, H. (1998). Introduction to Bion. In: *Yesterday, Today and Tomorrow* (pp. 211–218). London: Routledge, 2007.

Winnicott, D. W. (1971). *Playing and Reality*. London: Routledge, 2005.

CHAPTER 13

Democracy, parrhesia, and the psychoanalyst's freedom of thought

Eran J. Rolnik

Introduction

At the end of the First World War, Freud offered a poignant response to Sándor Ferenczi's lament over the disintegration of the Hungarian monarchy: "Withdraw your libido from your fatherland in a timely fashion and shelter it in psychoanalysis, or else you will have to feel uncomfortable" (Falzeder & Brabant, 1993).

In this chapter I want to explore the experience of practising psychoanalysis amid political upheaval. Though far from a new theme within psychoanalytic discourse, it is too often relegated to the past—as if it belonged to another era. For me, however, it became an increasingly pressing issue over the past few years. And I believe it will soon pose not only a philosophical or ethical, but also a technical challenge for analysts across the globe.

Although never explicitly acknowledged by its founding father, psychoanalysis has, from the outset, been a deeply political project. Its transformative potential lies in its ability to unearth latent infantile assumptions, expose unspoken tyrannies, and dismantle the internalised power structures that govern both individuals and collectives. As psychoanalysts we are often focused on interpreting the interplay of power between mental structures and the urges, fantasies, and demands of the mind, promoting the patients' liberation from the tyranny of the superego. However, the discipline has often neglected the influence of political and social conditions on the analyst's ability to perform their clinical task and societal role. This chapter reflects my ever-growing concern with the question of how much political reality psychoanalysis can bear, beginning with Freud's famous advice to Ferenczi: "Withdraw your libido from your fatherland and shelter it in psychoanalysis." By reflecting on political events in Israel, and my own experience as a part-time civil servant, of the government attack on freedom of speech and freedom of thought, I examine the intersection of psychoanalytic ethics, democratic values, and the capacity for free thought in the analytic setting. I propose that by forging links between the private and public spheres—the ontological, the psychological, and the technological—psychoanalysis offers a space in moments of political caesura where individual insight can become political action. It facilitates the relinquishing of primitive fantasies, illusions, and libidinal investments—those that masquerade as self-expression or freedom of will.

A functioning democracy is essential not only for societal well-being but also for the analytic process itself, as attacks on democracy mirror assaults on thinking and truth. This exploration concludes by positing that psychoanalysis and democratic principles are mutually reinforcing projects.

A historical lineage

Freud's advice, quoted above, urging Ferenczi to transfer his emotional investment from the turbulence of national politics to the steadiness of psychoanalysis, symbolised the emergence of a tradition and a professional identity at one and the same time. This tradition sought to prioritise analytic identity and solidarity over ethnic, religious, national, ideological, or political allegiances. Four years earlier, at the Great War's outbreak, Ernst Jones had written to Freud from London with a similarly striking sentiment: "if the future of psychoanalysis had to be weighed with the future of my own country, I should side with the former" (Paskauskas, 1993).

This view, that psychoanalytic science could and should remain insulated from the political contexts in which it developed, was not universally shared among early analysts. In 1933, when a colleague in Berlin asked Otto Fenichel what pressing issues lay at the heart of psychoanalytic research, Fenichel famously replied, "The question of if and when the Nazis will take power in Vienna." Fenichel, later dubbed a "political Freudian" (Jacoby, 1983; Rolnik, 2012), exemplified a contrasting approach that acknowledged the inextricable link between psychoanalysis and its sociopolitical environment.

The term "worldview" famously causes resentment in both scientific and therapeutic circles. Freud firmly objected to it in the lecture "The question of a *Weltanschauung*" (1933a) and many analysts to this day are also concerned that associating psychoanalysis with a worldview or a political affiliation is contradictory to rigorous scientific objectivity and analytic neutrality, a central tenet of psychoanalytic technique that can also be misused to silence opposition to a dominant ideology rather than question it. The early analysts' main concern was a politicisation of psychoanalysis following the ideological interpretations, mainly in socialist circles, of the theory of childhood sexuality and the Oedipus complex.

In the 1920s, Freud openly opposed the publishing of Wilhelm Reich's articles, which linked capitalism with a rise in the death drive. In the 1930s, he even had a hand in Reich's ousting from the International Psychoanalytical Association after Reich's attacks on German fascism that, in the opinion of Freud and his confidants, threatened the very survival of psychoanalysis in Germany.

These were the immediate social and political circumstances in which the discussion on a psychoanalytic worldview took place in the first half of the twentieth century. I believe that to this day, these circumstances still hide from us the fact that the relationship between psychoanalysis, history, and politics are a little bit more complex than those of other human sciences. Political culture sways a society's and the individual's notion of truth, conflict, resistance, and freedom of thought—all of which are central to the psychoanalytic enterprise. I will develop this claim further shortly.

Whether they practised in antisemitic imperial Vienna, colonial India, or mandatory Jewish Palestine; whether they gathered secretly under communist or fascist regimes in Europe, or under military dictatorships in Latin America—psychoanalysts throughout the twentieth century often viewed the analytic couch and their professional identity as sanctuaries, not merely from the tyranny of the individual superego but also from oppressive and blinding sociopolitical forces. Analysis was seen as an act of resistance against authoritarianism and chauvinism, a commitment to autonomy, individuality, sovereignty, interiority, and truth amid repressive conditions.

Interestingly, the enduring question of how much "political reality" the analytic process could endure—be that as a clinical practice or as a social institution—was often addressed from legalistic and technical angles. It was as though the analytic pair's unique communication and interaction could be secured solely through adherence to a rigorous framework: regular sessions, neutrality, abstinence, uncompromised confidentiality, and the like. It appears to me that analysts practising in liberal democracies by and large would perceive democracy as facilitating the analytic process by supporting the frame, the setting, and the ground rules of the psychoanalytic encounter rather than acknowledge the fact that attacks on democracy from without go to the very core of the mind's struggle with attacks on linking, on psychic space, and on psychic truth from within.

This argument can be unpacked as a series of questions:

1. Can the self or the mind truly reveal itself to the subject/analysand, even in the most rigorously held analytic setting, in an environment where individuals are deprived of the freedom to protest?
2. Can patients "freely associate" on the analytic couch while being denied the freedom to protest or the right for political association in the public sphere?
3. To what extent do the "analysing instrument" (Isakower, 1992) and the communicative process between patient and analyst depend on the existence of a benevolent social or political Third?

These questions underscore the complex interplay between psychoanalytic ethics and practice and the sociopolitical context in which they interact with each other.

Psychoanalytic perspectives on authoritarianism

Since the early contributions of Wilhelm Reich, Franz Alexander, Erich Fromm, and the Mitscherlichs on the psychic representation and personality structure brought about by capitalist, authoritarian, and nationalist political environments, a number of contemporary analysts have been giving serious thought to the social ramifications of our trade.

Christopher Bollas (1992) describes how individuals in a "fascist state of mind" may destroy parts of the self and internalised objects, blocking their capacity for doubt, uncertainty, and meaningful thought. Such archaic mental structures, perverse or psychotic in nature, suppress both thought and emotion. These dynamics are not limited to the clinical setting; they extend to societies and groups. A society functioning on a paranoid-schizoid level gravitates towards narcissistic and charismatic leadership, which fosters denial of internal and external realities—even to the point of self-destruction. In totalitarian regimes, individuals avoid independent thought, willingly blinding themselves to reality. They deny accessible knowledge and suppress critical thinking.

In her paper "Silence is the real crime" Hanna Segal (1987) called upon the analytic community to raise its voice against the nuclear arms race. She wrote: "We [psychoanalysts] are cognizant with the psychic mechanisms of denial, projection, magic thinking, etc. We should be able to contribute something to the overcoming of apathy and self-deception in ourselves and others."

That same atmosphere of apathy Segal was talking about is, I believe, very much palpable in Western societies. I sometimes think of it as "social media anesthesia". It may also be a testimony to the vicious cycle of helplessness and omnipotence, promoted by authoritarian politics, to the vicious circles between the death instincts and the defences against them that preclude integration and action (Rolnik, 2024a). Werner Bohleber (1992) argued that in fascist contexts, idealisation becomes destructive because it is built on splitting (good vs evil), dehumanisation of the "other", and denial of reality. Bohleber links this to the massive use of propaganda and the creation of "totalizing" narratives. Michael Šebek (1996) described the "totalitarian object" as an internalised superego, a product of collective projection that venerates submission, obedience, unity, and self-sacrifice, while elevating a singular, authoritative leader. David Bell (2004) sees democracy as a system, a mode of mental functioning, that thrives on ambivalence, internal conflict, and the capacity to bear difference—both internally (within the psyche) and socially.

In democratic societies, the distinction between prejudice and "facts of life" (Money-Kyrle, 1971) remains significant. Facts of life include not only empirical truths recognised by scientific consensus but also psychological truths that blend objective and subjective dimensions of human experience.

Few are those uniquely exceptional individuals whose humanity and integrity remains unharmed by an environment that surrenders itself to a selfish authoritarian leader, devoid of any moral inhibitions, who considers himself above the law. It is no coincidence that the process of Germany's de-Nazification went on for many years after the defeat of Nazism. Authoritarian, corrupt regimes also take hold of the souls of even those citizens who did not support them at the ballot box or consciously identify with their racist ideology and actions. National Socialism permeated the German language and insidiously took hold of psychoanalysis long after Nazism was defeated (Bohleber & Drews, 1991). In an authoritarian regime and a totalitarian society, people avoid independent thinking and blind themselves to reality "of their own free will". They deny knowledge when it is available to them.

In the last decade, many democracies have undergone a similar sequence: the delegitimisation of courts, the erosion of independent institutions, the systematic production of lies, the identification of political opponents as traitors, the militarisation of language. Israel provides a concrete case, though the phenomenon is not unique. The model is familiar: corruption becomes normalised, hatred is permitted to circulate, the public sphere is flooded with fantasies of purity and fantasies of omnipotence. In such conditions, the capacity to think is weakened. The link to reality is attacked. The distinction between fact and fiction becomes blurred. The result is not only political; it is psychic. The intimate world becomes infected by the collective hallucination.

The political and cultural spheres wield great influence on the quality of our search for truth in its many manifestations and a huge influence on psychic reality and our relationship with the life and death drives, the fundamental building blocks of the psyche. Politics influence the willingness of individuals and groups to incorporate more than one point of view into their interior psyche.

I first explored the intersection of psychoanalysis, history, and ideology in earlier publications, particularly in examining the migration of psychoanalysis from Central Europe during the interwar years and its reception in Palestine/Israel. Practising psychoanalysis at the frontier where early Zionist ideological collectivism often converges with its later forms of militant nationalism and religious fanaticism has long presented a unique challenge for those therapists committed to fostering their patients' personal agency and supporting their capacity to know themselves in order to think for themselves (Rolnik, 2012, 2025a). Over the past few years, these questions have become even more urgent for a number of Israeli psychoanalysts, as Israeli democracy has come under attack from an ultra-right-wing government, introducing a series of laws collectively referred to as "the judicial overhaul" (Rolnik, 2014, 2023a, 2023b, 2024a, 2025b).

Personal testimony

Israel has moved backwards in the past few years and reached the status of being a democracy only in terms of formality. Hamas' attack on October 7 was merely grist to the mill of religionisation, exclusion, disintegration, and brutalisation that Israeli society had already been undergoing. We live in a time when the large, overt fractures in the reality we therapists share with our patients get mixed up with the subjective, intimate ruptures of their internal world. This is one of the reasons why working at a psychoanalytic clinic, in which the interpretation of mental reality has a central role, has become harder than ever for therapists and patients alike (Rolnik, 2024b).

Initially, I was hesitant to alter my psychoanalytic technique in response to a political revolt occurring so close to my home and office. Then came the October 7 Hamas terror attack. In the aftermath, faced with the government's refusal to negotiate for the hostages' release, the brutality of the war in Gaza, and the growing radicalisation of Israeli public discourse, I found my analytic equilibrium beginning to unravel. My "evenly hovering attention" was further tested when I was summoned for interrogation by the Civil Service Commission's disciplinary enforcement department.

During several hours of questioning, I was interrogated about my journalistic writings and my involvement in the Kaplan civil protests. The investigator scrutinised a stack of highlighted printouts of articles I had published in *Haaretz*, reading passages aloud and asking me to confirm my statements. I was asked to sign each and every page of about a dozen opinion pieces I published over the years. I was questioned about my comments on Prime Minister Netanyahu and legislation promoted by the coalition. The investigator asked whether it was "appropriate" for someone in my position as a civil servant to attend protests, speak at rallies, and write about legislation concerning mental health and medical ethics. Interestingly, the investigation did not focus on articles that concerned the Israeli Palestinian conflict but on more recent op-eds that put into focus the judicial overhaul and the links between democracy and mental health.

In my defence, I explained that my public writing is part of my vocation as an author, mental health professional, and university teacher. I emphasised that my work in the civil service, as the medical director of the office for Holocaust Survivor Compensation, is deeply connected to protecting individual rights. I made it clear that I had no intention of ceasing my writing or public engagement. At one point, I even explained to my interrogator—a former police officer born and raised in a kibbutz—the intrinsic link between mental health and democracy and the distinctions between intellectual persecution, incitement, and patriotism.

The conversation oscillated between comical and bewildering. Our roles of prosecutor and defendant often felt reversed, each of us grappling with the other's perspectives on Israel's current state and its ongoing societal transformations. When I asked if similar interrogations had taken place since the war began, the investigator paused before mentioning that a recent case involved someone (an Israeli Arab doctor employed in a state-owned hospital) who had posted a picture of hostages alongside a Palestinian flag. "You, Doctor," he said, "are different. You clearly love your country. I don't think you have anything to worry about." Recently I was informed that the state intends to prosecute me after all because of my critical opinion pieces.

The responses of colleagues, patients, students, and supervisees to my interrogation and disciplinary trial—as reported in the press (Mack, 2025; Peleg, 2025)—were as varied and unexpected as one might imagine. While patients' reactions were, for the most part, shaped more by transference identifications than by political alignment, students and colleagues expressed a curious blend of solidarity and disbelief. There appears to be a significant difference between encountering your analyst or colleague as the author of a political op-ed and discovering that he has been summoned for questioning by the state because of it.

Although I did not experience this as persecution, I did feel compelled to attend to a newly emerging facet of my analytic identity—one marked by a less passionless state of mind. Particularly, I found myself more attuned to the state's impact on the psyche and on mental functioning in general.

In Plato's cave

Freedom is not a central concept in the psychoanalytic lexicon. Yet psychoanalysis teaches us that moral values, thinking, and internal reality are deeply intertwined. Human subjectivity requires not only individual mental and developmental conditions but also enabling social and political contexts. A society, like an individual, can live for extended periods without truly thinking, feeling, or dreaming.

Not all patients (or analysts) have a developed political consciousness, nor is it the role of the psychotherapist to turn a Democrat into a Republican, a long-time conservative into an enthusiastic liberal, or a right-winger into a leftist. Still, I think taking part in protests against the Netanyahu/Ben-Gvir coalition was during the past two years therapeutically important to quite a few patients I treated on an individual level, not just politically, because in the absence of a democratic regime, there is also an increase in internal dictatorial forces such as violent incestuous fantasies and vengeful impulses.

In times of political upheaval, the therapist must not only encourage the patient to recognise their dependency on the internal good object, make the connection between their mental inhibitions and their infantile unconscious fantasies, and generally "tend to their garden". As therapists, we should also take into account that a functioning democracy plays a role in the regulation of an individual's deepest impulses and fears, as well as in a society's ability to exist and adapt to changing historical realities.

Psychoanalytic ethics and democracy share a complex relationship. Psychoanalysis compels us to confront unconscious desires—such as the longing for an idealised leader or the avoidance of grief—that those autocratic regimes exploit. In this sense, fighting for democracy mirrors the psychoanalytic project: resisting the lure of idealisation, consensus, and false peace of mind offered by undemocratic forms of rule and the archaic object relations between the individual and society that they promote, as well as by the culture of perfection surrounding us.

Self-deception, denial of mental conflict and of psychic pain, the fantasy of omnipotence, and sadistic impulses are inherent to the human condition. Politics profoundly influences individuals' willingness to integrate multiple perspectives and accept complex realities both internally and externally. It shapes our capacity for thought, emotion, and the pursuit of truth. The analytic process, therefore, is more reliant on political realities than many analysts care to acknowledge. Both the patient's freedom of thought and the analysts' range of plumbing unconscious communication within the analytic setting are intertwined with the broader societal conditions of freedom.

In times of political upheaval, therapists cannot afford to remain detached or defensively entrenched in stereotyped analytic neutrality. Beyond fostering introspection and helping patients acknowledge their dependency needs, we must also attend to the distinct challenges faced by those no longer living in a functioning democracy. History teaches us that authoritarian regimes erode not only social institutions but also the psychic scaffolding that supports mental life, making sustained therapeutic work increasingly fragile—if not untenable.

A patient said to me recently: "I'm cracking up, but I can never know in advance if going to a demonstration will help me collect myself or just deepen my sense of helplessness and shame." I believe many analysts hold the conviction that by abstaining from public protest, they are not only preserving their own psychic integrity but also diligently maintaining a "sanitary corridor" between the consulting room and the impingements of external reality.

Consider Plato's allegory of the cave: Plato himself says the prisoners would kill anyone who would escape the cave to return wiser and more knowledgeable about reality. But Plato does not offer an explanation as to why would the prisoners wish to kill the philosopher who returned to the cave with this new liberating knowledge of the world. This is where psychoanalysis comes into the picture and attempts to explain this emotional and irrational aspect of our love-hate relationship with truth, which are very seldom regarded by science, philosophy, or politics.

It is the role of politics to protect the philosopher, the artist, and the scientist—and also the psychotherapist—to allow them to persevere in their search for truth for the benefit of all other dwellers of the cave. "To reject thought," writes Hannah Arendt in the prologue to her book *The Human Condition*, "does not mean to be stupid or unintelligent, but to become thoughtless, to prefer complacent repetition of empty and trivial truths" (Arendt, 1958, p. 5). Through her concept of the banality of evil, Arendt offered a historical-sociological analysis of the loss of ability to think and act morally, which in many ways complements Freud's, Lacan's, Klein's, and Bion's theories of thinking that are focused on internal emotional resistances we, as subjects, harbour against knowledge.

In "Lying in politics: Reflections on the Pentagon Papers", Arendt (1971) describes how modern bureaucracies did not merely lie to the public but constructed self-serving fictions that insulated policymakers from reality. These "image-making" operations reveal a fundamental resistance to facts: the refusal to bear their weight and disruptive power. Facts, for Arendt, are stubborn, uncomfortable, and unyielding qualities that echo Freud's sense of psychic truth as something the psyche continually resists. Psychoanalysis, both as a science and as a therapeutic practice, is oriented precisely towards these resistances to truth which are akin to resistance to internal reality and the distinction between the subjective and the objective dimension of human experience. Just as the state substitutes manufactured narratives for facts, the individual substitutes defensive constructions for intolerable psychic truths. In both domains, lying becomes not simply a tactical manoeuvre but a structural mode of avoiding reality and work of mourning over damaged good internal objects. Arendt warns that a polity that abolishes factual truth loses the ground of judgement; psychoanalysis shows that an individual who abolishes psychic truth loses the ground of self-understanding and mental development. Both realms require the patient labour of truth-work: in politics, the preservation of factual reality as a common world; in analysis, the working through of resistances to drive derivatives and unconscious fantasies so that hidden truths can be borne.

As human beings, we are not born democratic. We become democratic and truth-seeking subjects only if we live in a democracy and learn to contain and to work through our anxieties, fantasies, and prejudices democratically. The inner world of a person is an arena in which conflicting needs, archaic wishes, frustrations, primary anxieties, and impulses clash. Along with the desire for independence, freedom, and psychological separation, humans also have a tendency to sell their soul, to unite, and to merge with whatever will calm their anxieties. Along with curiosity and a desire to know the world, we are fearful of the new and the foreign and have a penchant for hating and denying whole swaths of inner and outer reality when experiencing situations of pain, anxiety, and uncertainty. A tyrannical, narcissistic leadership such as that in power in a large number of countries is adept at augmenting the innate human tendency to see the world in black and white.

A political climate of suspicion and exclusion, such as populist leaders are expert at creating, intensifies the fear not only of the Other but also of the encounter we have with our own inner reality. A group of people can conduct themselves and live for long periods without truly thinking and without truly feeling—even without truly dreaming. The result is a numbness of the senses, narrow-mindedness, and indifference that will be vividly recalled by anyone who has ever lived under a dictatorship. The schizo-paranoid gaze is already discernible in the streets of my Tel Aviv neighbourhood. People avoid eye contact, protect themselves from the threatening encounter with the Other. Soon no one will feel that this is their land—even those who in their arrogance believe that they are lords of the land.

A populist leadership and press use the truth to lie. They will see to it that the public is overfed with "alternative facts" in the guise of pluralism with the aim of sowing chaos and confusion regarding every single "fact of life", and regarding the very possibility of truly knowing anything about the world. In a psychic and media world in which, ostensibly, nothing can be known about anything and everything is at the mercy of narratives and subjective interpretation, the interest in scientific research, intellectual thought, and the exchange of opinions also declines. Most of our psychic resources become geared towards easily obtainable pleasures and getting rid of tension and anxiety. In undemocratic and populist regimes, priority will always be given to excitable sentimentality over meaningful emotion; to rash, violent action over thought. There is hardly any place left for shame, remorse, or feelings of guilt.

"A clear conscience is among the signs of bestiality," writes Wisława Szymborska (1995). Indeed, many of the titans of culture, capitalism, and politics of our day represent, for their admirers, the possibility of a guiltless, shameless world, not only in the intrapsychic, interpersonal context but also when it comes to the relations between man, nature, and environment.

For all these reasons, democracy is implicitly a frustrating, never-ending project that requires constant defence and courage—as does a lengthy therapeutic process. In an undemocratic regime, the pressure to become part of the collective persecutory experience and to adopt a strategy of projection and denial means that even sane, mentally healthy and "well-analysed" individuals find it difficult to distinguish between inner and outer reality, or to identify the danger lurking for their psyche. Mistrust of the media and the multitude of open sources of information may cause children to perceive the learning process as subversive.

Compassion, caring, and acceptance of inadequacy and dependence are supplanted by wickedness, omnipotence, contempt, and narrow-mindedness, which become a "cultural code": a means through which the authorities offer citizens an alternative social pact that overrides the "letter of the law". The state and its corrupt institutions signal to the public that "real life" occurs outside the law. This permits hatred, covetousness, oppression, and efforts to grab everything in sight, in order to dispel anxieties stemming from feelings of dependence and want, deficiency, ignorance, uncertainty, and loneliness.

Being a psychoanalyst means looking for the particular in the universal and vice versa. It means listening to the singular plight of an individual patient as embedded within their particular unconscious-phantasmal-sexual discontent and the historical-cultural-political discontent of the group and the polity this patient inhabits. Accordingly, it is important that dynamic therapists in this day and age develop and nurture profound thinking on what is taking place in society while listening to patients. The future of psychoanalytic practice and ethics—in Israel and across many other nations—is increasingly shaped by political and technological forces that extend well beyond the analytic discourse or the confines of the consulting room. Regardless of whether analysts are overtly engaged in political or social activism, their role, I believe, is to help individuals recognise the threats posed by the state to their psychic integrity:

the emergence of destructive impulses and tyrannical tendencies in response to governmental assaults on humanity, on the rule of law and its disregard for both its citizens and the international community.

In today's world, the therapist's mission extends beyond "speaking truth to power" within the analytic frame. It lies in occupying an intermediate position—one that integrates their own and their patients' capacities for self-analysis in pursuit of a psychic truth that is both psychological and political, personal and collective. This stance is aligned with the ancient Greek tradition of *parrhesia*, a key concept from ancient Greek political and philosophical thought. It entails the courage to speak candidly, not only to oneself and to a patient within the confines of the consulting room, but also on behalf of the common good—even at the risk of censure or unpopularity. This kind of "fearless speech" can be contrasted with rhetoric, which persuades without necessarily telling the truth. Such a commitment, I hope, merits being called a psychoanalytic *Weltanschauung* for our time. The analytic frame does not merely require democracy as external safeguard; rather, both analysis and democracy are parallel practices of truth-seeking, each threatened by denial and authoritarianism.

Coda: A clinical moment

Mrs B was unusually silent during the session. As I listened to the weight of her silence, I was wondering whether it had anything to do with yesterday's no-confidence motion passed by Netanyahu's cabinet against the attorney general and the head of Shin Bet (Secret Service).

Mrs B: It feels strange lying here on the couch this morning. I really don't know what can be said on such a day.

Analyst: I wonder what's happening today in other people's analyses.

Mrs B: You'd know better than I would how your other patients are feeling these days.

Analyst: What I'm curious about is how other analysts are listening to their patients. Somewhere in Israel, there must be an analyst who, unlike me, wouldn't rush to associate your silence this morning with the government renewed attacks on democracy.

References

Arendt, H. (1958). *The Human Condition*. Chicago, IL: University of Chicago Press.

Arendt, H. (1971). Lying in politics: Reflections on the Pentagon Papers. *New York Review of Books*, *17*(8): 30–39.

Bell, D. (2004). Psychoanalysis and the idea of democracy. *Free Associations*, *11*(57): 7–26.

Bollas, C. (1992). *Being a Character: Psychoanalysis and Self Experience*. London: Routledge.

Bohleber, W. (1992). Nationalismus, Fremdenhass und Antisemitismus: Psychoanalytische Überlegungen [Nationalism, xenophobia, and antisemitism: Psychoanalytic reflections]. *Psyche: Zeitschrift für Psychoanalyse und ihre Anwendungen*, *46*: 689–709.

Bohleber, W., & Drews, J. (1991). *Gift, das du unbewußt eintrinkst … Der Nationalsozialismus und die deutsche Sprache* [*Poison that You Unconsciously Drink … National Socialism and the German Language*]. Bielefeld, Germany: Aisthesis.

Falzeder, E., & Brabant, E. (1993). Letter from Sigmund Freud to Sándor Ferenczi, October 27, 1918. In: *The Correspondence of Sigmund Freud and Sándor Ferenczi, Volume 2, 1914–1919* (pp. 304–305). Cambridge, MA: Harvard University Press.

Freud, S. (1933a [1932]). "Lecture XXXV: The Question of a Weltanschauung." In: *New Introductory Lectures on Psycho-Analysis*. *S. E.*, *22*: 158–182. London: Hogarth.

Isakower, O. (1992). The analysing instrument in the teaching and conduct of the analytic process. *Journal of Clinical Psychoanalysis*, *1*: 181–222.

Jacoby, R. (1983). *The Political Freudians: From Freud to Reich*. New Haven, CT: Yale University Press.

Mack, E. (2025, September 1). The method of arbitrariness: How Netanyahu's regime fabricated a case against Dr Rolnik. The four stages of dealing with regime opponents, the Israeli version. *The Seventh Eye*.

Money-Kyrle, R. (1971). The aims of psychoanalysis. In: D. Meltzer (Ed.), *The Collected Papers of Roger Money-Kyrle* (pp. 442–449). Strathtay, UK: Clunie, 1978.

Paskauskas, R. A. (Ed.) (1993). *The Complete Correspondence of Sigmund Freud and Ernest Jones, 1909–1939* (p. 308). Cambridge, MA: Harvard University Press.

Peleg, B. (2025, July 22). Israeli civil servant faces disciplinary trial over *Haaretz* columns criticising Netanyahu and his government. *Haaretz*, English edition.

Rolnik, E. J. (2012). *Freud in Zion: Psychoanalysis and the Making of Modern Jewish Identity*. London: Karnac.

Rolnik, E. J. (2014, September 20). Can you leave Israel and still be a Zionist? *Haaretz*, English edition.

Rolnik, E. J. (2023a, November 8). Israel's slouching towards authoritarianism. *Haaretz*, English edition.

Rolnik, E. J. (2023b, September 15). Each act of protest against Netanyahu's coup is a therapy session. *Haaretz*, English edition.

Rolnik, E. J. (2024a, April 15). Israel's internal dictatorship keeps us from taking to the streets. *Haaretz*, English edition.

Rolnik, E. J. (2024b, July 2). How will the Gaza War change Israeli psychotherapy? *Haaretz*, English edition.

Rolnik, E. J. (2025a). Dreams and trauma: With Freud to Zion. In: S. Frosh & D. Baum (Eds.), *International Handbook for Psychoanalysis and Jewish Studies*. London: Routledge.

Rolnik, E. J. (2025b). *Psychoanalytic Objects Near and Far: Talking Cure*. London: Routledge.

Šebek, M. (1996). The fate of the totalitarian object. *International Forum of Psychoanalysis*, *5*: 289–294.

Segal, H. (1987). Silence is the real crime. *International Review of Psycho-Analysis*, *14*: 3–12.

Szymborska, W. (1995). In Praise of Feeling Bad About Yourself. S. Barańczak & C. Cavanagh (Trans.). In: *View with a Grain of Sand: Selected Poems* (pp. 67–69). San Diego, CA: Harcourt Brace.

CHAPTER 14

The poetic truth of the unconscious: Metaphor, meaning, and the analytic encounter

David Howell Morgan

Everywhere I go I find that a poet has been there before me.
— Freud, S. (1930)

In a letter to Stefan Zweig, Freud acknowledges that poets have often anticipated the insights of psychoanalysis through intuition and imagination. Zweig, in his psychological portraits and in his biographies of Freud—*The Right to Heresy* (1951) and *Healing Through the Spirit* (2021)—beautifully captures this admiration. Zweig—himself a humanist and a writer of psychological depth—saw Freud not as someone who invented the unconscious, but as someone who dared to study it systematically, to give shape to what poets, dramatists, and mystics had already intuited in metaphor and symbol.

Freud wrote in *Delusions and Dreams in Jensen's "Gradiva"* (1907a):

> Creative writers are valuable allies, and their testimony is highly prized, for they know a great deal between heaven and earth that our academic wisdom cannot yet dream of. In their mind, knowledge, they are far in advance of us, everyday people, because they draw upon sources we have not yet tapped for science. (pp. 33–34)

Here, Freud is saying that through symbol, image, dream, and drama, poets access truths that psychoanalysis can only later try to formulate. In a sense, they are the unconscious speaking for itself through form.

Shakespeare, Sophocles, Goethe, Dostoevsky, and Ibsen were all figures Freud returned to as dramatists of repression, guilt, and the tragic structure of the psyche. The Oedipus complex, the most famous Freudian idea, was not discovered but recognised in Sophocles. Freud assiduously followed the trail that art had already laid.

Zweig's insight lies in recognising that Freud was not simply a man of science, but a sort of lyrical investigator whose clinical vocabulary was deeply rooted in metaphor, myth, and the musical structure of language. Bion would later say, "Psychoanalysis is not a science, it is an art." I wholeheartedly agree with this view and see the link between the poet and the analyst as very clear; both listen for the unsaid, the layered, the concealed, both traffic in ambiguity, both trust that truth can appear through symbolisation. Psychoanalysis dissects metaphor, and poetry is the metaphor. As Zweig understood, Freud was among the few who could listen to both languages at once.

The nature of poetic truth

Poetry, metaphor, and psychoanalytic interpretation strike the same chord because they function as an articulation of the interior world, through which the unknown unconscious reaches consciousness; it links the unconscious fantasy life with the ego's effort to symbolise and bear truth in the here and now.

As Bion (1965) describes, truth has to be discovered, not manufactured; it enters psychic life only when the mind can tolerate contact with emotional reality. The poetic or metaphoric act thus becomes a moment of containment: a transformation of raw, unprocessed emotional experience (beta elements) into thinkable form (alpha function).

Winnicott, in agreement with Bion (1970), suggested that there can be an emergence of creativity within a "potential space" between the inner and outer worlds; he saw this as the very field where meaning can be born rather than imposed. In this way, I see metaphor as a mediating between unconscious phantasy and conscious thought, allowing the ego to perceive psychic reality without annihilation or denial.

As Segal (1952) argued, the capacity to symbolise rather than engage in concrete equations marks the movement from defensive omnipotence towards psychic truth. In the analytic setting, then, poetic language may reveal rather than conceal the unconscious: it offers a lived metaphor for the analyst's and patient's joint struggle to speak the unspeakable and to think the previously unthinkable.

For instance, in the poem "Tulips" (1961) by Sylvia Plath:

> The tulips are too red in the first place, they hurt me.
> Even through the gift paper I could hear them breathe
> Lightly, through their white swaddlings, like an awful baby.
> Their redness talks to my wound, it corresponds. (pp. 12–15)

We might posit that tulips here are like unprocessed emotional truths, beta elements, wanting containment corresponding to the speaker's "wound", a form of unassimilated trauma involving existence. Their redness represents an overwhelming vibrancy of life, the intensity of aesthetic beauty in Meltzer's (1989) sense.

In the analytic process, the analyst, rather like the tulips, may appear too alive, too invasive, too truthful, stirring what the patient's defences seek to keep out of mind. Yet, through this disturbance, symbolic contact is restored, the poem (like analysis) re-establishes the link between unconscious phantasy and conscious recognition. As Segal (1952) would suggest, metaphor here functions as a symbol rather than an equation, transforming persecutory anxiety into meaningful understanding.

Metaphor is emergence, its density reflects the patient's psychic world. It feels layered, ambivalent, and resistant to decoding, yet full of yearning to be understood. In that sense, the patient is deferring clarity but craving resonance. This resonates, of course, with Bion, who tells us that transformation is not about behavioural change or insight in the cognitive sense. It is about a deep, often preverbal shift in how emotional experience is metabolised, from the raw, chaotic, and unformulated (beta elements) into something that can be borne, symbolised, and shared (alpha function). This is the heart of psychic growth within our profession. There is a longing for a container: someone who can think the unthinkable thoughts, feel the unbearable feelings, and not evacuate or retaliate. That's Bion's reverie: the analyst's capacity to receive projected fragments, dream them internally, and return something transformed.

In Bion's terms, transformation often occurs silently, without announcement. A shift in tone, a moment when confusion becomes curiosity, or unbearable silence is felt as presence rather than absence (1965). The analyst, in this frame, is not a technician of answers. Still, a container for psychic digestion, who can tolerate uncertainty, resist premature interpretation, and allow truth to emerge in its own time.

A case illustrated this for me; it involved a young Spanish woman who was a hospital inpatient, who would fill her sessions with me, quoting large chunks of the poet Lorca from memory. I eventually learned, unfortunately from another source, that she was the child of a monk and a nun, who had left holy orders for parenthood after having an affair and becoming pregnant with her. How these facts manifested in her dramatic presentation stayed an elusive enigma, clearly indicative of her unlikely origins and her refusal to escape the bonds of her sacred narrative and find a metaphorical understanding of her actions. Indeed, my struggle to make sense of this dense material was and remained elusive for some time. For me, the history that led both parents to become chaste adherents of a religious ideology already appears as a form of dissociation—a withdrawal from sexuality and from ordinary life. This may reflect their respective family fantasies. The sacred ritual of the Mass, with its secret language and grandiosity, seemed echoed in her recitation of Lorca: a rarefied, elevated language invested with special, almost esoteric meaning. It also resonated for me that Lorca himself was a famous, openly gay poet, reviled by both the Catholic Church and Franco and eventually assassinated by the fascists.

Unfortunately, all these lofty thoughts made little difference to her need for concrete enactments. This was not simply a failure of metaphorical understanding on my part, but reflected a persistent pressure within her family system—her parents had stayed together in order to take care of her—and a repeated pattern of disappointment. It also challenged my youthful idealisation of being able to reach the unreachable, a fantasy that I now recognise, in retrospect, as tied to my own imagined sense of priestly knowledge and a special, almost sacred calling.

Whatever the communication, it moved something in me. At first it did not land as understanding at all; for some time it remained in my mind and body as indigestible material. Eventually, it entered my active imagination, where I began to make meaning from her utterances.

The space between patient and analyst changes; the room feels different. Something true arrives not as an explanation but in metaphorical form; its meaning is often opaque to both patient and analyst, yet it is generative of unknown thoughts and feelings.

Clinical encounters with metaphor

Woman underwater

A successful academic in her third month of analysis described a dream as follows: "I was underwater. I wasn't drowning exactly, but I couldn't breathe, and no one noticed." She dismissed it as stress. But sitting with the image—underwater, not drowning, unnoticed—the phrase took on weight. In the following sessions, metaphors recurred: "behind glass", "air too thin". Eventually saying, "I think I've always been underwater."

This became the beginning as metaphor and gradually allowed her to feel what could not be previously articulated—emotional submersion and performing competencies, while suffocating internally. Later, she dreamed of swimming, and rising to the surface, with waves breaking. The metaphoric world became transitional, allowing movement, and truth came not as insight but as image; my task was not translation, in the beginning at least, but bearing witness, becoming the container for a gradually evolving metaphorical truth.

Second ice age

For years, I saw a writer as an inpatient and then in an outpatient setting, whose symbolic functioning had become encased in ice. Her creativity dried up as a result, stuck in repeating themes of ice and apocalypse; she told me that she had harboured a lifelong fantasy that she could save the world from a coming second ice age, listening to BBC shipping forecasts for imaginary signals.

This messianic system defended against her internal world, dominated by a cold, post-puerperal, depressed mother. The first "ice age" was when she felt her experience; she created a delusional system where she was saviour, not victim, but this defence in older age was fading and the encroaching ice crowded out other imagery, inhibiting her creative work.

I worked with her before our current climate anxieties, but of course, I wondered whether her obsession was entirely delusional. Her "ice age" was a personal defence, a symbolic representation, and a prophetic recognition of civilisational crisis. The line between psychosis and prophecy blurs when the world itself has gone mad.

Therapeutic work involved not discarding her restricted metaphor or symbolic equation but helping it become flexible once again, and able to hold multiple meanings. The shift from concrete belief to living symbol was eventually a psychic movement, from frozen narrative to a breathing metaphor. Her ice became tears as she thawed in our work together. This early survival mechanism shifted through human contact, allowing the unspeakable to become spoken rather than enacted.

An obstetrician's termination

A deeply depressed obstetrician was hospitalised after taking part in a termination. She could hardly speak; holding her in our inpatient space was precarious due to her suicidal ideation. In the pregnant silence between us, I could only say that while she felt hopeless and dead, hope at least lived in me for both of us.

Months later, her story unfolded: about why this triggering event spoke so powerfully to her origins. We pieced together a narrative while tolerating repeated threats of termination of the therapy, which became her early narrative. The clinical metaphor had multiple meanings, involving her own origins as a survivor after her mother, having lost five babies due to a blood group issue, gave birth to her.

The poets as precursors: learning from literary voices

Seamus Heaney (1974) writes of "thoughts that waver and lift", that delicate moment when something unformulated begins taking shape, when unconscious edges into language. His poetics attend to what is appearing, the flicker of meaning beneath the surface, language's murmur before it solidifies. Heaney does not aim for conceptual precision but for resonance, rhythm, and felt sense arising when something true is felt but not quite named. His metaphors are vehicles of psychic movement, thresholds where past and present, private, and political, body and speech mingle.

Max Porter's *Grief Is the Thing with Feathers* (2015) stages grief not as a recovery process but as visitation. After sudden death, absence becomes presence, and Crow arrives as a voice, a creature, and a psychic double. Crow is grief itself: rude, irreverent, violent, and consoling. This makes Porter's work psychoanalytically resonant: grief becomes an internal object, an occupying force speaking in multiple registers. Crow functions as an aesthetic container, grotesque but essential, holding what the narrator cannot. Porter teaches us that grief does not heal but transforms; eventually Crow leaves, not because the pain has gone but because father and sons are changed towards it.

Ted Hughes' poems on the theme of "Father" in his collection *Birthday Letters* (1998) also express similar profound archaic object relations. The father is never symbolised but stays pre-symbolic, mythical, fused with nature and war. His version of the Crow poem (Hughes, 1970) holds unsymbolised grief that resists traditional elegy, giving voice to psychic states that resist and struggle against narrative form. Hughes builds a mythology of absence where loss is represented in landscape, mourning, echoing in wind, fox's blink, and crow's scream. This mourning does not end but transforms into an elemental voice, teaching us that grief sometimes explodes into a metaphor, monster, or animal, and we must resist the urge to tame it.

The analyst as poet: Method and ethics

Bion's "eschew memory and desire" is fundamentally a poetic stance, a call to presence, to sensibility. The analyst must wait without grasping, receive without defending, think without rushing to know. Like poets, we suspend our control to hear what language or psyche wants to say.

Sessions unfold not as a linear argument but as a fragmented, associative, recursive composition. Their form resembles the lyrical more than the logical, and patients return to images like refrains. Speech begins in prose but slips into broken poetics, faltering syntax, suspended clauses, and abrupt silences. The analyst's interpretation, when it comes, must land not as explanation but aesthetic truth, something patients recognise with body as much as mind. Well-timed interpretation, like poetry, does not explain problems but alters the psychic weather, creating new emotional affordance.

In psychoanalysis, metaphor is not merely illustrative but generative. Indeed, Freud recognised this: in dreams, jokes, and symptoms, the unconscious speaks through displacement and condensation mechanisms, metaphoric in structure, combining and translating psychic material more like poetry than prose. When patients say, "I feel like a puppet" or "There's a storm inside my chest" they offer metaphors carrying unformulated experience. These are often more precise than conceptual language, appearing from affect's depth and bypassing defence. Our task is not to interpret too quickly but to allow resonance and see where the metaphors lead.

A metaphor can evolve: "wall" becomes "fortress", then "prison", finally a "house with a door". The unconscious moves through these transformations, and analysis provides a space for such metamorphoses. Metaphor is the unconscious in motion, speaking, reaching, and trying to make some transformation.

Politics: The death of metaphor

In some corners of contemporary discourse this poetic sensibility and the role of metaphor are under threat. The current policing of language, especially around gender identity, pronouns, and political speech, is often framed as progressive. Still, at its most rigid, it begins to resemble a kind of collective surveillance superego formation that, for me, is punitive, humourless, and very anxious about nuance. This is becoming so endemic that I have sometimes wanted to create a syndrome called nuance anxiety. Words are no longer vessels of complexity but signify tokenistic allegiance. What cannot be instantly categorised becomes suspect, ambiguity is treated as evasion, and curiosity is treated as violence.

Psychoanalytically, this has the flavour of hysteria transposed onto the collective stage, the classical hysteria of Freud's day, but its modern form: a disorganised, persecutory anxiety about categories and borders. This anxiety fuels a kind of anti-poetic madness, where speech must be purified, intentions must be pre-certified, and any deviation is punishable.

Metaphor is lost like a man I saw who said, "I do not want therapy; I just want to get rid of my old man!" (cockney for penis). He had a strong transgender fantasy which he seemed determined to enact with the help of surgeons. I replied at some point, that by old man he may also have meant his father. He responded with absolute contempt, "I have not seen my father since the day after I was born." I could not help but respond as gently as I could, "Yes, he painfully cut you off." He was understandably furious with me for my crass attempt at linking his proposed enactment to something more symbolic. "Don't mutilate my mind with your crackpot theories," he replied. But we had moved here, at least to some extent, into metaphoric thinking; it was his mutilated mind, not his body, that he was at least now engaged with.

There is real suffering here, genuine trauma, and a profound longing to be seen and named. But instead of creating spaces for mourning, uncertainty, and exploration, some strands of activist culture would foreclose his complexity in the name of safety and superficial parity. The result is a totalitarian use of language in which words are stripped of resonance and pressed into service as ideological armour.

This is the opposite of the analytic and the poetic. It does not listen for the unsaid; it condemns it. It does not wait for truth to appear; it enforces a pre-approved version. In its most extreme form, it mirrors the dynamics of fascism, not in content but in structure. Anxiety is channelled into control, difference experienced as a threat, and the symbolic stripped of elasticity.

This is not a critique of trans people or trans rights, which, like all questions of identity, deserve analytic thought and, yes, poetic care. It is, for me, a critique of instrumental language, wherever it arises, and of the fantasy that the right word, perfectly chosen, will erase conflict or repair trauma. Psychoanalysis and poetry both resist this fantasy and recognise that language always fails and that something true may be beginning in its failure.

Trump: Anti-poetic mind and anti-metaphor

For me, Donald Trump stands for a psychic and rhetorical style fundamentally opposed to the poetic. Where poetry opens ambiguity, Trump forecloses it. Where the poet lingers in the unknown, Trump dominates with assertion, and where metaphor breathes, he bludgeons it to death with repetition. His language is not figurative, but compulsive; the tweet, slogan, and the chant are tools of identification, not reflection. He is the only president who has never had a poet at his inauguration, or, to my knowledge, has in place a poet laureate.

From a psychoanalytic perspective, Trump embodies traits associated with psychopathy: lack of empathy, shallow affect, manipulativeness, grandiosity, and impulsivity. But what may be more dangerous is the emptiness at the core, a self constructed not around any inner life but a mirrored reaction. As many analysts have seen, Trump does not reflect; he responds, does not mourn; he deflects. There is no psychic space in which thought or self-questioning might occur.

Bion wrote of the psychotic part of the personality, a psychic structure that attacks linking, that treats thinking itself as dangerous. To my mind, Trump performs this publicly, mocking complexity, punishing nuance, and celebrating binary certainty. In this, for me, he is the anti-analyst and anti-poet: he rejects depth in favour of spectacle, intimacy in favour of performance, accountability in favour of projection, and concrete delusional thinking over metaphor.

In a world shaped by leaders like Trump, the poetic becomes political, and speaking metaphorically resists this reduction. To listen analytically is to challenge the flattening of thought, and to bear witness, hold silence, preserve ambiguity, is to defend the unconscious itself from colonisation by propaganda.

Conclusion

At the heart of poetry and of psychoanalysis is a trust in ambiguity. Both recognise that language does not simply point to meaning; it unfolds it, so meaning is always provisional, felt, negotiated. A poem, like an analytic hour, is a space in which truth is not declared, but approached slowly, uncertainly, with room for contradiction and revision. Poetry and psychoanalysis both recognise that language fails, and, in that failure, something deeper begins to speak; in metaphor, in rhythm, in silence and structure, the unconscious finds a form in which it can live. The analyst's role, like the poet's, is not to explain away the suffering, but to offer a space in which it can be metabolised, symbolised, and mourned. This is the ethical demand of both practices, to hold the unformulated, to sit with the opacity, to wait for what emerges not as certainty, but as resonance. Poetry, as we have seen, often gets there first, not because it offers answers, but because it offers form without closure, and it allows the psyche to breathe.

In the quiet rooms where analysts and poets do their work, or where the poetry group meets, the interest is that what has no shape might find one, and that what was once unspeakable might be heard, not fully, not definitively, but enough.

So, this is not a treatise by me on poetics or a clinical manual, but my attempt at a meditation on what binds psychoanalysis and poetry together. If anything, it's their shared commitment to metaphor, the sayable and often the unsayable. The shared trust that truth does not arrive neatly and involves an ability to stay close to pain, or indeed joy, and not to interpret it away, but to find the form that might hold it.

So, this piece is a love letter to the analyst (indeed maybe my own) who waits in silence, and to the poets who I have come to love increasingly, who dare to speak in fragments, and to the patient (and analyst) who tries to name what they have never said before. I do not care about what psychoanalysis can teach poetry, or vice versa. I appreciate what they teach together about grief, about finding a voice, about the slow unfolding of meaning in the space between people, and what it might mean to write and listen as though the truth, for us all, is that we are all a poem still becoming.

Psychoanalysis shares this ethic, that is, a commitment not to rush the patient into knowing, but to stay with what stirs beneath. To wait, with reverence, for the thought to lift.

References

Bion, W. R. (1965). *Transformations: Change from Learning to Growth*. London: Heinemann.

Bion, W. R. (1970). *Attention and Interpretation*. London: Tavistock.

Freud, S. (1907a). *Delusions and Dreams in Jensen's "Gradiva". S. E., 9*: 141–154. London: Hogarth.

Freud, S. (1930). Letter to Stefan Zweig. In: P. Gay (Ed.), *Freud: A Life for Our Time*. New York: W. W. Norton, 1988.

Heaney, S. (1974). Feeling into words. In: *Preoccupations: Selected Prose 1968–1978*. London: Faber and Faber.

Hughes, T. (1970). *Crow: From the Life and Songs of the Crow*. London: Faber & Faber.

Hughes, T. (1998). *Birthday Letters*. London: Faber & Faber.

Meltzer, D. (1989). *The Apprehension of Beauty: The Role of Aesthetic Conflict in Development, Art and Violence*. Strathtay, UK: Clunie.

Plath, S. (1961). Tulips. (First published in *The New Yorker.*) In: *Ariel*. London: Faber & Faber, 1965.

Porter, M. (2015). *Grief Is the Thing with Feathers*. London: Faber & Faber.

Segal, H. (1952). A psycho-analytical approach to aesthetics. *International Journal of Psychoanalysis, 33*, 196–207.

Zweig, S. (1951). *The Right to Heresy: Castellio Against Calvin*. P. Eden & P. Cedar (Trans.). Boston, MA: Beacon.

Zweig, S. (2021). *The Healing Through the Spirit: Mesmer—Mary Baker-Eddy—Freud*. R. Boettcher (Trans.). Independently published.

CHAPTER 15

On self traumatisation

Christopher Bollas

Few psychoanalysts at work in the United States or the UK in the middle 1970s to mid 80s will forget the at times harrowing confrontations over reported episodes of child abuse. Experienced clinicians who had years of expertise assessing reports of child abuse and had developed profiles that allowed one to begin to differentiate fact from fiction were pushed to the side by state legislatures or government guidelines that mandated reporting any account of abuse to the authorities.

Recently qualified psychologists eager to make a mark for themselves became overnight experts on assessing reported episodes of child abuse while experienced clinicians left the clinics and hospitals where they had assessed children over the decades.

The experts left the field.

The opportunists filled the gap.

Sadly, those individuals who had been abused as children were overshadowed by people who claimed to be victims.

Why would people who may not have actually been victimised by child abuse claim to have been?

Because their "therapists" told them so. That they had come to this discovery while in therapy authenticated their accounts.

Eventually some of the allegations of abuse were discovered to be false and, in some cases—the McMartin School investigation in Los Angeles—led to public alarm over how scores of children and parents could report episodes of abuse that upon review proved to be inventions. As time passed, a new generation of lawyers and clinicians discovered that they could implant memories in jailed molesters that lead the individual to embellish the memory. What they remembered had not happened, but they believed so.

As accounts of falsely accused people going along with this injustice occurred there was a social chill when it came to prior knee-jerk support for anyone claiming abuse.

There were and still are many reasons to study this period in social history, but I shall only concentrate on one derivative of this era: the claims still being made about "trauma" to the point that this issue is likely the most common form of complaint from the patient community to this day.

Freud's view of trauma is not so well known and bears repeating again and again.

Focusing on a child's cognitive ability and psychology Freud argued that a child who was abused would only experience this as a shock.

What would that have meant?

A child being molested or mistreated would ordinarily not have the mental capacity to process the injustice of the situation or even to objectify it as so. Whereas a chronically abusive parent would instantiate recognition of this in the child victim, invasion of the self by molestation was often a one-off or series of "encounters" that were secretive, often silent, hard to figure.

It would not be until years later—adolescence and after, usually—that in the midst of an ordinary event, something in that happening would link to the childhood abuse. For example, in a restaurant while receiving a plate from the server, the diner is shocked when the waiter brushes against his shoulder and spills food on his trousers. He breaks out in a sweat, is trembling, and immediately leaves the restaurant.

He has no idea what has happened and why.

He seeks help and visits an expert in shock and trauma and after a while recovers a memory of being molested by a childminder when he was about eight. He has a very clear memory of the room and person as if etched on the walls of his brain.

Now imagine that this event is reported in the local news. A reader is very taken by this account and wonders if indeed he might have been abused as a child. He is haunted by the weight of this question and seeks help. It is affirmed in time that he shows all the symptoms of child abuse.

But wait.

How do we know that he was not the victim of abuse even if this was sprung by reading in a paper?

We don't know.

Although atypical, his trauma could be just as real as someone who had it clearly in memory but not activated affectively. Freud, writing in 1895, said the affects surrounding the shocks were deferred until later when cognition could process the emotional shock (1950a).

The above dilemma was and still is rightly challenging.

Clinicians do not have a clear view of the history behind these convictions.

And for many they never will.

However, there is one interesting clinical distinction having to do with "the presenting picture" or the demeanour and attitude of the person who is in trauma. The victim of shock and then trauma does not want to talk about the episode. If they do come to talk about it the first requisite is building a safe platform in consciousness where they can recall more of what happened and how it feels to do so.

These episodes are painful and haltingly difficult to narrate.

The feeling in the room that "this is hard to believe" dissipates as the affective struggle of the patient confirms the ideational recollection.

There is *no secondary gain* from telling this to the other.

And therein lies an important consideration.

While we take into account the exceptions to any rule, it would be rare for anyone to gain pleasure from narrating such an event, the sort of pleasure of secondary gain: of finding that in speaking one's anguish the pleasure of attentive care exceeds the need for resolution of the problem so that one can get on with one's life. In such a case the aim is to perpetually utilise the benefits of this narrative as they virtually guarantee solid affective support and almost supplicant-like adoration of what seems to be narrative courage.

Setting aside sociopathic opportunists, who trade in the tale of abuse—something very rare indeed but we mention it briefly—how do we help those who genuinely believe they have been molested and the tale of this abuse dominates their life? Or, if the person does indeed recall moments of parental cruelty or apparently bewildering "episodes" that seemed sexual it is imperative to treat them no differently than those where it has been clear for one reason or another that they were indeed victims of abuse.

Let us be a bit clearer.

Imagine that the story of abuse is indeed an embellishment. The clinician realises this or believes it to be true and the question is, "What does one say?"

The answer is surprisingly simple but often evades the consciousness of both clinician and patient.

The individual who *repeatedly* tells the account of his or her abuse is *unwittingly* engaged in the act of *self traumatisation.* Whether one has been abused or has not, the act of repeatedly telling this account to others, or of instantiating it as a life defining moment, aids and abets the act of abuse.

That individuals are self-abusive should be no surprise.

We may think of alcoholism, smoking, taking drugs, as the typical forms of self-abuse.

The narratives we select to tell our story do not seem high on the list of toxic objects that distress the soma.

But the individual who cannot end the narrative, indeed who capitalises on it, is engaged in a *malignant transgression*, passing on what the other did to the self now to what one is doing to one's self.

In many sessions, having heard the account of abuse, there may come a moment when it is clear the person is wedded to the narrative. Interpreting this is potentially transformational and liberating.

This is not a matter of telling the truth or lying. Human imagination is so powerful that anyone could believe something happened to them in childhood if they imagined so. To imagine is not to be wrong. It is simply another form of thinking.

But we also see people who do more than simply overidentify with victims of a trauma, a happening that is common and may take place for many reasons. Some assume the victim's identity which may be a form of pathological introjective identification that I elect to term *appropriative identification.* This envy-driven form of hate takes place when a person steals an other's identifying characteristics and lifestyles by imitation.

An example will help clarify this issue.

Robert is a well-known artist. He meets a lesser artist Zeno—unknown and not original in his works—who is nonetheless a lot of fun and good company. Over the first two years of friendship Robert notes that when he introduces Zeno to his other friends that Zeno "rolodexes them": he always writes to the newcomers in his life and invites them to meet up.

Zeno has also convinced Robert to help him flog some of his work in differing galleries which oblige, but it becomes uneasy when the only galleries he picks are ones where Robert's work had been hung.

By the third year of friendship Zeno had "absorbed" all of Robert's world and overdeveloped it. For example, Robert had a close but respectful relation to a leading gallery owner who was something of a mentor. Zeno—who came from the same country as the gallery owner—invited the owner to his home and to join him at different venues in differing countries.

This same appropriation of Robert's friends was taking place with many people to the point that some were now concerned that Zeno always managed to include a somewhat disparaging comment about Robert.

One day, a close friend told Robert what Zeno had been doing, and both had to consider the fact that Zeno was trying to appropriate Robert's life.

To complicate matters further, Zeno had casually informed Robert that close friends of Robert had made disparaging and malignant comments about him, thus damaging Robert's internal objects of close friends. Zeno had mentioned in passing, "Oh, I heard at a party that X said you were a selfish pig," or "I understand from Y that he never said to you that you were mistaken about your distress with Z."

Such asides voiced over a rather long period of time—thus not eliciting immediate alarm in Robert—were dismissed by Robert as just unfortunate outbursts by close friends.

It was only when Robert realised that Zeno had poisoned all of his friendships through salacious false "gossip" did Robert then realise that Zeno had invented these accusations in order to try to destroy Robert's relations to his friends.

As Robert realised this, he also recognised that he had indeed backed away from the friends and finally built the courage to ask a friend if, indeed,

Zeno's report of this friend's alleged criticism of Robert was correct. The friend stated that he had never said what Zeno reported and with a minimum of investigation of the other reports it was clear that Zeno had falsified all the accounts in order to try to destroy Robert's friendships and as importantly, Robert's relation to his internal objects.

Wisely, Robert slowly backed away from his relation to Zeno even though this did have further consequences.

Appropriative identification is a form of psychotic invasion of another's "person". It is driven by envy and evoked by disparity between the subject's creativity and the other who is the object of envy. By splitting the self into identity fragments, which Leslie Sohn (1985) termed "identificates", this sociopath is able to house a multitude of stolen identities which for the unwitting seem remarkably charming.

Is this not simply "identity theft"?

It is a form of such theft, for sure.

But appropriative identification refers to a total unconscious absorption of another person to the point of *intersubjective fusion.* These often gregarious, enthusiastic, and fun-loving individuals attach themselves to accomplished or gifted people and take over their social world.

Ultimately, if played out, it can be *a form* of homicide.

And the rage upon confrontation can be endangering.

As it is a *form* of murder it is a risk to confront the sociopath who has committed a relational felony. Indeed, by the time the victim of this theft becomes aware of what has taken place—and for some time the thief's actions may simply seem to be a form of affection and friendship—the question of "what does one do" arises.

If this arises in analysis the better way forward is to help the victim of this form of murder step back, not to engage in a "talking cure" with the other, as that would not only be counterproductive but dangerous as it might only feed his murderous intent.

In analytical work, however, Robert's relations to his siblings became of crucial focus. The elder child, he survived extreme parental discord which affected his siblings. Looking back over his life he could see that he did accept "brotherhoods" from damaged people; indeed, he unconsciously welcomed them into his life. When those relations failed—he could not provide them with what they sought—he turned a blind eye to their appropriation of his world. This endowed him with responsibility and agency. Why had he done this?

Why allow any other to damage himself?

Because in his unconscious to do so was to offer himself as sacrificial object to allay his survival guilt.

When facing the question of what to do about Zeno, Robert realised a crucial fact. One can make reparation for one's own destructiveness, but no one can repair the other's damage to one's self. Reparation theory is a one-person psychology. Robert had repeatedly sent Zeno "let's forget this" cards but to no avail. Ironically but not surprisingly Robert was left to feel the projectively identified guilt.

In place of the impossible—one cannot help the damaging other repair damage done to one's self—the individual can accept this fate without confrontational rancour which is an act of true sister- or brotherhood.

The victim of actual sexual abuse may suffer another appropriation as individuals identifying with the trauma assume they have suffered this as well. More often than not these are not malignant hysterics but usually young people, often bereft from family conflict, who have met with a trauma "counsellor" who snatches out of very thin air the certainty that the client's state is derived from abuse.

Ironically, this "therapist"—a modern con artist—appropriates the identity of the experienced and expert psychoanalyst or psychotherapist and leaves such identity theft as a social and political issue for the future.

References

Freud, S. (1950a). A project for a scientific psychology. *S. E., 1*: 283–397. London: Hogarth.

Sohn, L. (1985). Narcissistic organization, projective identification, and the formation of the identificate. *International Journal of Psychoanalysis, 66*: 201–213.

CHAPTER 16

The truth will set you free: Explorations into psychoanalytic truth and freedom*

Jean Arundale

Introduction

The concept of freedom and the aims and values of psychoanalysis share precepts that are central to them both: aspirations towards autonomy, dignity, and self-determination. The European liberal tradition and psychoanalysis both developed from Enlightenment values that were shaped by roots in ancient Greece and Rome and that were influential in the development of Western civilisation.

In this chapter I shall try to show the ways in which personal and social freedom and psychoanalysis are linked with truth, how lies can enslave, and how personal emancipation from the grip of false narratives, unnecessary anxieties, the infiltration of traumas from the past, and from the inducements of internal and external propaganda, can liberate the individual.

The fascinating thread of the history of freedom, echoing the values of psychoanalysis, can only be barely touched on here: the Renaissance rekindled the idea of individual potential, and the rise of Protestantism

* This chapter was originally presented at the 2025 Annual Conference of the European Psychoanalytical Federation at the Maritim Hotel & Internationales Congress Center in Dresden, Germany, 5 April 2025.

furthered this by challenging religious authority, promoting personal faith and individual freedom of conscience. The Enlightenment era marked a significant turning point in the conceptualisation of freedom, claiming it as an inherent human right that is fundamental to human existence.

Later, the socialist movement and liberal democracy synthesised these ideals, striving for individual liberty and social justice through democratic governance. The desire for freedom swept through the colonial world, leading to decolonisation, and the Universal Declaration of Human Rights, adopted by the United Nations in 1948, reflected the global consensus, affirming rights to liberty, security, and freedom of expression.

Soon after, in the 1960s, a cultural shift took place that saw freedom as an absence of constraint: the youth wanted to "do their own thing", and to express themselves freely. There was free love, the birth control pill, and the feminist movement.

In a democratic society, our freedoms are encoded in laws, reflecting the mandate of the people, but at the present time our precious freedoms appear under threat. Populist political groups seeking power, aiming towards autocratic rule, are misusing free speech, spreading lies, and showing contempt for the truth. Power and money have become the driving force.

The "Age of Information" has become the "Age of Disinformation", a so-called "post-truth era", in which "fake news" has corrupted the political discourse, and moreover, has infected the general public like a virus, normalising lies. This has created an alarming distrust of truthfulness that has cast doubt on all our institutions: journalism, science, the courts, the professions, the pillars of our society.

George Orwell (1949), addressing the themes of freedom and truth, foreshadowed this in his party slogans in *Nineteen Eighty-Four*, sent out by the Ministry of Truth: "War is peace. Freedom is slavery. Ignorance is strength". In these slogans, Orwell's satire succinctly captures the manipulation and propaganda used by charismatic authoritarian groups to control the populace. We find ourselves now in a world that is moving towards authoritarianism, the closure of our freedoms.

These are dangerous times. Around the edges of the campfires of freedom are circling the wolves of autocracy, dictatorship, and fascism. Truth needs to be restored to protect our freedoms.

Does truth really make one free?

The quotation, "The truth will set you free" has ancient origins, biblical and Buddhist, and has been used for many purposes, saintly and perverse.

Its message, however, cannot be universally applied. Occasionally there are valid reasons to maintain false narratives, for example, to protect children from the more unsavoury truths in life, the violence and horror of which humans are capable. How much truth can an individual bear? Doctors used to withhold the truth of cancer diagnoses to protect patients from what felt like a death sentence.

Psychotic phantasies might need to be allowed to go unchallenged by the truth in some individuals, thus preventing psychotic breakdown or disfigurement of the personality.

There are people whose entire lives are built on false belief systems who can be utterly crushed when faced with reality. An example of this can be found in Ibsen's play, *The Wild Duck* (1884). Can the truth be therapeutic if it is destructive of all one's values and beliefs?

Personal freedom

While a democratic society can attempt to preserve social, political, and economic freedoms, to be free we require something else, something more: personal freedom, an internal capacity to think, to feel, and to choose in order to negotiate our lives.

However, Freud (1920g), the neurologist, showed us that there are unconscious patterns directing us, limitations to freedom that can thwart us: false selves, the repetition compulsion, denial, projection, inhibition, rationalisation, identification, repression, the many ways used to avoid facing painful truths, not wanting to know, "turning a blind eye", what Wilfred Bion (1962, p. 47) termed –K, the repudiation and denial of truth, or the destructive attachment to it. To become free from internal barriers and unconscious limitations, the truth, both psychic and external, needs to be faced and understood.

Freud stated in "Analysis terminable and interminable": "we must not forget that the analytic relationship is based on a love of the truth—that is, recognition of reality—and that it precludes any kind of sham or deceit" (1937c, p. 248).

Melanie Klein (2017) was known for her unfailing desire to ascertain the truth, while at the same time maintaining that no truth is final or absolute. Bion (1962) placed truth-seeking at the very centre of his innovative work, famously stating that, "healthy mental growth seems to depend on truth as the living organism depends on food. If it is lacking or deficient the personality deteriorates" (pp. 144–146). In "On arrogance" (1958) Bion wrote of Oedipus' relentless search for the truth, regardless of the consequences, even at the risk of catastrophic change. This passion for truth is our foremost weapon against being determined by the past and the repetition compulsion.

Bion (1965, p. 38) appeared to believe it is the truth itself that is transformative, that the movement in consciousness from preconception to conception to realisation in his logico-deductive grid system, what he labelled "transformation in K", is sufficient to bring about change. This is arguable; for most of us, it takes effort to combat old patterns and to implement our "pearls of intent".

Psychoanalytic truth

Hanna Segal wrote specifically about truth and freedom within the context of psychoanalytic theory and practice. Crucial for psychological growth and mental freedom, she said: "Freedom is not an easy thing to achieve because it requires the individual to confront and accept the truth about themselves, no matter how painful that truth might be" (1978, p. 213).

In our work, we endeavour to help our patients to gain what one might call "a taste for psychic truth", involving curiosity and the epistemophilic spirit, that fuels their investigation into the repressed unconscious.

Clinical material

I will turn to the clinical cases.

Case 1—Clara

From the start, Clara was eager to let me know that she was already knowledgeable about psychoanalysis and knew the theories. She also knew herself, so didn't really need analysis. Moreover, she informed me that she felt her personality and character had been formed in childhood and could not be changed. She was only submitting to treatment because eventually she wanted to train.

Clara's intellectual skills were in fact quite impressive, but they formed a formidable intellectual defence. The only symptom that she admitted to having was hypochondria: anytime she had a headache, or a pain somewhere in her body, she would become terrorised, convinced that she had a brain tumour or terminal cancer, and could only calm down after she was examined by a doctor and assured that nothing was wrong. Emotionally, her mind was organised in terms of black and white; if she didn't feel 100 per cent healthy and pain-free, she felt in imminent danger of dying.

It was only after some time into the analysis that she could let me know how severely she suffered from the panic attacks and that from childhood she had believed there was something wrong deep inside her. Whatever this bad object was, her terror was extreme, would take her over and nearly paralyse her; she would shake violently on her way to the doctor's surgery. These panic attacks she associated with ones she had had in adolescence before going to university; she was given strong anxiolytic medication, which meant her first year at university was experienced as a sleepy fog.

Clara often described herself as a plucky and determined little girl who would just get on with things despite the difficult family set-up. Father was often away working, leaving her older brother and her with what she described as their histrionic, volatile, and critical mother. She told me about their frequent fights when her mother would slap or hit her when she complained, which she often did, particularly in vigorous protest that mother adored her brother and neglected her; boys were important and valuable in mother's eyes, girls were insignificant, and this infuriated Clara. She concluded that it was not only a penis that she was missing, but there must be something bad inside her that she could not comprehend; why else would mother treat her so badly? Her foremost desire was to gain her mother's love. In the transference I became the bad mother who always criticised her, while during her analysis her relationship with her mother improved.

Like the many patients whose mothers were unable to connect emotionally with them, to contain their anxieties, and without a securely internalised good object, Clara had formed an omnipotent defence, compensating for states of infantile helplessness and existential vulnerability in the face of maternal unavailability, created to soothe her terror of abandonment by a phantasy that she could survive without mother and that she possessed inside her everything she needed to survive. Afraid of dependency, she couldn't really trust me or let me in. Like the doctors she went to for reassurance, she wanted me to reassure her, to pronounce her as mentally fine, just fine as she is.

Clara often complained that I didn't praise her or speak about her good qualities, that I only criticised her; she managed to twist everything I said into a criticism. Her response to transference interpretations was to say that, yes, as her analyst I was just like her mother, she had never been good enough. When I spoke of her positive qualities and assets, it was as if she couldn't hear me.

Clara was a closed shop, having a "no entry" system of defences, so-named by Gianna Williams (1997), within which she sustained the belief that she possessed everything she needed and anything new was not welcome; clearly, letting me in was highly problematic. A few dream fragments about men attempting but failing to break into her house, first from the front door and then from the rear, illustrated my difficulty in the transference. I felt rejected and abandoned, just as she felt as a child in relation to her inaccessible mother. Allowing her husband to penetrate her in sexual intercourse also was forbidden, another no-go area, just as she kept me out in verbal intercourse: she waited politely for me to finish speaking then carried on with what she wanted to say, or responded with, no …, but …, or yes, but … as she pushed me away. I frequently pointed out how she wasn't listening or letting me in, but no matter how gently or diplomatically I tried to speak, she always heard me as a critic, not as her analyst trying to understand her. Speaking the truth, introducing the patient to herself as Bion put it, is a difficult proposition when coming up against narcissistic defences in a patient in the paranoid/schizoid position (Bion, 1962, pp. 21–45).

After speaking to her more about food for thought, space to think, and her fear of swallowing my thoughts, this exchange took place:

P: I felt very happy yesterday, the sun was shining and everything felt good. Then at night I had that painful tension in my throat [she had been speaking for two sessions in a strangulated voice]. It's a familiar thing for me; whenever I feel good, I feel afraid something bad will happen.

A: You're telling me you don't like to allow yourself to feel happy, something in you will spoil it.

P: Something disrupts the good feeling, something in my throat restricts my swallowing.

I thought of *globus hystericus* and how she resembles Freud's classic hysteric. I responded: "That's the mind-body split you were speaking about yesterday. Something is blocking your throat, preventing things going in and out; you don't want to listen to me and swallow what I say for fear it will spoil your good mood. It's hard for you to trust me and to take in my words and think about them, maybe even digest them."

P: But I do listen to you, I do try to hear what you're saying, I want to listen to you.

At this point, I took up her ambivalence: partly she does want to listen to me and take in what we find out in our sessions, but partly she doesn't want to let me see her and know her.

Clara appeared to be terrified of her unconscious, what was hidden in her internal world, and this could be seen particularly in her refusal to remember dreams. She came session after session to say that she'd had a dream or several dreams but could not remember then; I began to push, to consistently point out that she was so frightened of her dreams that she refused to try to remember them. Eventually, her defences loosened; she began to tell me dreams, although with much trepidation.

P: I was with R [her husband], and we were in a sort of camp. I could feel there was something wrong with me and I felt down in the space between my belly button and vagina; there were chocolates that had accumulated there, stuck on my skin. I peeled one off and under it was a sore and a kind of hole. It was disgusting!

This dream set loose a stream of associations in me: the passages in her between inside and outside are blocked, there is sweetness trying to get in, her husband is affectionate and makes sexual advances, but she finds her vagina and sex to be disgusting. The orifice on her belly might be to eliminate poo or wee and be confused with other orifices and erotogenic zones causing anxiety about taking in toxins, by mouth, by ears or eyes, thus needing to obstruct the passages.

She went on with the dream: "R and I went into a small room; in it on the wall was a sculpture, made of canvas but it was like skin, weird. It was moving strangely, it was something supernatural, absolutely terrifying." She said she felt the sculpture represented something unbearably bad, a feeling inside her that must be avoided at all costs, and she went on to assign external reasons for having such a frightening dream: getting sunburned yesterday, meeting her work group in which there were bad people, unpleasant exchanges with a client. Any exploration of the bad feelings inside was too much to face or to think about. This was consistent with her magical belief she told me of several times, that to speak about something bad will make it happen.

The next day she told me another dream, a familiar dream that she was being injecting with something that was contaminated. I responded, saying she is afraid I put into her dangerous or contaminated food for thought, poisonous words. She said:

P: I don't really think that of you but maybe unconsciously. I don't like to focus on myself. Yesterday I said lots about me. I'm finished now; today I want to concentrate on my clients. I can't do two jobs at once. I don't really want to know about myself or my dreams.

A: It's hard for you to think about the scary feelings inside from when you were a frightened little girl.

P: Yes. I know that a psychotic area is there, but I don't want to go there, I don't want to know.

Despite her resistance, her evasions and avoidances, her mistrust of me, Clara never missed a session, wrestling with the analytic work. She brought a vivid dream that clearly showed how threatening she found the analytic process. She dreamt she was on the edge of a cliff top, looking down into the valley in which there was a pool with people swimming around; it was a cult, and the people had been brainwashed. A strong force was pulling her down into the valley, and she was clinging to the edge of the cliff in terror. I interpreted the dream as how frightened she was to give herself over to analysis, that she was afraid I wanted to brainwash her, that she felt instead of helping her, analysis would cause her to lose her identity. Her response to this was a bemused hmmm …, a part acknowledgement this might be so.

It is hard to tell if my interpretations connect with her and alleviate her internal terror, as her dreams of very bad objects continue: a vampire came into her bedroom and was biting her neck, not to suck blood but to put poison into her. Yet, she told me with some reluctance, not wanting to give me or psychoanalysis too much credit, that actually she feels less anxious in her day-to-day life and has fewer frightening psychosomatic incidents compared to before starting analysis.

It appears that, despite her defences, some psychic truth has seeped through to free her a bit from panic, from the prison of black and white thinking, and a bit freer from the fear of her internal malignant bad objects.

Case 2—Mr T

Giuseppe Civitarese (2016), with an acute understanding of the deep interconnections between truth, freedom, and the unconscious in psychoanalysis, emphasises the uncovering of psychic truths as the way to achieve individual authenticity and freedom. Civitarese writes of how seeking and accepting internal truth can liberate individuals from psychological constraints, allowing them to achieve a more genuine sense of self, although the process, he notes, can be painful, meeting with strong resistance. Brenman (2006) too was acutely aware of the difficulties, stating: "the process of psychoanalysis aiming at the discovery of the truth about ourselves is a mixed blessing, by no means always welcome."

Accepting the truth was a painful struggle for the second patient I will discuss, Mr T. At the time of his referral, he had been in bed for a month with a depressive breakdown, having heard news of the near-death of a family member, a devastating blow. The family was, in Mr T's mind, fused together into one unit; this enmeshment meant that illness or threat involving one member brought the whole unit into jeopardy; moreover, the shadow of death had appeared, disturbing his omnipotent phantasy of immortality.

Mr T idealised his mother as a goddess, brilliant, exciting, beautiful, and indeed, in his descriptions, she was. As he entered the analytic process, his associations were without emotion, consisting of repetitive stories about his failed relationships with girlfriends. Having denied, split off, projected, or otherwise disposed with his emotions, any momentary glimpse of anger or criticism of his mother in the analytic process set into motion denials and rationalisations that excused her from any shortcoming as a mother. Yet the truth of what had happened slowly emerged: how mother had given all her attention to his sickly twin sister, turning over the care of her undemanding, uncomplaining little infant boy to his cool and distant grandmother for most of his first year. Mother often reiterated to the family and to guests when he was present that she never wanted a third child, wanting only a girl when the twins were born. Mother ignored and overlooked him, intensely involved with his chronically ill sister, and as they grew up, she blamed him for the sister's misbehaviours and naughtiness. He was never given the feeling that he counted or was valued, or that he was allowed thoughts or emotions of his own. Mother used him as a container for her marital unhappiness, then later as an errand boy and slave, refusing to let him grow up.

In the transference, as I interpreted his idealisation of me, the idealising transference faded after a couple of years, but deeper transference phantasies appeared, usually at the beginning of sessions, hidden in his associations of infant wishes to move into my house, to be looked after 100 per cent, to be supplied with everything he needed without his having to make an effort. To have an analyst/mother who did not comply with this agenda, and was not available in this way, he admitted, was a failure of mine. Throughout his analysis, phantasies would appear of his wish for me to be his goddess mother who would eventually supply him with all his needs, to be available to him whenever he wanted; a frightened, helpless, neglected baby with an unavailable mother.

Prior to entering analysis, Mr T's *modus operandi* was to give others whatever they wanted from him while he remained oblivious and out of touch. He reflected: "I still haven't started to live my own life." But as the analytic work went on, his split-off emotions began to return. He slowly began to feel, to learn what he liked and what he didn't like, what was good for him and what wasn't. He began to be interested in his authentic self. These movements were transformative.

When Mr T reflected on his phantasy of immortality, he could see that it was an omnipotent phantasy that protected him from the unbearable truth: that death was inevitable, that his family members and he could not escape the end of life. In a particularly poignant session, he said: "I've always thought I was a hyper-rationalist; how could I deny something like death? How could I? I'm not going to lie to myself anymore;

what's the point of having intelligence if it's based on lies. I declare an era in which lying is over. I hate lying in other people, why do I tolerate it in myself?"

He went on to speak of his denial of the painful truth about his mother, that he had not been honest with himself about how she treats him, that being with her evokes in him feelings of worthlessness and insignificance, and that it was not good for him to be around her. He had tolerated so much, forever hoping to get her respect and love, but also to prevent himself from experiencing the pain of helplessness, the pain of not having the mother he so needed and wanted. He slowly began to grasp the notion that he could not make her into what he wanted her to be.

These were extremely painful truths to bear, the pain of truth and the truth of pain. Having always imagined his family as a single eternal unit, a family with no individuals, his perceptions changed. He could see a truer picture: his identification with an ideal mother-goddess who was actually a tyrant, his helpless, unkind sister, his brother who ignored him despite his repeated attempts to befriend him, his withdrawn but quietly caring father, who despite a successful medical career (significantly, as an anaesthesiologist), was sidelined and impotent in the family, not able to set boundaries or rules, a vital constituent of the paternal function. He remembered furious quarrels between his parents that often reached the level of "character assassination"; he remembered as a small boy sitting on the stairs at night listening to battles between his parents that terrified him, particularly when he heard his mother threaten to walk out and leave the family.

Rarely did he dream, but recently he had a terrifying science-fiction dream, reminiscent of the film *War of the Worlds*, representing his terror about the future. He could see in the dream how, in the battleground that was his family, his entanglement with his mother and sister had caused him damage, how his life was in danger of being destroyed. He had always felt it was his responsibility above all to protect them, and he feared he would continue to sacrifice his life for them.

The dream had a strong effect on him, and he was deeply shaken; he wanted a life of his own. He slowly began to separate internally from his family and began to put effort into his own life. He contacted old friends and made new ones, having dinner parties and a more active social life. Often speaking of worry about his health and how he had never looked after himself, he regularly started going to the gym with a personal trainer, is seeing a dietitian, and has stopped putting on weight.

Having always shunned doctors, he allowed himself to be diagnosed as diabetic and to take medication.

As the unconscious truth was revealed, he slowly and reluctantly accepted the true story of his childhood and family relations; he was able to be in touch with his rage. As I continued interpreting in the transference his rage towards his analyst/mother, who has failed to deliver the 100 per cent care he wants and how he was still waiting for me to magically fulfil his wishes, he accepted this, in tiny increments. Building a good internal object out of the fragments in his mind and his experience in analysis, Mr T told me that he had taken inside and established within himself a figure that represents me and our work together that will last. It is now up to him, he said, to make choices for himself, free now to conduct his own life. The shift of position from dependency to taking responsibility for his own life was easier said than done; this was sometimes true, but often slipped away, a work in progress.

To some extent, facing the truth for both patients has enabled a greater freedom.

References

Bion, W. R. (1958). On arrogance. *International Journal of Psychoanalysis, 39*: 144–146.

Bion, W. R. (1962). *Learning from Experience.* London: Karnac.

Bion, W. R. (1965). *Transformations: Change from Learning to Growth.* London: Heinemann.

Brenman, E. (2006). *Recovery of the Lost Good Object.* London: Routledge.

Civitarese, G. (2016). *Truth and the Unconscious in Psychoanalysis.* London: Routledge.

Freud, S. (1920g). *Beyond the Pleasure Principle. S. E., 18.* London: Hogarth.

Freud, S. (1937c). Analysis terminable and interminable. *S. E., 23.* London: Hogarth.

Ibsen, H. (1884). *The Wild Duck.* Una Ellis-Fermor (Trans.). In: *Ibsen: Six Plays.* London: Oxford University Press, 1960.

Klein, M. (2017). The technique of analysis. In: J. Steiner (Ed.), *Lectures on Technique by Melanie Klein.* London: Routledge.

Orwell, G. (1949). *Nineteen Eighty-Four.* London: Secker & Warburg.

Segal, H. (1978). *Psychoanalysis and Freedom of Thought.* London: H. K. Lewis.

Williams, G. (1997). The no-entry system of defences: Reflections on the assessment of adolescents suffering from eating disorders. In: *Internal Landscapes and Foreign Bodies: Eating Disorders and Other Pathologies* (pp. 115–122). London: Routledge.

Index